WITHDRAWN

Madrid
Shortlist

timeout.com / madrid

Contents

ABOUT THE GUIDE

The *Time Out Madrid Shortlist* is one of a series of pocket guides to cities around the globe. Drawing on the expertise of local authors, it distils their knowledge into a handy, easy-to-use format that ensures you get the most from your trip, whether you're a first-time or return visitor.

Time Out Madrid Shortlist is divided into four sections:

Welcome to Madrid introduces the city and provides inspiration for your visit.

Madrid Day by Day helps you plan your trip with an events calendar and customised itineraries.

Madrid by Area is the main visitor section of the guide. It includes detailed listings and reviews for the very best sights and museums, restaurants ⑩, tapas bars ⑩, cafés and bars ⑩, shops and services ⑩ and entertainment venues ⑩, all organised by area with a corresponding street map. To help navigation, each area of Madrid has been assigned its own colour.

Madrid Essentials provides practical visitor information, including accommodation options and details of public transport.

Shortlists & highlights

We have selected a Shortlist of stand-out venues in each area, which are marked with a heart ♥ in the text. The very best of these appear in the Highlights feature (*see p10*) and receive extended coverage in the guide.

Maps

There's an overview map on *p8* and individual street maps for each area of the city. Venues featured in the guide have been given a grid reference so that you can find them easily on the maps and on the ground.

Prices

All our **restaurant listings** are marked with a euro symbol category from budget to blow-out (€-€€€€), indicating the price you should expect to pay for an average main course: € = under €10; €€ = €10-€20; €€€ = €20-€30; €€€€ = over €30.

A similar system is used in our **Accommodation** chapter based on the hotel's standard prices for one night in a double room: **Budget** = under €100; **Moderate** = €100-€150; **Expensive** = €150-€200; **Luxury** = over €200.

Introduction

Madrid has few residents who can call themselves *madrileño*, yet the presence of migrants from all over the country makes the capital what it is. Andalucía may be the birthplace of flamenco, but Madrid has the top-class venues, and sooner or later the best artists all make their way here; similarly, any aspiring *torero* must make his debut in Las Ventas bullring. The city may be far from the sea, but it has long boasted the best fish and seafood in Europe. Unable to provide its own produce, Madrid demands and pays for the choicest pickings.

In the euphoria of newly democratic Spain, when anything seemed possible, Madrid filled with artists, actors, musicians and filmmakers, creating the much-lauded Movida cultural movement. Since then, political infighting and the recession have taken their toll on this bouncy optimism, but the vital café and club society endures, and Madrid today offers a greater variety of nightlife than any other European city. Sure, there are challenges aplenty, but it is still possible to get caught up in that same uplifting swirl of energy that the city first experienced way back in the 1980s.

Welcome to Madrid

Plaza de Colón

CHAMBERÍ

MALASAÑA

CHUECA & MALASAÑA

GRAN VÍA

SOL & GRAN VÍA

SOL

SANT ANA

LOS AUSTRIAS & LA LATINA

LA LATINA

RASTRO

LAVAPIÉS & THE RASTRO

600m

600 yds

8

© Copyright Time Out Group 2018

C/Santa Engracia

C/Sagasta

Rubén Darío

Museo Arte Público de Madrid

Museo Lázaro Galdiano

Núñez de Balboa

Los Doce Apóstoles

Fundación Juan March

C/Príncipe de Vergara

Alonso Martínez
Plaza de Alonso Martínez

C/Génova

Colón

SALAMANCA

Museo del Romanticismo
Palacio Longoria

Palacio de Justicia

Fernán Gómez Centro Cultural de la Villa

Serrano

Velázquez

Palacio de Buenavista

Jardines del Descubrimiento

THE RETIRO & SALAMANCA

HUECA

Chueca

Museo de la Biblioteca Nacional
Museo Arqueológico Nacional

Palacio Benevolista
Banco de España

Palacio de Linares

Retiro

C/Alcalá

Príncipe de Vergara

Gran Vía

C/Alcalá

Puerta de Alcalá

C/O'Donnell

RETIRO

villa
Círculo de Bellas Artes

Banco de España

CentroCentro

Glorieta El Salvador

Ibiza

Museo Colecciones Instituto de Crédito Oficial
Congreso

Museo Naval

Museo de Artes Decorativas

Museo Thyssen-Bornemisza

Bolsa de Comercio

Glorieta de la Sardina

Barrio de las Letras

HUERTAS & SANTA ANA

Paseo del Prado

Palacio de Velázquez

Jardines de Cecilio Rodríguez

El Retiro

HUERTAS

Museo Nacional del Prado

Palacio de Cristal

Antón Martín

Sociedad Cervantina

Caixa Forum

Conservatorio de Música

C/Alfonso XII

LAVAPIÉS

Centro de Arte Reina Sofía

Atocha

Ministerio de Educación y Ciencia

Plaza del Emperador Carlos V

Ministerio de Agricultura, Pesca y Alimentación

Viveros Municipales

Museo Nacional de Antropología

Ronda de Atocha

Vieja Estación de Atocha

Atocha Renfe

Real Observatorio Nacional

Avenida de Menéndez Pelayo

Estación de Atocha

Museo de Ferrocarril

Paseo de la Infanta

Paseo de la Reina Cristina

Paseo de Santa María de la Cabeza
Paseo de las Delicias
C/Méndez Álvaro

A. de la Ciudad de Barcelona

Real Fábrica de Tapices

Highlights

From the vast art palace of the Museo del Prado to the sounds and smells of the Rastro flea market, Madrid has something for every taste. This is just a selection of some of its greatest sights and events.

Museo Nacional del Prado *p142*

This iconic gallery houses the greatest collection of religious art in the world, and is an essential stop on any Madrid circuit. The focus is on paintings from the 15th to the 17th centuries – most notably with the works of Velázquez – but fans of Goya, Hieronymous Bosch, Rubens and many other major artists will not leave disappointed.

02

Museo Thyssen-Bornemisza *p96*

Home to an unparalleled private collection of art, this gallery offers an impressive number and range of significant artists and movements – from Tintoretto to Kandinsky, from Flemish old masters to cubism. It has the feel of a highly personal selection, which clearly displays the occasionally quirky tastes of the late Baron Hans-Heinrich Thyssen-Bornemisza and his wife.

03

Plaza Mayor *p75*

The handsome, arcaded Plaza Mayor has been a hub of city life since the 15th century, when it was a market square. It was spectacularly overhauled according to a commission from Philip III (who is represented in the equestrian statue at its centre) in the 16th century, and it has had many impressive buildings added since.

04

Palacio Real *p70*

The Royal Palace has an unfathomable 3,000 rooms, many of which are open to the public and are decorated with exquisite frescoes and reliefs, and filled with glorious statuary and paintings. Highlights include the throne room and the armoury, where you can see the same armour that El Cid wore into battle.

05

Museo Nacional Centro de Arte Reina Sofía *p108*

Though it doesn't claim the same clout as the Prado or the Thyssen, the Reina Sofía boasts as its showpiece Picasso's *Guernica*, a vast outpouring of grief and rage at the horrors of war. Most other important Spanish artists are represented, too, and you'll see further works by Picasso, as well as art by Miró and Dalí.

06

The Retiro *p136*

The Retiro in the early evening after the punishing temperatures of a hot summer's day is a sight not to be missed. Families and couples turn out to stroll arm in arm along the park's manicured pathways under its numerous trees or to take a boat for a turn on its pretty lake.

07

The Rastro *p111*

Madrid's beloved flea market is less of a shopping experience and more of a Sunday tradition. Turn up early for any chance of a bargain, or simply stroll among the stalls soaking up the atmosphere, and make the most of the many nearby cafés that have sprung up to cater for the leisurely brunch crowd.

08

CaixaForum Madrid *p139*

Housed in the former Mediodía Electric Power Station, and remodelled by architects Herzog & de Meuron to striking effect, this cutting-edge cultural centre runs a lively programme of events and exhibitions. Contemporary and traditional temporary art exhibitions are run alongside engaging and stimulating music and poetry events, as well as lectures, debates and workshops.

09

Museo Lázaro Galdiano *p148*

This wonderfully eclectic private collection includes 15,000 artworks (including a couple of typically eerie paintings by Goya, and work from Bosch, El Greco and Constable), as well as ancient jewellery, armour and weaponry, illuminated manuscripts, ceramics and furniture. The former home of art collector Lázaro Galdiano, the building itself is worth the trip uptown.

10

Real Monasterio de las Descalzas Reales *p86*

The favoured convent of barefoot (*descalza*) novices from the aristocracy, and benefitting from royal patronage, the wildly baroque Descalzas Reales was bequeathed many great works of art over the years, including paintings by Titian and Breughel. Most of the art is on show to the public today, and a cloistered community of nuns still lives here.

11

Museo de la Real Academia de Bellas Artes de San Fernando *p85*

Oft overlooked thanks to rivalry from Madrid's major art museums, the Bellas Artes has a fantastic collection of paintings, including 13 important works by Goya, as well as work by Velázquez, Rubens and Zurbarán. It also houses an engravings museum that has original plates used by Goya for his etchings.

12

Barrio de las Letras *p100*

The area around Plaza Santa Ana and Calle Huertas is known as the 'District of Letters' for the playwrights, poets and men of words that once walked these streets. Quotes from their better-known works are inlaid in the pavements in bronze. Today, this is still the city's main theatre district, with the landmark Teatro Español and Teatro de la Zarzuela.

13

Mercado de San Miguel *p72*

This elegant market, with a restored 19th-century wrought-iron facade, has been a huge success story since reopening in 2009 and was one of the first of a number of gastro markets to open all over Spain. It's a good place to pick up local delicacies to take home as souvenirs, or to just crawl the many tapas bars.

14

San Isidro *p59*

There is no shortage of festivals in Madrid but none is more riotous than the Fiestas de San Isidro in mid May, celebrating the city's patron saint. There is a series of concerts, shows and performances in venues and squares all over the city, and families go on a pilgrimage to the Ermita de San Isidro in traditional *castizo* costume.

15

Parque El Capricho de la Alameda de Osuna *p157*

Outside the centre but accessible by metro, the Parque El Capricho is a real delight, with rose gardens, lakes and replica classical temples. It was the 18th-century country estate of the Duke and Duchess of Osuna, who had its theatrically designed gardens designed as a meeting place for the great artistic minds of the time, as well as more enlightened members of the aristocracy.

16

Casa de Campo *p155*

This huge slice of parkland is close to the centre but feels like the countryside, providing a much-needed green lung to the city. In addition to its vast expanses of grass and network of wooded pathways, it has a boating lake lined with cafés, a zoo, swimming pools and a funfair. You can get here on the Teleférico de Madrid cable car.

17

Museo de Historia *p120*

The History Museum lay virtually empty for many years, but has been superbly revamped to house a collection of paintings, scale models, furniture, interesting artefacts and old photos of Madrid. It now provides an informative and enjoyable introduction to the history of the city, starting from the beginning of its importance in the 16th century.

18

Matadero Madrid *p163*

This vibrant cultural centre is situated in the improbably handsome surroundings of a former slaughterhouse (*matadero*). As well as some of the most exciting artistic, cinematic and musical programming in the city, the rambling complex is a great place for lunch in its restaurant in the former boilerhouse, or for a drink under the stars in summer.

19

Mad Cool *p62*

It has only been around for a couple of years, but the Mad Cool music festival is already one of the most talked-about in the country, and pulls in big names from the UK and US as well as more local acts. Massive Attack, Depeche Mode, Jack Johnson and Fleet Foxes all feature in the line-up for 2018.

20

Museo del Ferrocarril de Madrid *p164*

In a city of such grand attractions and with an abundance of high culture, the appeal of this modest little railway museum – with its interesting collection of old locomotives, clocks, models and train-related paraphernalia – is curiously enduring. Something of a sleeper hit, you might say.

COME HERE, YOU

Get to know the Madrid attractions with pulling power, and book them for less with Time Out.

Sightseeing

The old city, with its narrow medieval streets, contains Madrid's most atmospheric and well-defined *barrios*, as well as its best eating, drinking and nightlife options and many of its landmark buildings. Most visitors spend the bulk of their time here – whether enjoying the Habsburg and Bourbon splendour of Los Austrias, the laid-back tapas bars of La Latina, the alternative cultural scene of Lavapiés, or the heady nightlife and hip cafés of Malasaña and Chueca. The heart of the area is the Puerta del Sol, and much of old Madrid converges on this square. Plaza Mayor, the heart of Golden Age Madrid, lies south-west of here, along C/Mayor, while two art museums from Madrid's 'Golden Triangle' – the Reina Sofía and the Thyssen-Bornemisza – lie to the east, bordering the Paseo del Prado.

Best art museums
Museo Nacional Centro de Arte
Reina Sofía *p108*
Museo Nacional del Prado *p142*
Museo Thyssen-Bornemisza *p96*

Best boating lakes
Casa de Campo *p155*
Retiro *p136*

Best views
Faro de Moncloa *p154*
Teleférico de Madrid *p155*

Best squares
Parque de Atracciones *p155*
Plaza de Oriente *p67*

Best Bourbon hangouts
Catedral de la Almudena *p68*
Palacio Real *p70*

Best convents
Convento de la Encarnación *p84*
Real Monasterio de las Descalzas
Reales *p86*

An overview of the city

Madrid is a surprisingly walkable city and most
neighbourhoods of interest lie within a 20-minute stroll
of the Puerta del Sol. This is literally the centre of the city,
in that all street numbers in Madrid count outwards from
Sol and it contains *kilómetro cero* (marked by a plaque
in the pavement), from which distances to the rest of
Spain are measured.

Seen from the air, or on a map, two of Madrid's main
features immediately stand out: one is the immensely
long Paseo de la Castellana, a north–south arterial
avenue that slices Madrid in two and links the old city
with its newer northern business districts. To the east
of the Castellana are the gridiron-patterned streets of
Salamanca (*see pp145-152*). The second unmissable
feature is the cramped old city with its maze of rambling
streets, sliced in two from east to west by the Gran Vía.

Neighbourhoods – defined here according to the
overview map on *p8* – mostly have quite distinct
flavours, with marked differences both architecturally
and in terms of the types of restaurants, bars and shops
that dominate. In this guide, we've split the old city into
five districts. Just south-west of **Sol** (*see pp81-92*),

along C/Mayor, lies the Habsburg city (**Los Austrias**, *see pp66-80*), including Plaza Mayor, the heart of Golden Age Madrid, while south of the square is Madrid's most multicultural barrio, **Lavapiés** (*see pp105-114*). Plaza **Santa Ana** and **Huertas** (*see pp93-104*) are to the south-east. Running east from Sol is C/Alcalá, which connects the square with the Plaza de Cibeles, the junction with the Castellana that leads to modern Madrid. Just north of Sol, the historic but buzzing areas of **Chueca** and **Malasaña** (*see pp115-132*) border on the Gran Vía.

Finally, we've listed some of Madrid's outlying districts as **Beyond the Centre** (*see pp153-164*). Though the neighbourhoods themselves are not particularly exciting, they do contain a handful of the city's most inspiring attractions.

Retiro park

Paseo del Arte

The art triumvirate of the Prado, the Thyssen and the Reina Sofía

In the **Prado** (*see p142*), the **Thyssen** (*see p96*) and the **Reina Sofía** (*see p108*), Madrid has three art palaces that are quite simply world-class. You'll find them dotted along Paseo del Prado, in what has increasingly, and slightly facetiously, come to be known as the 'Golden Triangle'. This formidable trio of museums has made Madrid the world's capital of art for many people in the know, and with extensive revamps of all three museums over the past decade (reckoned to have cost some €150 million in total), this label is only set to stick more firmly.

The city council initiative known as the **Paseo del Arte** ('art stroll') takes advantage of the proximity of the three art collections, promoting the fact that they are barely ten minutes' walk from one another. The idea echoes Berlin's Museum Island and London's Museum District. The axis that unites the big three – as well as avant-garde newcomer the **CaixaForum** (*see p139*) – is the Paseo del Prado.

Of course, it would be far too tiring to approach the Paseo del Arte as a one-day itinerary – a visit to just one of the three museums is likely to take up several hours, and plenty of energy. The idea is more to familiarise visitors with the area – which is becoming more and more pedestrian-friendly – so that the museums can be understood within a historical, geographical and cultural context, and for visits to then be undertaken at one's leisure.

Tickets

A joint ticket, the **Paseo del Arte**, gives entry to the Prado, the Reina Sofía and the Thyssen-Bornemisza for €29.60. It is available from the ticket desks at all three museums; after visiting one you can visit the other two at any time in the same calendar year. Each museum also has its own 'friends' tickets, giving unlimited entry for a year, which are more expensive and more widely publicised. A better deal is the €36 annual museum ticket (Tarjeta Anual de Museos Estatales), available from any state-run museum, which gives unlimited entry to all the main museums (except the Thyssen).

The Dream (Franz Marc, 1912), Thyssen-Bornemisza

Getting around

While much of Madrid can be navigated on foot, the metro system is reasonably efficient and covers most areas of interest. The bus is useful for journeys up the Castellana, but otherwise it's probably simpler to stick to the metro. For more information on getting around and fares on public transport, *see p171*.

Sights & museums

Madrid's most famous attractions are, of course, its world-class art museums: the **Prado** (*see p142*), the **Reina Sofía** (*see p108*) and the **Thyssen-Bornemisza** (*see p96*), but these have been joined in recent years by the **CaixaForum Madrid** (*see p139*), which has a limited permanent collection, but some of the best temporary programming in the city. Thanks to this spectacular quartet, some of the other collections are unjustly overlooked, such as the superb paintings spanning a range of eras and styles at the **Museo de la Real Academia de Bellas Artes de San Fernando** (*see p85*), or the collections within the many convents and monasteries, such as those at the **Real Monasterio de la Encarnación** (*see p84*) and the **Real Monasterio de las Descalzas Reales** (*see p86*). In the same area, you'll find the magnificent **Palacio Real** (*see p70*).

Though art is the principal player, Madrid also has a fine selection of thematic museums, such as history (**Museo de Historia**, *see p120*); archaeology (**Museo Arqueológico Nacional**, *see p146*); ships (**Museo Naval**, *see p140*); clothing (**Museo del Traje**, *see p159*); and trains (**Museo del Ferrocarril**, *see p164*). It's worth putting aside some time for some of its kookier museums, however; something that Madrid excels in. A couple of the most charming are the **Museo Lázaro Galdiano** (*see p148*) and the **Museo del Romanticismo** (*see p116*).

Finally, when the weather is right (because Madrid can get blisteringly hot and bitterly cold), don't miss the two main parks – the vast **Casa de Campo** (*see p155*) and the elegant **Retiro** (*see p136*).

Tourist information

The **Centros de Turismo**, run by the city council, and the tourist office, run by the regional authority (Comunidad de Madrid), provide similar basic information on Madrid and the surrounding region, plus free maps. The city also runs a phone information line for locals, 010, which can be useful to visitors. For details of this number plus more on Centros de Turismo, *see p183*. Tourist offices do not make hotel bookings but can advise on vacancies.

Full information on what's on is in local papers and listings magazines.

Tours

If you prefer to see the city independently, but need extra guidance, then the website www.madridenruta.com has a large number of suggested routes and guided maps you can print out.

Puerta del Sol

Key Events

All the Madrid dates that matter

c860 AD Madrid founded during the reign of Emir Mohammed I of Córdoba.

1085-6 Alfonso VI of Castile conquers Toledo and Madrid.

1109 Madrid besieged by Moorish army.

1212 Battle of Navas de Tolosa: decisive defeat of Muslims in Spain.

1476 Isabella becomes unchallenged Queen of Castile after battle of Toro.

1492 Conquest of Granada; expulsion of Jews from Spain; discovery of America.

1547 Birth of Cervantes in Alcalá de Henares.

1561 Philip II moves the Court to Madrid from Toledo.

1563-84 Building of El Escorial.

1599-1600 Plague and famine in Castile.

1601-6 Court moved to Valldolid.

1605, 1615 *Don Quixote* published.

1609 Expulsion of former Muslims from Spain.

1617-9 Completion of Plaza Mayor.

1632-40 Buen Retiro Palace built.

1702-14 War of the Spanish Succession: Philip V becomes first Bourbon King of Spain.

1734 Alcázar of Madrid destroyed by fire.

1778 Goya moves to Madrid from Aragon.

1808-12 Madrid under French occupation.

1812 Cortes in Cádiz agrees first Spanish constitution; disastrous famine in Madrid.

1833 Carlist Wars begin on death of Fernando VII; constitutional government established in Madrid, with limited powers.

1836 Main decree on Disentailment of Monasteries.

1851 The railway to Aranjuez is inaugurated.

1858 Revolution overthrows Isabel II.

1868 The Canal de Isabel II water system is inaugurated.

1871 Amadeo of Savoy becomes King of Spain. First trams in Madrid, drawn by mules.

1898 Spanish-American War: a disaster for Spain. Madrid's tramlines electrified.

1910 Building of Gran Vía initiated.

1919 First Madrid metro line opened.

1923-1930 Primo de Rivera dictatorship.

1931 Proclamation of Second Republic.

1936 February: elections won by Popular Front. July: military uprising against left-wing government. November: Francoist forces launch assault on Madrid.

1939 1 April: Franco declares war over.

1946-50 UN imposes sanctions on Spain.

1959 Stabilisation Plan opens up the Spanish economy.

1970 Juan Carlos declared as General Franco's successor.

1975 20 November: death of Franco.

1977 15 June: Spain's first democratic general election.

1986 1 January: Spain joins the EEC.

2004 11 March: terrorist attacks kill 192.

2014 Juan Carlos abdicates; succeeded by his son King Felipe VI.

2016 PP wins second term after general elections.

2017 Illegal independence referendum in Catalunya results in Mariano Rajoy imposing direct rule.

Plaza Mayor

All the guides at **Carpetania Madrid** (91 531 40 18, www. carpetaniamadrid.com, 2 hr tours €9-€12) are art history specialists. As well as city walking routes, they offer expert guided tours around art exhibitions. With over 100 different itineraries (by bus and on foot), **Madrid En Ruta** (mobile 648 078 568, www.madridenruta.com, tickets on foot €5.90, by bike €6.90, under-5s free) is run by the tourist board and offers tours focusing on architecture, literature and history. **MadWay to Madrid** (www.madwaytomadrid.com) has alternative and eco-friendly tours on foot or by bike, in English, Dutch, Spanish, French or Italian.

Offering city bus tours and/or trips focused on bullfights, flamenco and so on, as well as tours of Toledo, Ávila, Segovia and other towns around Madrid, are **Juliá Travel** (91 559 96 05, www.juliatravel.com) and **Trapsatur** (91 542 66 66, www.trapsatur.com). **Madrid City Tour** (902 02 47 58) is a city-owned tour bus service with two routes. You can purchase tickets online, by phone, at the Madrid City Tour information office next to the Prado, at the tourist office, or through Juliá Travel (*see above*).

Callos

Eating & Drinking

Not so long ago dishes from Asturias were thought exotic here in the capital. But today, thanks in no small part to immigration, *madrileños* have become Spain's unlikely flag-bearers for culinary globalisation. Mexican, of course, has been around for a long time, and Asian food now features strongly too. Add in Italian, French, Cuban, Middle Eastern, Thai and Japanese, and you start to wonder about the future of paella. Whereas the dining scene used to be all red-checked tablecloths or old-style elegance, now those who fancy chic and minimal have a place to go. Finally, vegetarians can smile too – the options are no longer limited to tortilla or green beans with the ham picked out.

❤ **Shortlist**

Best restaurants
Ribeira do Miño *p121*
Sacha *p161*
El Sobrino de Botín *p71*
TriCiclo *p99*

Best tapas bars
Casa Alberto *p99*
Casa Labra *p88*
José Luis *p150*
Juanalaloca *p80*
La Taberna de Antonio
Sánchez *p112*
Taberna Matritum *p80*

Best cocktail bars
Hemingway *p89*
Museo Chicote *p89*
Salmón Guru *p103*

Best breakfast
Café Gijón *p150*
Los Chuchis *p113*
La Mallorquina *p89*
Meat *p121*

Best desserts
La Casa de las Torrijas *p88*
Chocolatería San Ginés *p73*

Capital mainstays

The famous *cocido madrileño* – a stew of various bits of meat, offal and vegetables served up in three courses – is still eaten religiously, particularly at weekends. The down-home *casas de comida* (eating houses) are packed daily with regulars who are perfectly happy with a plain *ensalada mixta* followed by a greasy pork chop and the ubiquitous *flan* for dessert. Even young hipsters are faithful to the less expensive classic *mesones* (old-style taverns), while the most upscale traditional places still require you to join a waiting list.

Most traditional *madrileño* cuisine is found in the area around Los Austrias and La Latina – particularly along C/Cava Baja, leading south from the Plaza Mayor. Chueca and Huertas are packed with stylish restaurants offering both international and Spanish cuisine (many of which offer great value at lunchtime). The city's most upmarket restaurants can be found in the Salamanca area.

Timing & prices

Rule number one for visitors to Madrid: don't go out too early. *Madrileños* rarely eat lunch before 2pm. Consequently, dinner is usually eaten late as well –

around 10pm, and even later in summer. It's advisable to book a table in most places for Friday and Saturday nights, and at other times if you're in a big group. Many restaurants close on Sunday evening and all day Monday. August is livelier than it used to be, but most restaurants still close for at least two weeks. Where possible, we've indicated this, but it's best to ring and check.

While the *menú del día* is aimed at workers looking for a cheap three-course lunch, the concept also works well for hungry tourists after a morning's sightseeing. It can be a great way to eat cheaply and well, and usually consists of a starter, main course, dessert, bread and wine. Dishes cost much less than they would do à la carte (although portions tend to be smaller) and the *menú del día* also provides a chance to sample upmarket places on a budget. Standard Spanish restaurants tend to offer typical *comida casera* (home cooking), though, so don't expect fireworks. The *menú del día* should not be confused with the *menú degustación*, a tasting menu.

Tipping is something of a grey area – around five per cent is a reasonable rule of thumb. In a bar you'd just leave the small change given back to you, while in restaurants, a couple of euros will suffice – though don't be shy about tipping more if you're impressed.

Casa Alberto

In the know
Price categories

All our restaurant listings are marked with a euro symbol category, indicating the price you should expect to pay for a standard main course. The final bill will of course depend on the number of courses and drinks consumed.

€ = under €10

€€ = €10-€20

€€€ = €20-€30

€€€€ = over €30

Tapas tips

In their more fanciful moments, Spaniards will describe them as 'the world on a plate'. They will tell you that the eating of tapas is proof of the country's gregarious nature, its need to share and the importance it places on spending time in good company. Thanks to the *tapa*, it's possible to spend the whole night in a bar without requiring help to get home. This is the point so often missed by those outside the country, those who reproduce them for dinner parties or nibble them in expensive restaurants in London. For the Spanish, it's not about what you eat, it's about how you eat.

Tapas vary from region to region, and examples of most can be found in Madrid. Galician bars highlight octopus, prawns and seafood, served in ceramic bowls, traditionally with white Ribeiro wine. In Extremaduran bars you'll find *migas* (crumbs), fried and mixed with chorizo. Asturian bars specialise in *sidra* (cider), theatrically poured from above the head to separate out sediment, accompanied by blood sausage (*morcilla*) or blue cabrales cheese.

Andalucían bars offer dry fino sherry with *mojama* (dry-cured tuna) or sardines. Madrid's own specialities are *patatas bravas*, offal (particularly *callos*, tripe), and snails in a hot sauce.

Tapas have become more sophisticated and consequently more expensive in recent times, and an evening's *tapeo* can cost more than a full meal in a restaurant.

What to drink

A *café con leche* is a largeish milky coffee. An espresso is a *café solo*; the same with a dash of milk is *un cortado*, while *un americano* is black, diluted with twice the normal amount of water. A *carajillo* is usually a *solo* with a shot of *coñac*, and you can equally ask for a *carajillo de whisky*, *de ron* (rum), *de Bailey's* (pronounced 'bye-lees'), *de anís* or anything else you fancy. Decaffeinated coffee is *descafeinado*, and you will normally be asked if you want it from a sachet (*de sobre*) or the machine (*de máquina*). In summer, a great alternative is *café con hielo* – iced coffee.

Tea in bars is usually awful and, unless you specifically request otherwise, will often come as a glass of hot milk with a teabag on the side. Very popular, however, are herbal teas (*infusiones*), such as *menta* (mint) or *manzanilla* (camomile). Hot chocolate is also popular and comes thick as tar, all the better for dipping *churros*, deep-fried batter sticks.

Draught beer is served in *cañas*, a small measure that varies but is less than half a pint.

Museo Chicote

In the know
Local etiquette

To attract a waiter's attention, try a firm, but questioning, '*oiga*' (literally, 'hear me', a perfectly polite way of attracting someone's attention). Once you've got him/her, ask '¿*Me pones un...?*' ('Could you bring me a...?').

Food Glossary

Understanding the menu

Basics

Primer plato (**entrante**) first course; **segundo plato** second or main course; **postre** dessert; **plato combinado** quick, one-course meal, with several ingredients served on the same plate; **aceite y vinagre** oil and vinegar; **agua** water (**con gas/sin gas** fizzy/still); **pan** bread; **vino** wine (**tinto** red, **blanco** white, **rosado** rosé); **cerveza** beer; **la cuenta** the bill; **servicio incluído** service included; **propina** tip.

Cooking styles and techniques

Adobado marinated; **al ajillo** with olive oil and garlic; **al chilindrón** (usually chicken or lamb) cooked in a spicy tomato, pepper, ham, onion and garlic sauce; **a la marinera** (fish or shellfish) cooked with garlic, onions and white wine; **a la parrilla** charcoal-grilled; **al pil-pil** (Basque) flash-fried in sizzling oil and garlic; **a la plancha** grilled directly on a hot metal plate; **al vapor** steamed; **asado** (**al horno de leña**) roast (in a wood-fired oven); **crudo** raw; **en salsa** in a sauce or gravy; **escabechado, en escabeche** marinated in vinegar with bay leaves and garlic; **estofado** braised; **frito** fried; **guisado** stewed; **hervido** boiled; (**en**) **pepitoria** casserole dish, usually of chicken or game, with egg, wine and almonds; **relleno** stuffed.

Sopas y potajes (soups and stews)

Caldo (**gallego**) broth of pork and greens; **fabada** rich Asturian stew of beans, chorizo and *morcilla* (black blood sausage); **gazpacho** cold soup, usually of tomatoes, red pepper and cucumber; **purrusalda** (Basque) soup of salt cod, leeks and potatoes; **sopa de ajo** garlic soup; **sopa castellana** garlic soup with poached egg and chickpeas; **sopa de fideos** noodle soup.

Huevos (eggs)

Huevos fritos fried eggs (sometimes served with chorizo); **revuelto** scrambled eggs; **tortilla asturiana** omelette with tomato, tuna and onion; **tortilla francesa** plain omelette; **tortilla de patatas** Spanish potato omelette.

Pescado y mariscos (fish & shellfish)

Almejas clams; **atún, bonito** tuna; **bacalao** salt cod; **besugo** sea bream; **bogavante** lobster; **caballa** mackerel; **calamares** squid; **camarones** small shrimps; **cangrejo, buey de mar** crab; **cangrejo de río** freshwater crayfish; **dorada** gilthead bream; **gambas** prawns; **kokotxas** (Basque) hake cheeks; **langosta** spiny lobster; **langostinos** langoustines; **lubina** sea bass; **mejillones** mussels; **mero** grouper; **merluza** hake; **ostras** oysters; **pescadilla** whiting; **pescaditos** whitebait; **pulpo** octopus; **rape** monkfish; **rodaballo** turbot; **salmonete** red mullet; **sardinas** sardines; **sepia** cuttlefish; **trucha** trout; **ventresca de bonito** tuna fillet; **vieiras** scallops.

Carne, aves, caza y embutidos (meat, poultry, game & charcuterie)

Bistec steak; **buey, vacuno** (cuts: **solomillo, entrecot**) beef; **butifarra** Catalan sausage; **callos** tripe; **capón** capon; **cerdo** pork, pig; **chorizo** spicy sausage, served cooked or cold; **choto** kid; **chuletas, chuletones, chuletillas** chops; **cochinillo** roast suckling pig; **cocido** traditional stew of Madrid; **codillo** knuckle (normally ham); **codornices** quails; **conejo** rabbit; **cordero** lamb; **costillas** ribs; **estofado de ternera** beef stew; **faisán** pheasant; **gallina** chicken; **hígado** liver; **jabalí** wild boar; **jamón ibérico** cured ham from Iberian pigs; **jamón serrano** cured ham; **jamón york** cooked ham; **lacón** gammon ham; **lechazo, cordero lechal** milk-fed baby lamb; **liebre** hare; **lomo (de cerdo)** loin of pork; **morcilla** black blood sausage; **pato** duck; **pavo** turkey; **perdiz** partridge; **pollo** chicken; **riñones** kidneys; **salchichas** frying sausages; **sesos** brains; **ternera** veal (in Spain it is slaughtered much later than most veal, so is more accurately young beef).

Arroz y legumbres (rice & pulses)
Alubias, judías white beans; **arroz a banda** rice cooked in shellfish stock; **arroz negro** black rice cooked in squid ink; **fideuà** seafood dish similar to a paella, but made with noodles instead of rice; **fríjoles** red kidney beans; **garbanzos** chickpeas; **judiones** large haricot beans; **lentejas** lentils; **pochas (caparrones)** new-season kidney beans.

Verduras (vegetables)
Acelgas Swiss chard; **alcachofas** artichokes; **berenjena** aubergine/eggplant; **calabacines** courgettes/zucchini; **cebolla** onion; **champiñones** mushrooms; **col** cabbage; **ensalada mixta** basic salad of lettuce, tomato and onion; **ensalada verde** green salad, without tomato; **espárragos** asparagus; **espinacas** spinach; **grelos** turnip leaves; **guisantes** peas; **habas** broad beans; **judías verdes** green beans; **lechuga** lettuce; **menestra** braised mixed vegetables; **patatas fritas** chips; **pepino** cucumber; **pimientos** sweet peppers; **pimientos de piquillo** slightly hot red peppers; **pisto** mixture of cooked vegetables, similar to ratatouille; **setas** oyster mushrooms; **tomate** tomato; **zanahoria** carrot.

Fruta (fruit)
Arándanos cranberries, blueberries, redcurrants or blackcurrants; **cerezas** cherries; **ciruelas** plums; **fresas** strawberries; **higos** figs; **macedonia** fruit salad; **manzana** apple; **melocotón** peach; **melón** melon; **moras** blackberries; **naranja** orange; **pera** pear; **piña** pineapple; **plátano** banana; **sandía** watermelon; **uvas** grapes.

Postres (desserts)
Arroz con leche rice pudding; **bizcocho** sponge cake; **brazo de gitano** swiss roll; **cuajada** junket (served with honey); **flan** crème caramel; **helado** ice-cream; **leche frita** custard fried in breadcrumbs; **membrillo** quince jelly (often served with cheese); **tarta** cake; **tarta de Santiago** sponge-like almond cake; **torrijas** sweet bread fritters.

Quesos (cheeses)
Burgos, **villalón**, **requesón** white, cottage-like cheeses, often eaten as dessert; **cabrales** strong blue Asturian goat's cheese; **idiazábal** Basque sheep's milk cheese; **mahón** cow's milk cheese from Menorca; **manchego (tierno, añejo, semi, seco)** hard sheep's-milk cheese (young, mature, semi-soft, dry); **tetilla** soft cow's milk cheese; **torta del casar** tangy sheep's milk cheese from Extremadura.

Octopus and mussels

Some places even serve *pintas* (pints), often in a *jarra*, a large, heavy glass with a handle – but be warned that Spanish lagers are usually strong. Spain produces some good-quality beers. In Madrid, the favourite is the local Mahou, with two basic varieties – green label Mahou Clásica and stronger red label Cinco Estrellas. San Miguel is less common, while Andalucían favourite Cruzcampo is growing in popularity. A darker Mahou beer (*negra*) is also available. Shandy is *clara*, and is made with bitter lemon. Imported beers are now common, too, and craft beers can be found in many bars around town.

All bars have a sturdy, cheap red wine (*tinto*) on offer, and usually there's a white (*blanco*) and a rosé as well (*rosado*). Madrid's traditional summer drink is *tinto de verano* (red in a tall glass over ice, with a slice of lemon and topped up with lemonade).

Low- and alcohol-free beers (Laiker, Buckler, Kaliber) have an important niche in the market; other favourites for non-alcohol drinkers are the Campari-like but booze-free Bitter Kas, and plain tonic (*una tónica*) with ice and lemon. Fresh orange juice, *zumo de naranja*, is often available. Mineral water (*agua mineral*) can be ordered anywhere, either sparkling (*con gas*) or still (*sin gas*).

La Taberna de Antonio Sánchez *p112*

Shopping

The high streets of Madrid have undeniably taken on the identikit look of most European capitals, albeit with Spanish chains – Zara, Mango, Bershka – proliferating; but get off those thoroughfares and what strikes you is the curious mix of the traditional and the new. Here the chains and international franchises rub shoulders with museum-piece, family-run businesses and ancient shops dedicated to just one product – espadrilles, maybe, or Spanish ceramics.

Visitors from cities with cutting-edge fashion scenes, such as London, New York and Berlin, are sometimes disappointed by Madrid's clothes shops; however, the scattering of independent boutiques that have opened around Malasaña, Conde Duque and Alonso Martínez is starting to raise consumer expectations.

❤ **Shortlist**

Best bookshops
J&J Books & Coffee *p131*
Ocho y Medio *p125*

Best for fashion
Agatha Ruiz de la Prada *p151*
La Antigua *p131*
Antigua Casa Crespo *p131*
Custo Barcelona *p123*
¡Oh, qué Luna! *p152*

Best accessories
Guantes Luque *p90*
Taller Puntera *p74*

Best for crafts and gifts
Antigua Casa Talavera *p89*
Popland *p131*

Best food and drink
Cacao Sampaka *p123*
Lavinia *p152*
Mantequerías Bravo *p152*
El Riojano *p74*

Best souvenirs
Casa de Diego *p89*
Museo del Prado *p142*

Where to shop

Madrid isn't a large city, and its main shopping
areas break down into several distinctive zones, all
conveniently within walking distance – or a short metro
ride – of one another. A short walk from the Puerta del
Sol, C/Preciados and C/Carmen are always bustling
with shoppers, and offer a mix of chains and smaller
stores selling cheap and mid-price clothes, shoes and
accessories. Several branches of **El Corte Inglés** are in
this area. Gran Vía itself is given over to the flagship
stores of many a household name, like **Zara**, the **Nike
Store** and many more.

After battling through the crowds of dawdling
shoppers on the Gran Vía, the tranquil area of Los
Austrias comes as a welcome respite, with its musical
instrument stores, bohemian gift shops and troves
of decorative items. Chueca houses a host of hip
independents, such as **Bunkha** (*see p131*), **Isolée** (C/
Infantas 19, 91 522 81 38, www.isolee.com) and bookshop
Panta Rhei (C/Hernán Cortés 7, 91 319 89 02, www.panta-
rhei.es), as well as the youth-orientated brands of C/
Fuencarral (home to **Diesel** and **Puma**, as well as Spanish

brand **Hoss Intropia**). Also on C/Fuencarral are branches of upmarket international cosmetics and skincare brands, such as **MAC** and **Kiehls**.

For shoes, head down C/Augusto Figueroa, and then continue north up C/Barquillo for the more refined fashion boutiques, most of which are squeezed into the area between C/Argensola and Plaza Santa Barbara.

West of here, the trendy triangle called triBall – just west of where C/Fuencarral meets Gran Vía – and the area around C/Conde Duque are now home to some of the city's most interesting boutiques.

If you're all about labels, then Salamanca is the place to be, in particular C/Serrano, where on the same block you will find **Loewe**, **Yves Saint Laurent** and **La Perla**, as well as smaller designer boutiques throughout the area. Lots of upmarket, specialist antique dealers can be found on and around C/Claudio Coello.

Loewe, Calle de Serrano

The Rastro

Market day

Madrid's markets are a noisy, colourful way to stock up on cheap food – and to get close to the locals. They offer a vast range of fruit and veg, meat, fish, cheese, charcuterie and offal. Markets are usually open from around 9am to 2pm and 5 to 8pm during the week, and 9am to 2pm on Saturdays.

The city's biggest flea market, the **Rastro** (*see p111*) is an obligatory visit, but more for the atmosphere than the goods – you will almost certainly walk away empty-handed.

Some markets are now better known for their eating options than their fresh produce, including the atmospheric **Mercado de San Miguel** (*see p72*) in Los Austrias, with its gourmet specialists, and the **Mercado de San Antón** (*see p122*) gastro

In the know
End of the line

Spaniards do queue (although it may not look like it) – just ask '*¿Quién es el último/la última?*' ('Who's last in the queue?') before joining.

Cuesta de Moyano *p134*

market in Chueca. To sample more delicacies, head along to **Magerit**, stand no.20/21 in **La Cebada** market in the Plaza de la Cebada in La Latina – it's an excellent place to buy cheese. For olives of all varieties, **Fillanas**, stalls no. 33-44 in the **Mercado de Chamberí** (www.mercadodechamberi.es, C/Alonso Cano 10), is a good bet.

Back to basics

Opening times are changing, as is the traditional August break. While smaller stores will still close for two or three hours at lunch and stay shut on Saturday afternoons, some mid-size and nearly all large outlets will remain open all day. If you have yet to get used to a 2pm lunch and can face the heat in the summer, head to the bigger stores in the early afternoon and you will miss the crowds. Pressure from large retailers brought about a relaxation of the laws on Sunday opening too, all amid much grumbling from small businesses, who find it very hard to compete with such timetables.

> **In the know**
> **Supermarkets**
>
> Hypermarkets are mostly to be found on the main roads around the edge of the city, and are mainly accessible only by car. If you're mobile and need to stock up, look for ads for **Alcampo**, **Carrefour** or **Hipercor**. Many branches of **El Corte Inglés** also have (pricey) supermarkets. For information on Sunday opening, *see p180*. In town, keep your eye out for branches of **Carrefour Express** (www.carrefour.es), **Mercadona** (www.mercadona.es) and **Lidl** (www.lidl.es).

As a result, large retailers can – and do – open every first Sunday of the month. As revenue from tourists becomes more vital to the shopkeepers of Madrid, August is no longer a month when the city closes down.

Sales are usually on through January and February, and then in July and August. Non-EU residents can claim refund cheques for purchases over the value of €90.16. The VAT can be reclaimed at the **Global Blue** (www.globalblue.com) offices in C/Claudio Coello, Western Union on Gran Vía, Exact Exchange in Puerta del Sol, and Barajas airport terminals 1, 2 and 4. Look out for the Tax-Free sticker in the window of participating outlets.

In the know
Museum shops

Madrid's 'Paseo del Arte' museums all have excellent bookshops and souvenir shops. The shop in **Reina Sofía** (see p108) is particularly good for books, while the **Prado** (see p142) is great for a Hieronymous Bosch t-shirt or Goya notebook. The **CaixaForum** cultural centre (see p139) is great for quirky gifts and useful gadgets.

Madrid al Cubo

Entertainment

Madrid's cultural clout has steadily increased in recent years, with the city finally shaking off a reputation for producing stuffy composers, mainstream theatre and a reactionary public. Gran Vía is littered with Broadway and West End hand-me-downs – Spain's fervent passion for the blockbuster musical has not wavered – but little theatres soldier on in the face of local government and city council limits on licences and funds.

While the pace of Madrid's nightlife scene may have slowed down somewhat from its early noughties heyday, *madrileños* still party harder – and later – than most. And they do so in spite of interference from the local council, which fails to see the value of the capital's after-dark antics, though that gives the whole scene an underground feel. Many Madrid clubs double up as gig venues too,

Best for night owls
Medias Puri *p114*
Teatro Kapital *p104*

Best classical music venues
Teatro Real *p76*
Teatro de la Zarzuela *p92*

Best flamenco
Café de Chinitas *p90*
Cardamomo *p104*
Casa Patas *p114*

Best live music
Café Central *p104*
La Riviera *p162*
El Sol *p92*
Terraza Atenas *p77*

Best theatre
Teatro Español *p104*

Best LGBT spots
Escape *p123*
Gymage *p129*

giving much-needed space to the city's up-and-coming bands. Its LGBT scene is also legendary, with the *barrio* of Chueca as its dazzling, rainbow-hued epicentre.

Classical music & opera

Traditionally, the scene orbits around three main venues: the modern and austere (and arguably best-quality classical venue in Europe) **Auditorio Nacional de Música**; the grand hosting opera; and the **Teatro de la Zarzuela** for a decent selection of classical concerts (as well as for *zarzuela*, Madrid's traditional operetta art form).

Zarzuela – Spain's early answer to Italian opera, but shorter and funnier and incorporating elements of theatre, slapstick and dance – is an ineffable part of *madrileño* culture, though tricky for the outsider to get a grip on. It's full of local jokes (usually rhyming and rattled off at speed) and traditional songs with which the public will sing along, so be prepared. Catch it in its home ground of the Teatro de la Zarzuela, in the Centro Cultural de la Villa in July or August, or at a summer open-air performance.

Theatre & dance

Look beyond the heavyweights, such as the **Teatro Español** and the **Teatro María Guerrero**, and you'll find that Madrid has an active fringe scene, with the key players being the **Teatro del Barrio** and **Cuarta Pared**, the oldest of the *salas alternativas*. Other theatres to look for include **Teatro Cofidis Alcázar** (C/Alcalá 20, 91 532 06 16, www.teatrocofidis. com), **Teatro Caser Calderón** (C/Atocha 18, 91 429 40 85 teatrocalderon.com), and **Teatro Lara** (Corredera Baja de San Pablo 15, 91 523 90 27, www.teatrolara.com) for family entertainment along with other shows.

Three major dance companies are based in Madrid: the contemporary, but far from radical, **Compañía Nacional de Danza**; the state **Ballet Nacional de España**, which specialises in Spanish styles of dance; and **Victor Ullate Ballet – Comunidad de Madrid**.

As ever, contemporary dance teeters on an economic knife-edge, but spaces such as the **Teatro Pradillo** (C/Pradillo 12, Chamartín, 91 416 90 11, www.teatropradillo. com) continue to show good work. Among the main

Teatro Español

Corral de la Morería p74

contemporary dance companies are **Provisional Danza** (www.provisionaldanza.com), one of the pioneers of contemporary dance in Spain since 1987. It's also worth noting that the **Teatro Real** (*see p76*) often stages dance productions, notably with the Ballet Nacional de España and the Compañía Nacional de Danza.

Flamenco

The most authentic flamenco inhabits a closed world and is proud of it; but if you know where to go and are lucky on the night, you might be granted a peek. Where people are most likely to see flamenco, though, is at a *tablao*, of which there are several in Madrid; below is a selection of those with more genuine performances. As well as the show, you can dine or just drink; both are

In the know
Flamenco tours

It's very easy to catch bad flamenco as a tourist, and the help of an insider is invaluable. Passionate enthusiast Yoly Martín makes a great guide, bursting with knowledge and the low-down on where to rub elbows with performers and where to catch the most authentic (and often underground) experiences. Book one of her tours and read her blog on www.theflamencoguide.com.

appallingly expensive, but if you stay until closing you may get your money's worth. The fun really starts around midnight, when most tourists go off to bed and the major artists appear; until then you may just get the kitsch jollity of the *cuadro de la casa* (the house musicians and dancers). Flamenco purists are notoriously snobbish about what's on offer in Madrid, but even they are thrilled by the performances at **Casa Patas**, where guitarists are skilled, dancers ooze power and grace, and singers are as they should be – bloody terrifying.

Seasons & festivals

The **Festival de Otoño a Primavera** (*see p63*) is the biggest event for theatre, dance and puppetry, attracting major international names and sometimes putting on shows in English. The summer **Veranos de la Villa** (*see p61*) offers even more outdoor performances, or for a trip out of town, don't miss the **Festival Internacional de Teatro Clásico** (call 91 521 07 20 or visit festivaldealmagro.com for details) in Almagro every July. The event pays tribute to Lope de Vega, Molière, Shakespeare et al with plays, workshops and street performances. FITEC, the **Festival Internacional de Teatro de Calle** (91 601 83 23, festivalfitec.com), features

In the know
The price is right

Monday and Wednesday are often *días del espectador* ('spectator days'), offering special discounts, though every cinema has its own policy on price reductions.

Teatro Kapital p104

street art, music, theatre and dance in the Getafe suburb. The **Madrid en Danza** festival, held for three weeks in November and December, is one of the most prestigious Spanish dance events, and attracts outstanding national and international performers.

Nightlife

Nightlife here has distinct stages. In the early evening, from 6pm until midnight, teenagers take to the streets. Most of them congregate in parks and squares, and engage in what is known as the *botellón*.

At around 11pm, a more mature crowd starts to spill out of the restaurants and hits the bars. Generally, bars break down into a few distinct categories. *Bares de copas* sell spirit-based drinks with or without a DJ in the corner. Next come the *discobares*, which may require a cover charge and bang out international and Spanish pop, perfect for their alcohol-fuelled clientele. Then there are the funkier pre-club bars, often with a house DJ warming you up for a night on the town. City legislation says that bars must close at around 3am: precisely the moment when the clubs or *discotecas* start to fill up. (*Discoteca* carries no cheesy connotations in Spanish; in fact, be

Ocho y Medio DJs *p125*

careful what you ask for when talking to locals – *club* in Spanish usually means brothel.)

The late-night clubs start closing their doors at around 6am, but the night's still not over. Plenty of clubbers spill out into what are commonly referred to as 'old men's bars' for a few early morning beers, before finally staggering home. But those with energy to burn seek out the after-hours bars (*los afters*). There aren't as many as there used to be, but they are out there; you just need to ask around.

Apart from the **Palacio de Deportes** (Av. Felipe II, 91 444 99 49, www.wizinkcenter.es), concert venues are mostly small, intimate affairs in the centre of the city, with bigger acts usually requiring a trip out to the suburbs. Venues listed don't charge admission unless otherwise stated. These days, smaller bands

In the know
Price to party

The ticket you're given on the door of a club is almost always valid for a drink, so don't toss it away. Spain has recently seen a hike in prices across the board and some of the swankier clubs will charge you as much as €15 for a long drink, and €10 for a beer. Remember, though, measures for long drinks are huge, so if you're on a tight budget, stick to the rum and Coke. Before you head out, it's also worth checking club websites for printable flyers or guest lists that'll get you in for a discount.

usually pay to play in venues, with the take on the door going directly to them – along with a cut of the bar take, too, if they're lucky. Few venues accept credit cards on the door, although many will at the bar. To make licensing issues easier, a lot of listed venues stay open as nightclubs after the concerts.

LGBT Madrid

The throbbing heart of the LGBT scene (*el ambiente*) is the Plaza de Chueca. Tightly packed around what is an otherwise nondescript square in the centre of town, the dazzling array of bars and services are aimed almost exclusively at one of Madrid's most vociferous and dynamic communities. With bars, cafés, hotels, saunas, travel agencies and bookshops, the formerly run-down neighbourhood has emerged as one of the city's liveliest and trendiest areas. But Chueca has become, perhaps, a victim of its own success, because in recent years its hip hangouts have started attracting a non-gay crowd. Now, many want their ghetto back, at least for cruising, and plenty of shag-and-go male-only bars have popped up all over the place. Special events aimed at specific subcultures are a growth industry, too: there are camping weekends for bears in the nearby mountains, an action-packed 'Sleazy Madrid' long weekend every spring, plus lesbian raves with dyke-y darkrooms, body-shaving bashes and sloppy mud parties.

In the know
Information and tickets

Check venue websites for current and future seasons, as well as any last-minute changes or cancellations. You can pick up leaflets from most venues or check the **Guía del Ocio**, or a listings supplement such as *La Luna de Metropolí*, which comes out Fridays with the *El Mundo* newspaper. Tickets can usually be purchased over the phone, via the venue website or from **Ticketea** (www.ticketea.com) or **Ticketmaster** (902 150 025, www. ticketmaster.es). Tickets for state-run venues such as the Auditorio Nacional de Música and Teatro de la Zarzuela are sold at the venue box offices, online at www.entradasinaem. es or by phone (902 22 49 49).

Madrid
Day by Day

Paseo del Prado

Itineraries

For such a grand and sprawling city, Madrid is surprisingly quick and easy to get around, and many of the following routes can be covered on foot. Some of its museums and churches merit a couple of hours' lingering, however, and the seductive bars and restaurants can be hard to leave. These itineraries should be seen as ideas only – sometimes the city itself calls the shots.

▶ *Budgets include transport, meals and admission prices, but not accommodation and shopping.*

ESSENTIAL WEEKEND

Budget €340 for two (€325 with the Paseo del Arte ticket, *p22*)
Getting around Walking

DAY 1

Morning

Start the day in the **Puerta del Sol** (*see p81*), Madrid's official centre, by enjoying a coffee and a pastry in **La Mallorquina** (*see p89*) – something of a Madrid institution.

Head south-east down the Carrera de San Jerónimo until you reach the **Paseo del Prado**. Madrid's three world-famous art museums – the Thyssen, the Prado and the Reina Sofía – are all in the vicinity, but we don't suggest you try to tackle them all. The **Museo Nacional del Prado** (*see p142*), based on Spain's royal collections, is the absolute don't-miss. Buy a ticket from the machine outside to skip the queues, and head to the Goya rooms. Other highlights include Bosch's *Garden of Earthly Delights* and Velázquez's *Las Meninas*.

Museo Nacional del Prado

CaixaForum Madrid

Afternoon

Estado Puro (*see p99*), not far from the Prado, is a good bet if you're looking for local cuisine in a chic space. Then enjoy a post-meal stroll south down the Paseo, taking in the façade of the **CaixaForum Madrid** (*see p139*) on the right – its vertical garden is now one of the most photographed spots in town.

After a morning of culture, you might like to enjoy some of Madrid's green highlights; the restful **Jardín Botánico** (*see p140*) lies just off the Paseo del Prado, while the **Retiro** park (*see p136*), with its shady avenues, is reached via the pedestrianised **Cuesta de Moyano** (*see p134*), lined with high-quality second-hand book stalls.

Taller Puntera

DAY 2

Morning

Environmentally minded mayor Manuela Carmena is changing the face of Madrid and nowhere is this more apparent than in **Gran Vía**, with its newly pedestrianised status. Strolling down here, you can now properly appreciate the grandiose architecture, little changed over the decades and beloved of various film directors. Head east until it merges with C/Alcalá, at the spectacular **Edificio Metrópolis**, and cross the road to the elegant **Círculo de Bellas Artes** (*see p84*) for coffee. Suitably fuelled, walk a couple of blocks south to the **Museo Thyssen-Bornemisza** (*see p96*) for a morning walking among artistic treasures from almost every major movement.

Evening

After a few hours relaxing in the park, head north-west to the historic *barrio* of Los Austrias. In Madrid, afternoon shopping hours are 4pm to around 9pm, and in Plaza del Conde de Barajas, near the Plaza Mayor, you'll find **Taller Puntera** (*see p74*), Madrid's best shop for artisan leather products. After flexing the credit card, head round the corner to the **Mercado de San Miguel** (*see p72*) for some upmarket tapas – it's a great spot to witness *madrileños* doing what they do best: enjoying food and drink in sociable surroundings.

Círculo de Bellas Artes

Salmón Guru

Museo Nacional Centro de Arte Reina Sofía

Sociedad Cervantina

Afternoon

The area just south-west of here has seen a recent explosion in cool, independent bistros, particularly in the streets around C/Huertas. The best might just be **TriCiclo** (see p99), or – if it's full – its little sister **Tandem** (see p99), down the road. This was the favoured *barrio* of Madrid's men of letters during Spain's Golden Age of literature, and you might want to visit one of its quirky little sights, such as the **Sociedad Cervantina** printing press (see p100), where the first edition of *Don Quixote* was created. Alternatively, and depending on energy levels, you could walk down to the city's third art palace, the **Reina Sofía** (see p108).

Evening

Bars and restaurants around the Reina Sofía are largely aimed at the sightseeing public, but if you head back up to C/Huertas, you will eventually arrive at the elegant Plaza Santa Ana, ringed with café terraces. To walk in Hemingway's footsteps, have a beer at his old haunt, the **Cervecería Alemana** (see p102) and follow it up with a light supper at lively **Ana La Santa** (see p98) on the same square. The area also lays claim to Madrid's new, coolest cocktail joint, **Salmón Guru** (see p103), the ideal spot for the final nightcap.

BUDGET BREAK

Budget €55 for two
Getting around Walking

Morning

Malasaña was the focus of the post-Franco counter-cultural movement known as **La Movida Madrileña**. Although the movement is well and truly over, the neighbourhood retains an atmospheric, grungy feel, with boho cafés and music-led bars. Soak up the vibe with a late breakfast at **Levadura Madre** (*C/Pez 1, 91 058 65 68, www. levaduramadre. es*) or **Lolina Vintage Café** (*see p130*).

After fuelling up for the day ahead, take a wander around the neighbourhood's laid-back streets. Some of Madrid's best small shops are to be found in this area, including **J&J Books & Coffee** (*see p131*) and espadrilles-specialist **Antigua Casa Crespo** (*see p131*). The area is home to the **Centro Cultural Conde Duque** (*see p126*) – both the building and the contemporary art museum within it) are worth a visit – and the newly renovated **Museo de Historia** (*see p120*), which, like all municipally run museums, is free to enter.

Centro Cultural Conde Duque

Afternoon

Although there are plenty of good restaurants in Malasaña, to get a sense of the distinctness of Madrid's different neighbourhoods, cross over Calle de Fuencarral into Chueca for lunch. The famously gay *barrio* has several good, and chic, restaurants, but if money is an object, try the ineffable **Tienda de Vinos** (also known as El Comunista, *see p121*), for cheap and cheerful Spanish grub in an unbeatably old-school atmosphere.

After a leisurely lunch, you'll have time to explore more of Madrid's *barrios*. The city's compact size means that its central neighbourhoods are all within walking distance. Head south of Gran Vía, through the Puerta del Sol, until you reach Lavapiés, the city's most multicultural *barrio*. It begins at the spruced-up **Plaza Tirso de Molina** (*see p106*).

Evening

A stroll through Lavapiés brings you to Calle de Santa Isabel, home to Madrid's national film theatre in the art nouveau **Cine Doré** (*see p114*). The place has featured in films by Pedro Almodóvar, a key Movida figure, and its café is a lively meeting spot for film buffs before a cheap (€2.50) screening – perhaps of a silent movie, or a classic from the national archives.

On the same street as the Cine Doré lies one of Madrid's best tapas bars, **La Musa de Espronceda** (*C/Santa Isabel 17, 91 539 12 84*), a great starting point for a bar crawl.

FAMILY DAY OUT

Budget €340 for two adults, two children
Getting around Cable car, walking

Morning

In Madrid, modes of transport can be as much fun for kids as the destinations themselves, and none provides as much exhilaration as the cable car, or **Teleférico** (*see p155*), to the **Casa de Campo** park (*see p155*), a spine-tingling ride over the tree tops. Once there, the Casa de Campo itself is a giant playground, with swimming pools, a zoo and play areas for little ones, but the main draw is the **Parque de Atracciones** funfair (*see p155*), which has some properly scary rides – along with some beautifully sedate ones.

Teleférico

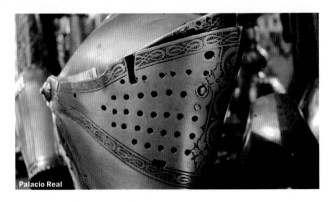

Palacio Real

Afternoon

Unless you've organised a picnic, eating options are fairly poor in the park, but the return trip on the cable car brings you close to **Casa Mingo** (*see p160*), a huge, noisy and family-friendly place, where chicken and chips is the order of the day. Stroll it off afterwards via the **Plaza de Oriente** (*see p67*) and head for the **Palacio Real** (*see p70*), loved by kids for its spectacular collection of armour. From here it's a five- to ten-minute walk to **Chocolatería San Ginés** (*see p73*), for a much-needed energy boost in the form of *churros* dipped in hot chocolate.

Evening

Fifty metres or so south of here is the stunning **Plaza Mayor** (*see p75*), a huge arcaded square where children can wander about, gazing at the human statues, buskers and hawkers until hunger strikes again. The square is a great place for parents to sip on a beer, meanwhile, but not really to eat – better to head south to any of the many tapas bars along C/Cava Baja or C/Cava Alta. Though *madrileños* wouldn't dream of eating before 9pm, most will be serving food well before that, and the earlier you go, the better chance of the little ones getting a seat.

Plaza Mayor

Diary

Practically all year round – apart from perhaps during the late winter lull (when everybody is worn out and broke from Christmas, New Year and Reyes celebrations) and at the end of summer – anyone coming to the Spanish capital is likely to encounter some sort of arts festival, music festival, *fiesta* or themed film season.

Events and festivals that receive official sponsorship come under the aegis of either the Ayuntamiento (city council) or the Comunidad de Madrid (regional government), and the influence of politics, inevitably, is felt in culture. Other events, such as the annual photographic extravaganza PHotoEspaña, are independent and still more are semi-independent, functioning with a mix of public and private money.

Spring

A Madrid spring can be unpredictable, weather-wise – bring clothes for all eventualities – but at its best will be warm, with blue skies. **Easter** week can be very busy (and hotel prices astronomical), and April normally sees some rain, though this rarely lasts long. The grand event of the season is the festival of **San Isidro** (*see p59*) in mid May, in which the entire city spills out on to the streets.

Mar-Apr Festival de Arte Sacro
www.madrid.org
This two-month festival of music, dance, theatre, poetry, movies and conferences focuses on the role of religion in art, music, dance and film through the centuries.

8 Mar Día de la Mujer/ Semana de la Mujer
International Women's Day is celebrated with a march through central Madrid (the route changes from year to year). Some of the many other related events taking place over the week include short film seasons and concerts.

Semana Santa

Mar Teatralia
www.madrid.org/teatralia
A regional jamboree of performing arts, including theatre, puppet shows, circus and dance, as well as workshops and other activities aimed at children and young people.

Mar/Apr Semana Santa (Holy Week)
www.esmadrid.com
Easter is usually a good time to be in Madrid, as many *madrileños* get out of town for the long weekend, and the weather can be fine. In Madrid and nearby towns there are many parish processions in which hooded *penitentes* schlep figures of Christ and the Virgin around. The most impressive one is considered to be Jesús Nazareño El Pobre from San Pedro El Viejo and around La Latina.

Late Apr-early May Dos de Mayo
www.somosmalasana.com
Commemorating the fateful day in 1808 when the people of Madrid rose up against Napoleon's occupying troops and paid for their audacity by being massacred, 2 May is now the region's official holiday and kick-starts a nearly continuous series of *fiestas* that go on throughout the rest of the spring and summer. Things get going in the Malasaña neighbourhood – named after the uprising's teenage heroine, Manuela Malasaña – in the Plaza Dos de Mayo.

Late Apr-early May Feria del Libro Antiguo y de Ocasión
www.feriadeprimavera.com
This antiquarian and second-hand book fair, spanning a week either side of the San Isidro weekend, has been held annually for more than 40 years. Here you may stumble across rare treasures, out-of-print editions or recent remainders. Don't expect much in English.

💙 San Isidro

Plaza Mayor, Los Austrias & all over Madrid (91 578 78 10 & 010, www.sanisidromadrid.com). **Date** *few days around 15 May.*

For a few days around 15 May, you can see *madrileños* doing what they do best: taking to the streets and having a rollicking good knees-up. The *fiestas* celebrate San Isidro, Madrid's patron saint, a humble 12th-century labourer and well-digger to whom all manner of miracles are attributed and whose wife, María de la Cabeza, was also canonised, making them the only sainted couple in history.

The action centres on the Plaza Mayor, where nightly gigs are held, including *zarzuela* performances and the odd classical concert. There is more music and dancing in Las Vistillas park; music, theatre, painting workshops and more are put on for kids at parks throughout Madrid. An associated event is the Feria de la Cacharrería, a ceramics market, held in the Plaza de las Comendadoras, close to Conde Duque. Also on offer is Documenta (*see p60*), a short season of international documentary films, and Universimad (universimad. org), a rock festival at the Pradera de San Isidro.

Throughout the week there are also numerous religious ceremonies in various churches. The 15th itself sees a procession of vintage cars in the Castellana. Possibly most fun of all is the traditional *romería* (pilgrimage) in and around the Ermita de San Isidro, in the park of the same name; families in traditional castizo garb, looking like something out of a Goya painting, drink from wine skins and stuff themselves with traditional *madrileño* delicacies such as chorizo, morcilla and other offal dishes.

1 May Fiesta del Trabajo (May Day)

The largest May Day march, attracting upwards of 60,000 people, is organised by the communist-led CCOO and the socialist UGT unions, which converge on Sol. Smaller in scale but quite animated is the anarcho-syndicalist CGT's march from Atocha to Plaza Jacinto Benavente. The anarchist purists CNT/AIT, meanwhile, march up C/Bravo Murillo from Cuatro Caminos. Many of the participants then head to the Casa de Campo where the UGT organises a lively party.

Early-mid May Documenta Madrid

www.documentamadrid.com
This popular international documentary film festival, which is organised by the Ayuntamiento de Madrid, celebrated its 14th year in 2017. It consists of screenings, workshops and related activities, in high-profile venues such as Matadero Madrid (also the festival's main office; *see p178*), Cine Doré (the Filmoteca; *see p114*) and cultural centres.

Summer

It used to the be case that Madrid was deserted in summer and hotels were practically giving away rooms, but this has changed in recent years with rising visitor numbers and more of a focus on summer activities (along with a huge increase in hotel swimming pools). It's still a good time for accommodation bargains, however, with even five-star rooms going for a song. The summer kicks off with the month-long **Suma Flamenca** festival (*see p60*) in May and June, followed by the wonderful, all-encompassing **Veranos de la Villa** (*see p61*), with its concerts, theatre, fireworks and outdoor movies. New music festival **Mad Cool** (*see p62*) in July is a must for indie fans.

May & June Suma Flamenca

www.madrid.org/sumaflamenca
The month-long Suma Flamenca is Madrid's high-profile flamenco festival, a feast of music, dance and intense emotion. Concert venues include Teatros del Canal (Sala Roja) and Pavón Cultural Kamikaze in Embajadores, plus a host of other buildings and theatres.

Late May-June La Feria del Libro (Book Fair)

www.ferialibromadrid.com
First celebrated in 1933, the Book Fair is now a major international event. Hundreds of publishers are present and well-known writers show up to sign copies of their works.

May-Aug PHotoEspaña

www.phe.es
Every spring/summer since 1998, PHotoEspaña has swept through Madrid's major museums and galleries, redefining the city as an international photography epicentre. In recent years, the retinue of photographic stars has included Anders Petersen, Karlheinz Weinberger, Adam Broomberg and Pierre Molinier. PHotoEspaña also puts on projections at the Real Jardín Botánico (*see p140*). As well as exhibitions, there are workshops, courses, talks and competitions related to photography and the visual arts.

9-13 June San Antonio de la Florida

One of the first of the summer's biggest street parties, these celebrations can trace their history back a very long way; 13 June is the feast day of San Antonio, the patron saint of seamstresses. Single women used to place 13 pins in the baptismal font of the hermitage. If one stuck to her finger she would marry within a year. The main party, including events for kids, takes place across the Paseo de la Florida, in the Parque de la Bombilla.

Late June-early July
LGBT Pride
www.orgullolgtb.org
One week of partying in Chueca, Madrid's gay neighbourhood, and a huge parade on the Saturday that runs from Puerta de Alcalá to Plaza de España. There's also film, theatre, exhibitions and other cultural activities.

Late June-early Sept
Veranos de la Villa
www.veranosdelavilla.com
As part of the 'Summers in the City' festival, a good selection of top names have appeared on the patio of the Centro Cultural Conde Duque, which acts as the festival's main stage. While the big names have been scaled down of late, you can still expect a range of decent acts. In 2017 these included Susana Baca and Bonnie Prince

LGBT Pride

Billy. Elsewhere, *zarzuelas* are programmed in both the Centro Cultural de la Villa and in the Sabatini Gardens, the 'Titirilandia' puppet season for kids takes place in the Retiro, while theatre productions may be seen outdoors beside the Muralla Árabe and in the Centro Cultural Galileo.

Early July-late Aug
Magnetic Terrace
www.lacasaencendida.es
Concerts and low-cost films are hosted outdoors on the rooftop terrace of the Casa Encendida cultural centre during its summer programme.

Mid July-mid Aug
Urban Beach Cinema
condeduquemadrid.es
Every summer, the Conde Duque Cultural Centre (*see p126*) organises the Urban Beach Cinema. It features outdoor film screenings, along with hammocks, a sandy fake 'beach', cafés, food trucks and weekend market stalls selling jewellery, clothes and homeware.

July-Sept Cibeles de Cine
sunsetcinema.es
This movie festival screens film classics under the grand glass roof of the Palacio de Cibeles. Also on offer are film-themed events with exhibitions and DJs.

July-Sept Fescinal (Cine de Verano)
www.fescinal.es
This open-air night-time venue in Parque de la Bombilla shows double bills of mainstream films during the Veranos de la Villa festival. As well as the massive screen (with wayward sound), Fescinal also offers a smaller one for kids, plus the opportunity to munch on *bocadillos* washed down with *cerveza*. Some of the films are dubbed – check out the website for details.

❤ Mad Cool

Espacio Mad Cool, Valdebebas-Ifema (www.madcoolfestival.es). RENFE Valdebebas. **Date** *3 days July.*

Mad Cool crashed on to the scene in 2016, with a line-up that ranged from old-timers such as Neil Young and The Who to hi-energy EDM acts such as Die Antwoord and a whole bunch of bands in between (The Prodigy, it seems, are back). The following year pulled in Foo Fighters, Green Day, Wilco, MIA, Alt-J, the Manics, Savages and a whole lot more. Bands play across five stages: the two main stages are outdoors and close to one another, so that audiences don't need to do more than sidle from one to another between acts – and smaller stages are indoors. It's not just about music – there are

art exhibitions, theatre, and documentary screenings.

The space itself has a Coachella look to it, with a big wheel, towering art installations and an awful lot of neon, and the crowd, similarly, has a glam-hippie California vibe. Various areas are entirely carpeted in Instagram-friendly Astroturf, and consequently there's always somewhere non-muddy to sit. Rows of food trucks cater to every taste, and the payment system (credit loaded on to bracelets), means that the queues are bearable.

As ever, though, tips for maximum comfort include good shoes, sun cream and something to throw over your shoulders in the evening – Madrid can get very hot during the day, but it cools down a lot at night.

Savages

6-15 Aug Verbenas de San Cayetano, San Lorenzo & La Paloma

www.madrid.es

This is Madrid popular culture at its best – the streets and squares of the Lavapiés, Rastro and La Latina neighbourhoods are dolled up with flowers and bunting and the locals don their *castizo* gear for some serious street partying. San Cayetano is first, on 2-8 August, followed by San Lorenzo on the 9-11 and La Paloma on the 12-15. Daytime sees parades and events for kids; by night there are organ grinders, traditional *chotis* dancing, the aroma of grilled chorizo and *churros*, sangría by the bucketful and a lot of good fun.

Verbenas de San Cayetano

Autumn

Autumn tends to be the time when the big-hitting exhibitions are launched, as *madrileños* trail back into town from their mountain retreats. The 'big three' art museums are good bets for this, but it's also worth checking the websites for the **Fundación Mapfre** (*see p146*) and the **CaixaForum** (*see p139*). The weather is mostly mild, and it's worth bringing an umbrella in October (though rain is far from guaranteed).

Late Sept Estampa

www.estampa.org

A firm fixture on the arts calendar, Estampa is a well-attended contemporary art fair that brings together galleries and collectors from around the world to exhibit prints and other artworks.

Late Sept-early Oct Fiesta del Partido Comunista

www.fiesta.pce.es

Now in the political minority, the Spanish Communist Party still has enough clout to stage this three-day *fiesta*. There are performances by flamenco and rock bands, stalls run by political groups, debates on many political and social issues, and lots of regional cuisine.

Late Oct Luna de Octubre

www.esmadrid.com/agenda/luna-de-octubre

Formerly known as La Noche en Blanco, La Luna de Octubre was repurposed and renamed in 2017, with a focus on light, including light installations and video mapping on iconic buildings. To have '*una noche en blanco*' means to spend a sleepless night, and this is insomniac heaven. In Madrid, as in other Spanish cities like Seville, Granada and Malaga, as well as Paris, Brussels and Riga, for one night only you can wander from exhibition centre to museum, from fashion show to concert all night long and all for free.

Oct-June Festival de Otoño a Primavera

www.madrid.org

Named, somewhat clunkily, the 'Autumn to Spring Festival', this event offers numerous Shakespearean, contemporary theatre, dance and music spectacles, and is one of the city's major performing arts events.

Winter

Madrid does winter well, and its finest dishes are warming, hearty stews, best eaten in cosy, traditional restaurants such as **La Bola Taberna** (*see p87*) or **Casa Lucio** (*see p79*). The twinkling **Christmas market** in the Plaza Mayor is not be missed, and if you possibly can, try and catch the Three Kings' parade along C/Alcalá for **Epiphany** on 5 January.

Early Dec-5 Jan
Feria de Artesanía
www.esmadrid.com

This large and crowded crafts fair is an ideal place to look for original presents and coincides with Christmas, New Year and Reyes.

25 Dec Navidad (Christmas)

Christmas in Spain is less important than Epiphany (Reyes; *see p64*), so you are not reminded of the number of shopping days left until Christmas at every turn. However, Father Christmas, tinsel and baubles are more evident than a few decades ago. The big family blow-out is usually on Nochebuena (Christmas Eve) with shrimps, red cabbage and either roast lamb, sea bream or both.

31 Dec Nochevieja
(New Year's Eve)

New Year's Eve is celebrated with gusto, usually *en familia*, and involves another blow-out meal, litres of cava and the curious tradition of eating 12 grapes as the clock chimes midnight. Ever resourceful, many supermarkets now sell seedless grapes pre-packed in dozens for the occasion. The Puerta del Sol is where thousands throng.

5-6 Jan Reyes (Three Kings)

On the evening of 5 January, Noche de Reyes, thousands of children and their parents line up along C/Alcalá to watch the annual *cabalgata* (parade), which is also televised. Dozens of elaborate floats pass by and the riders hurl sweets to the children. Later, most families have a big dinner, and the following day presents await those who have been good. Those who haven't get a piece of coal.

Feb/Mar Carnaval

Carnival is a very good excuse for dressing up and partying, either in the street or in Madrid's many bars and clubs. It opens in the Plaza Mayor, followed by a parade around old Madrid. On Ash Wednesday, the last day, there is a ribald ceremony during which a fish is carted around to the strains of a marching band, before being interred. It's known as the 'Burial of the Sardine', and was famously depicted by Goya in his painting of the same name.

Nochevieja, Puerta del Sol

Madrid
by Area

Iglesia-Catedral de San Isidro

Los Austrias & La Latina

The oldest part of the city, site of the Muslim town and of most of medieval Madrid, falls between Plaza de la Cebada, Plaza Mayor and the Palacio Real and was for centuries the seat of power. Even though most of the streets still follow their original medieval lines, this may not be immediately apparent today. Like several other parts of the Old City, this area has been smartened up over the past decade, and is now home to a slew of wine bars and expensive restaurants.

Best squares
The elegant Plaza de Oriente (*p67*) and the historical palimpsest that is the Plaza de la Villa (*p68*).

Best churches
The Catedral de la Almudena (*p68*) is the royal favourite, but the domed Basílica de San Francisco el Grande (*p77*) is a Madrid landmark.

Best sights
The impossibly huge Palacio Real (*p70*) is a short walk from the grand, arcaded Plaza Mayor (*p75*).

Best restaurants
El Sobrino de Botín (*p71*) was Hemingway's favourite, but Casa Lucio (*p79*) has attracted every sort of celebrity over the decades.

Best for souvenirs
Taller Puntera (*p74*) for hand-stitched leather bags, and Belloso (*p74*) for religious fripperies.

Best tapas
Graze through the stalls at the Mercado de San Miguel (*p72*) or *tapear* with the hip at Juanalaloca (*p80*).

Los Austrias

At the area's core is the **Plaza Mayor** (*see p75*), an archetypal creation of Castilian Baroque. To the east, leading on from the C/ Cava de San Miguel, is the **Arco de los Cuchilleros** (Knifemakers' Arch), which runs from the south-west corner of the square via a spectacular bank of steps leading down through C/Cuchilleros to the **Plaza de la Puerta Cerrada**, the walls of which are decorated with some engaging 1970s murals.

Just above C/Mayor is the 12th-century **San Nicolás de los Servitas**, while just off it is the **Plaza de la Villa**, Madrid's oldest square and home to the city hall, the **Casa de la Villa**. In pre-Habsburg times, the square was also the preferred place of residence for the elite; one such residence, the **Torre de los Lujanes**, can still be seen there.

Along with the **Casa de Cisneros**, also on the square, the buildings make up a compendium of the history of the city from provincial town to the imperial capital it was to become.

Ópera, the area between Plaza Mayor and the **Palacio Real** (*see p70*), is named after the **Teatro Real** opera house at its centre. As well as containing some of the city's most important buildings (the **cathedral** among them), this is one of the most elegant areas of Madrid. A tunnel whisks traffic under the stately **Plaza de Oriente**, so named because it sits just east of the palace, making it one of the most pleasant spots for a coffee.

Behind the palace, the delightful **Campo del Moro** gardens run down towards the Manzanares and the Paseo de la Florida.

➜ **Getting around**
The rambling streets of Madrid de Los Austrias are best explored on foot and have the Ópera metro station (L2, L5) at their heart. The district of La Latina is best reached by metro to the station of the same name (L5) and, again, is very easy to walk around.

Sights & museums

Campo del Moro

Paseo de la Virgen del Puerto (91 454 88 00). Metro Príncipe Pío. **Open** *Oct-Mar 10am-6pm Mon-Sat; 9am-6pm Sun. Apr-Sept 10am-8pm daily.* **Map** *p69 D14.*

This vast garden was named after a Muslim leader in the Middle Ages, Ali Ben Yusut, who attempted to capture the fortress that is now the Palacio Real. Unfortunately, it is only accessible from the Paseo de la Virgen del Puerto side, requiring a fairly long walk down Cuesta de San Vicente or Cuesta de la Vega. As a reward, however, you will see two fine monumental fountains. Nearest the palace is Los Tritones, originally made in 1657 for the palace in Aranjuez; the other is Las Conchas, designed in the 18th century by Ventura Rodríguez. Both were moved here in the 1890s.

♥ Catedral de la Almudena

C/Bailén 10 (91 542 22 00, www. catedraldelaalmudena.es). Metro Ópera. **Open** *9am-8.30pm daily.* **Admission** *Cathedral free (suggested donation €1). Museum & dome €6; €4 reductions.* **Map** *p69 E15.*

This is not Spain's most impressive cathedral, and it's something of a miracle that it exists at all. For centuries, Church and State could not agree on whether Madrid should have a cathedral; once they did, it took 110 years to complete it. Work began in 1883 on a neo-Gothic design by the Marqués de Cubas, but this scheme went off course after only the crypt was completed. Another architect, Fernando Chueca Goitia, took over in 1944, and introduced a neoclassical style. Although the cathedral has failed to win much affection over the years, it was finally finished in 1993 and visited by the Pope. The site once contained the church of Santa María de la Almudena, formerly the main mosque of Muslim Madrid (the name comes from the Arabic *al mudin*, 'the mill') until it was knocked down by liberal reformers in 1870. One of its more interesting pieces is the 13th-century polychromatic funerary chest of San Isidro.

♥ Plaza de la Villa

Metro Ópera or Sol. **Map** *p69 G15.*

Madrid's oldest square, home to the city's main marketplace in Muslim and early medieval times, contains three noteworthy buildings. Dominant is the Casa de la Villa, or City Hall, designed in Castilian-Baroque style by Juan Gómez de Mora in 1630, although not completed until 1695. The façade was also altered by Juan de Villanueva in the 1780s. It contrasts nicely with the Casa de Cisneros, which was built as a palace by a relative of the great Cardinal Cisneros in 1537. Restored in 1910, it now also houses municipal offices. Opposite the Casa de la Villa is the simple Torre de los Lujanes, from the 1460s, where one of Madrid's aristocratic families once resided. It is believed that King Francis I of France was kept prisoner in the tower by Charles V after his capture in 1525.

San Nicolás de los Servitas

Plaza San Nicolás (91 559 40 64). Metro Ópera. **Open** *8.30am-1.30pm, 5.30-8pm Mon; 8.30-9am, 6.30-8pm Tue-Sat; 10-10.30am, 6.30-8.30pm Sun.* **Map** *p69 F15.*

The oldest surviving church in Madrid stands a few minutes from Plaza de Oriente. Its 12th-century tower is one of two Mudéjar towers, built by Muslim craftsmen living under Christian rule, in the city. Most of the rest of the church was rebuilt later, during the 15th and 16th centuries. There is no entry during mass.

❤ Palacio Real (Palacio de Oriente)

*Plaza de Oriente, C/Bailén (91 454 88 00). Metro Ópera. **Open** Oct-Mar 10am-6pm daily. Apr-Sept 10am-8pm daily. **Admission** €10; €5 reductions. Incl guided tour €14; €9 reductions; free under-4s. Free to EU citizens Oct-Mar 4-6pm & Apr-Sept 6-8pm Mon-Thur. **Map** p69 E14.*

Commissioned by Philip V after the earlier Alcázar was lost to a fire in 1734, the Royal Palace is rarely used by the royal family, and many of its 3,000 rooms are open to view. The architects principally responsible for the final design, which reflects the taste of the Spanish Bourbons, were Italian – Giambattista Sacchetti and Francesco Sabatini – with contributions by the Spaniard Ventura Rodríguez. Completed in 1764, the late-Baroque palace is built almost entirely of granite and white Colmenar stone and, surrounded as it is by majestic gardens, contributes to the splendour of the city.

Inside, you must keep to a fixed route, but are free to set your own pace rather than follow a tour. The entrance into the palace is awe-inspiring: you pass up a truly vast staircase and then through the main state rooms, with soaring ceilings and frescoes by Corrado Giaquinto and Giambattista Tiepolo. In the grand Throne Room there are some fine 17th-century sculptures commissioned by Velázquez, which were saved from the earlier Alcázar. Other highlights are the extravagantly ornate private apartments of the palace's first resident, Charles

III, again decorated by Italians. Particularly striking are the king's dressing room, covered in mosaics and rococo stuccoes by Mattia Gasparini; and the Porcelain Room, its walls covered entirely in porcelain reliefs. A later addition is another giant: the State Dining Room, still used for official banquets. There are also imposing collections of tapestries, table porcelain, gold and silver plates, and finally clocks, a particular passion of the little-admired King Charles IV.

One of the highlights is the Real Armería (Royal Armoury), with a superb collection of ceremonial

armour, much of it worn by Charles V and other Habsburgs. Look out, too, for the suits of armour worn by El Cid and his horse – displayed on life-size statues. On the other side of the courtyard, the Royal Pharmacy is also worth a visit. One of the oldest in Europe, it was wholly dedicated to attending to the many ailments of Spain's crowned heads over several centuries.

On the first Wednesday of each month the Royal Guard stages a ceremonial Changing of the Guard in the courtyard, at noon. There are tours of the Palace throughout the day.

Restaurants

Casa Ciriaco €€€

C/Mayor 84 (91 548 06 20). Metro Ópera or Sol. **Open** *1-4pm, 8pm-12.30am Mon, Tue, Thur-Sun. Closed Aug.* **Map** *p69 F15* ❶
Castilian

Pick your way down to a deep dining room hung with pictures of visiting royals and celebrities, along with rather grimmer photos of the 1906 bombing of the wedding procession for Alfonso XIII and his English wife Victoria Eugenie – which happened right outside. Undamaged and still going strong, Casa Ciriaco was a meeting place for the intelligentsia in pre-Civil War days and although it no longer attracts many thinkers, the Castilian fare is a taste of days gone by. *Gallina en pepitoria* (chicken in an almond and white wine sauce) is the speciality.

❤ El Sobrino de Botín €€€

C/Cuchilleros 17 (91 366 42 17, 91 366 30 26, www.botin.es). Metro Sol. **Open** *1-4pm, 8pm-midnight daily.* **Map** *p69 G15* ❷ *Castilian*
The world's oldest restaurant is still coming up with the goods after nearly 300 years. For all its popularity as a tourist destination, its nooks and crannies add up to an atmospheric – if cramped – dining spot over several floors. Ask for a table in the vaulted cellar for the full effect. Order the suckling pig or the lamb, which are roasted in a huge wood-fired oven. And yes, since you asked, Hemingway did come here.

Tapas bars

Bodegas Ricla

C/Cuchilleros 6 (91 365 20 69). Metro Ópera. **Open** *1-4pm, 7pm-midnight Mon, Wed, Thur; 1-4pm, 7pm-1am Fri, Sat; 1-5pm Sun.* **No cards.** **Map** *p69 G15* ❶

LOS AUSTRIAS & LA LATINA

❤ Mercado de San Miguel

Plaza de San Miguel (www. mercadode sanmiguel.es). Metro Sol. **Open** *10am-midnight Mon-Wed, Sun; 10am-2am Thur-Sat.* **Map** *p69 G15* ❷

The 1915 wrought-iron and glass structure of the Mercado de San Miguel, with boutique-style food stands inside, has created a culinary buzz in the city and heaves with people day and night. Some say it's lost some of its original soul and that it's overpriced, yet the slick operation – one of the few covered markets in the city – is always rammed with smart-looking *madrileños* and tourists enjoying *pinchos de bacalao* (salt cod on bruschetta), oysters, tortillas, wine, sherry, vermouth and, just as important, conversation.

An excellent starting point is also one of San Miguel's best-loved spots: La Hora del Vermut (lahoradelvermut.wordpress.com). With 15 different types of vermút, it's an excellent place to initiate yourself in the quintessential *madrileño* tradition. Sherry is also taken seriously here.

Once you've whet your appetite, you'll want to move on to more

solid fodder. Salt cod specialist La Casa de Bacalao (www. lacasadebacalao.es) offers some of the market's most popular tapas: *pinchos* (small rounds of toast) topped with puréed *bacalao* in a range of different guises, such as with caviar. At around €1 per pincho, it's tempting to order several, but be sure to save room for the market's other temptations.

Two more stands not to be missed are upmarket Lhardy, on the opposite side to La Casa de Bacalao, and, a little way along, the oyster stand Ostra Sorlut (www.ostrasorlut.com), a great spot in which to undertake the oyster rite of passage.

The Carro de Croquetas is a stall on wheels that's always to be found somewhere in the market – it sells Basque croquettes (filled with salt cod, mushroom, leek and so on).

Whichever option you go for, the market is an excellent place to people-watch and marvel at *madrileños* doing what they do best: enjoying food in a civilised fashion, and being social – as if it were a duty, a passion and a performance, all rolled into one.

Café de Oriente

A tiny, bright and friendly mother-and-son operation, Bodegas Ricla does a great line in garlicky *boquerones* and an incongruous one in soft rock. Cheap but good wine and sherry are available by the litre, poured from tall clay urns, or there is vermouth on tap. Also worth trying are the *cecina* (thin slices of cured venison) and Cabrales cheese in cider.

Cafés & bars

Café de Oriente

Plaza de Oriente 2 (91 541 39 74, www.cafedeoriente.es). Metro Ópera. Open 8.30am-1am Mon-Sat; 9am-1am Sun. Map p69 F14 ❶
The belle époque interior is entirely fake yet entirely convincing, making this one of the most peaceful and elegant spots to flick through the newspapers or recover from the exertions of the Palacio Real opposite. Despite its location, with tables outside on the stunning Plaza de Oriente, the café seems to be more popular with locals than tourists, who are perhaps put off by its air of grandeur.

Café del Real

Plaza de Isabel II 2 (91 547 21 24). Metro Ópera. Open 9am-midnight Mon-Thur; 9am-1am Fri; 10am-1am Sat; 10am-11pm Sun. No cards. Map p69 G14 ❷
This likeable, cramped café with a lovely façade is a good place for coffee and cake (chocolate or carrot), though prices are a tad on the high side. Head upstairs to a low-beamed room with red leather chairs and old opera posters, overlooking the *plaza*. The café was a favourite haunt of intellectuals, artists and actors in the 1980s, but it's popular with a more varied crowd these days.

Chocolatería San Ginés

Pasadizo de San Ginés 5 (91 365 65 46). Metro Ópera or Sol. Open 24hrs daily. Map p69 H14 ❸
Serving chocolate and *churros* (deep-fried batter sticks) to the city night and day since 1894, this veritable institution has had to introduce a ticketing system – pay before you order – to deal with the 5am queues of exhausted clubbers and chipper old ladies. The lighting is a bit much if you fall into the former category, but at least there are tables outside.

La Fontanilla

Plaza Puerta Cerrada 13 (91 365 22 91). Metro La Latina. **Open** *1pm-2am Mon-Thur; noon-2am Fri-Sun.* **Map** *p69 G15* ❹
La Fontanilla claims to be not the biggest or the best or the oldest, but the smallest Irish pub in Madrid. There's no disputing this singular claim, but the place does manage to cram in a couple of wooden tables alongside wide hatches opening on to the street. The myriad beers racked up on the walls are sadly not for sale, but there is Murphy's and Guinness.

Shops & services

♥ Belloso

C/Mayor 23 (mobile 629 328 644, www.belloso.es). Metro Sol. **Open** *10am-1.30pm, 4.30-8pm Mon-Fri; 10am-1.30pm Sat.* **Map** *p69 H15* ❶ *Gifts & souvenirs*
This neighbourhood has an abundance of shops selling Catholic paraphernalia, but Belloso is one of the best. The gear on offer covers a huge range, including rosaries, crucifixes and statues of the Virgin.

El Riojano

C/Mayor 10 (91 366 44 82, www.confiteriaelriojano.com). Metro Sol. **Open** *10am-2pm, 5-9pm daily.* **Map** *p69 H14* ❷ *Food & drink*
El Riojano has been in business since 1885, selling irresistible cakes, pastries, meringues and seasonal goodies. All are made in the traditional way, with meringues a particular speciality. Enjoy one with a coffee in the café out back.

♥ Taller Puntera

Plaza Conde de Barajas 4 (91 364 29 26, www.puntera.com). Metro Tirso de Molina. **Open** *10am-2.30pm, 4-8.30pm Mon-Sat.* **Map** *p69 G15* ❸ *Fashion*
This lovely leather accessories shop/workshop makes simple but stylish bags, satchels, rucksacks, wallets, notebooks and more, all in top-quality leather, and available in a range of tasteful colours. Each 'piece' has a story behind it, and you can personalise most of them (dependent on the kind of leather) by getting your name engraved for free. What's more, the staff are genuinely friendly and the prices are excellent for this level of workmanship. A gem.

Tiempos Modernos

C/Arrieta 17 (91 542 85 94, www.tiempos-modernos.com). Metro Ópera. **Open** *11am-8pm Mon-Fri; 11am-2pm Sat. Closed 3wks Aug.* **Map** *p69 F13* ❹ *Antiques*
Tiempos Modernos deals in modern Spanish painting, and hosts temporary shows and exhibitions of photography and artwork. The main line of business, though, is the great range of 1940s, '50s and '60s furniture.

Entertainment

Corral de la Morería

C/Morería 17 (91 365 84 46, www.corraldelamoreria.com). Metro La Latina. **Open** *8pm-12.30am daily.* **Performances** *9pm, 11pm daily.* **Admission** *(incl 1 drink) €47.* **Map** *p69 E16* ❶ *Flamenco*
This longstanding *tablao* sports seemingly authentic Arab decor and an atmosphere to match. A relaxed mix of tourists, fans (Hemingway, Che Guevara and Picasso all paid a visit) and professionals enjoy a solid, expensive and sometimes exhilarating show.

♥ Plaza Mayor

Metro Sol. **Map** p69 H15.

Plaza Mayor began life in the 15th century as a humble market square, then known as the Plaza del Arrabal ('Square outside the Walls'). In the 1560s, after Madrid was made capital of Spain by Philip II, architect Juan de Herrera drew up plans for it to be completely rebuilt, but the only part constructed immediately was the Casa de la Panadería ('the Bakery'). Finished under the direction of Diego Sillero in 1590, it's typical of the Herreran style, with grey slate roofs, spiky pinnacles and two towers that dominate the square. In the early 1990s, in a move unlikely to be contemplated in most other countries, this historic edifice was decorated with colourful psychedelic murals. The rest of the *plaza* was built by Juan Gómez de Mora for Philip III and completed in 1619,

although large sections were destroyed by fire in 1790 and had to be rebuilt. Bullfights, carnivals and all the great ceremonies of imperial Madrid were held here. At its centre is a statue from 1616 of Philip III on horseback by Giambologna and Pietro Tacca, which stood originally in the Casa de Campo and was moved here in the 19th century.

The square is still an important hub, with most Madrid-wide celebrations, such as the Veranos de la Villa or San Isidro festivals, centred here, along with a traditional Christmas fair in December. Best enjoyed on quiet weekday mornings, Plaza Mayor has plenty of pavement cafés from which to contemplate its graceful architecture. On Sunday mornings the *plaza* bustles with a stamp and coin market. On the north side of the *plaza* is the city's main tourist office.

Teatro Real

Marula

C/Caños Viejos 3 (91 366 15 96,
www.marulacafe.com). Metro La
Latina. **Open** *11pm-6am Tue-Sun.*
Admission *varies. No cards.* **Map**
p69 F16 ❷ *Live music*

This small venue serves as bar,
club and live music venue. There
are gigs on weekday nights (check
the website for details), followed
by DJ sessions. But the place really
hots up at weekends, attracting
DJ sessions from local talent such
as Antonio Requena, Casbah 73
and Comandante Kwenya. The
summertime terrace is a big
pull, filling up by midnight and
staying that way.

Teatro Real

Plaza de Isabel II, Los Austrias
(information 902 24 48 48,
box office 91 516 06 60, www.
teatro-real.com). Metro Opera.
Box office *9.15am-8pm Mon-Fri*
(10am-8pm Sat performance days).
Visits 9.30am-3.30pm daily (with
audioguide); 10am-1pm (guided
tours). **Tickets** *Ballet €20-€180.*
Opera €20-€449. **Visits** *€7/€6*
reductions (with audioguide);
€7/€6 reductions (guided tours).
Map *p69 G14* ❸ *Opera*

Shaped like a compressed oval, the
interior of the city's opera house is
breathtakingly ornate compared
with its sombre façade, and it's

one of the most technologically advanced in Europe. Productions are impressive – with complicated revolving sets and attention to detail in costumes and props – and the acoustics are excellent. Projection screens at either side of the stage show the full action, though this doesn't quite compensate for the poor sightlines at the far ends of the top galleries (the *tribunas* and part of the *anfiteatro*). There's also a screen above the stage showing Spanish surtitles for non-Spanish operas.

The annual Festival de Verano runs alongside the theatre's regular programme in June and July but offers a more orchestra- and dance-orientated programme, as well as children's shows (tickets for these events are much cheaper and easier to obtain). Guided tours last 50 minutes, and a minimum of ten people are required for a guided tour to take place (call 91 516 06 96 for all tour enquiries/ bookings).

Performances usually begin at 8pm, or 6pm on Sundays, with ballet and family opera matinées at noon. Tickets go on sale approximately ten days before the première and standby tickets are available on the day. With the cheapest tickets, for rows F and G, vision is seriously restricted; check the website for a detailed plan.

Terraza Atenas
C/Segovia & C/Cuesta de la Vega (91 161 01 37, 91 868 422 24, www. terrazaatenas.com). Metro Ópera or Puerta del Ángel. **Open** *6pm-3am daily. Closed Nov-Mar.* **Admission** *free. No cards.* **Map** *p69 D15* ❹ *Live music*
A super-cool *terraza* that's set in its own small park. The plentiful tables in the front bar are filled by midnight and the overflow swells on to the surrounding gentle grass slope. With no neighbours to worry about, the crowd can enjoy the easy sounds of soul, funk and lounge long after other *terrazas* have called it a night. There are live gigs on Thursday nights.

La Latina

The **C/Cava Baja**, home to many of the most celebrated *mesones*, temples to Madrid's traditional cuisine, runs south from the Plaza Mayor and leads to the squares (**Plaza de San Andrés**, **Plaza del Humilladero** and **Plaza de la Paja**) that are prime territory for the traditional Sunday La Latina tapas bar crawl. The district is relatively quiet except during its grand *fiestas*, around the time of **La Paloma** (*see p63*) in August.

The area is mostly known for its wide range of restaurants and bars, but contains several important sights, such as the Mudéjar tower of the 14th-century **San Pedro el Viejo**; the lofty, neoclassical **Basílica de San Francisco el Grande**; the **Museo de San Isidro**, and the church of **San Andrés**. Close to here is the **Plaza de la Cebada**, where, in former times, executions often took place.

Sights & museums

♥ Basílica de San Francisco el Grande
Plaza de San Francisco (91 365 38 00). Metro La Latina. **Open** *Sept-June 10.30am-12.30pm, 4-6pm Tue-Sat. July, Aug 10.30am-12.30pm, 5-7pm Tue-Sun. Last admission half hour before closing.* **Admission** *(guided tour only) €3; €2 reductions; free under-4s.* **Map** *p69 E17.*
This huge, multi-tiered church between Puerta de Toledo and the Palacio Real is difficult to miss. A monastery on the site, reputedly founded by St Francis of Assisi, was knocked down in 1760; between

1761 and 1784 Francisco Cabezas and later Francesco Sabatini built this neoclassical church in its place. Most challenging was the construction of the spectacular dome, with a diameter of 33m (108ft). The dome was restored fairly recently, and work on the rest of the basilica has also now been completed. Inside there is an early Goya, *The Sermon of San Bernardino of Siena* (1781), and several frescoes by other artists.

Museo de San Isidro (Casa de San Isidro)

*Plaza de San Andrés 2 (91 366 74 15, www.madrid.es/museosanisidro). Metro La Latina. **Open** mid Sept-mid June 9.30am-8pm Tue-Sun. Mid June-mid Sept 10am-7pm Tue-Sun. **Admission** free. **Map** p69 F16.*

Dedicated to the city's patron saint, the well-digger and labourer San Isidro, this museum sits on the spot where he supposedly lived and performed one of his most famous miracles: when his son, Illán, fell into a well, Isidro made the water rise and thus was able to rescue the unfortunate lad. The well – or *a* well, anyway – is preserved inside the house, as is the chapel built in 1663 on the spot where Isidro allegedly died. According to legend, he was originally buried here, too. This is, then, a museum that deals in legends as much as in solid artefacts, and the current material on show is a little limited. More interesting are the finds from local archaeological digs, formerly kept in the Museo de Historia and now in the basement here. They include items from lower-Palaeolithic settlements in the area, as well as artefacts from the Roman villas along the Manzanares river, and from the Muslim era.

San Andrés, Capilla del Obispo & Capilla de San Isidro

*Plaza de San Andrés 1 (91 365 48 71). Metro La Latina. **Open** 9am-1pm, 6-8pm Mon-Sat; for services only Sun. **Capilla del Obispo** 12.30pm-1.15pm, 6.30-8.30pm Mon-Sat; guided tours (€2) 10am-12.30pm Tue, 4-5.30pm Thur. **Admission** free. **Map** p69 F16.*

The large church of San Andrés dates from the 16th century, but was badly damaged in the Civil War in 1936 and later rebuilt in a relatively simple style. Attached to it (but with separate entrances) are two of Madrid's most historic early church buildings. The Capilla del Obispo (Bishop's Chapel, 1520-35),

Basílica de San Francisco el Grande *p77*

with its entrance on Plaza de la Paja, is the best-preserved Gothic building in the city. It contains finely carved tombs and a 1550 altarpiece by Francisco Giralte. Further towards Plaza de los Carros is the Capilla de San Isidro, built in 1642-69 by Pedro de la Torre to house the remains of the saint, which were later transferred to the Iglesia-Catedral de San Isidro.

Restaurants

La Botillería de Maxi €

C/Cava Alta 4 (91 365 12 49, www. labotilleriademaxi.com). Metro La Latina. **Open** *12.30-4pm, 8.30pm-12.30am Tue-Sat; 12.30-6pm Sun. Closed last 2wks Aug.* **No cards.** **Map** *p69 G16* ❸ *Spanish*
Fashionably scruffy young waiting staff and blaring flamenco in a no-frills classic setting make for an unpretentious blend of old and new. While the *callos a la madrileña* (tripe in a spicy sauce) is acknowledged as the best in town, there's no shame in going for the *pisto manchego* (aubergine, courgette, pepper and tomato stew) with fried eggs, or the partridge pâté or the *mojama* (air-dried tuna).

❤ Casa Lucio €€€

C/Cava Baja 35 (91 365 82 17, www. casalucio.es). Metro La Latina. **Open** *1-4pm, 8.30-11.30pm daily. Closed Aug.* **Map** *p69 G16* ❹ *Spanish*
A restaurant unsurpassed by any other in Madrid for its famous patrons: the former king Juan Carlos, Bill Clinton and Penélope Cruz among them. This is the place of historical rendezvous, where Aznar and Bush's wives did lunch back when alliances were in the making. It also knows how to cook up one cracking *solomillo* (beef). The key to Lucio's glory is the use of a coal-fired oven and the best olive oil. Another star dish is a starter of lightly fried eggs laid on top of a bed of crisp, thinly cut chips – Juan Carlos always orders it. Be sure to ask for a table on the first floor.

El Estragón €€

Costanilla de San Andrés 10, Plaza de la Paja (91 365 89 82, www. elestragonvegetariano.com). Metro La Latina. **Open** *1pm-midnight Mon-Thur, Sun; 1pm-1am Fri, Sat.* **Map** *p69 F16* ❺ *Vegetarian*
El Estragón's underlying concept appears to be 'vegetarian food for meat-eaters', and thus there is no shortage of soya 'meatballs', 'hamburgers' and so on. Where this place really excels, however, is in its straightforward vegetarian dishes, such as a fabulous towering heap of *risotto verde* containing every green vegetable you can think of, topped with stringy Emmental. It's a delightful spot, with terracotta tiles, blue-and-white gingham and views over Plaza de la Paja, where tables are set out in summer.

La Musa Latina €

Costanilla San Andrés 12 (91 354 02 55, www.grupolamusa.com). Metro La Latina. **Open** *10am-1am Mon, Tue, Sat, Sun; 10am-1.30am Wed; 10am-2am Thur, Fri (kitchen open from 1pm).* **Map** *p69 F16* ❻ *Global*

In the know
La Latina Sundays

La Latina remains a popular Sunday outing for *madrileños* of all stripes. The tradition is to start at El Rastro flea market, and then head to the tapas bars around Cava Baja, Plaza de la Paja, Plaza San Andrés and Calle Humilladero for an aperitif of vermouth and some tapas. The hedonistic, sociable affair continues all day long, with some bars resembling scenes normally associated with late-night antics.

A laid-back vibe, tasty tapas and stir-fries, and a great location on Plaza de la Paja all contribute towards making La Musa Latina into a tempting package. Try the fried green tomatoes and the prawn tempura with avocado. There are plenty of indulgent desserts – go for the chocolate brownie or the *dulce de leche* panna cotta. Waiters are super cool but friendly, and the diners well-heeled and hip (note the Junk Club downstairs). There is a sister restaurant in Malasaña, but this one is roomier. **Other locations** La Musa, C/Manuela Malasaña 18, Malasaña (91 448 75 58); Ojalá, C/San Andrés 1 (91 523 27 47); Cafetería HD, C/Guzman el Bueno 67 (91 544 23 82).

Tapas bars

♥ Juanalaloca

Plaza Puerta de Moros 4 (91 364 05 25). Metro La Latina. **Open** *8pm-midnight Mon; 1-5pm, 8pm-midnight Tue-Thur; 1-5pm, 8pm-1am Fri; 1pm-1am Sat; 1pm-midnight Sun.* **Map** *p69 F17* ❸

Where the hip go to *tapear*, this Uruguayan-run tapas bar attracts a stylish mix of Argentinians, Uruguayans, locals and tourists. It's kind of pricey, but offers undeniably creative cooking – such as wild mushroom and truffle croquettes and tuna carpaccio with almond oil and rice. Its tortilla is also renowned.

Taberna Matritum

C/Cava Alta 17 (91 365 82 37, www. tabernamatritum.es). Metro La Latina. **Open** *1.30-4pm Tue; 1.30-4pm, 8pm-midnight Wed-Sun.* **Map** *p69 G16* ❹

Its name is Latin for 'Madrid', but Matritum has a great selection of tapas and wine from other regions of Spain, principally Catalonia. Try the *gambas all cremat* (prawns with burnt garlic) or fabulous canapés such as Cabrales cheese with apple compôte. The wine list, too, is dominated by Catalan labels, with many notably good bottles from the Penedès.

Cafés & bars

Almacén de Vinos (Casa Gerardo)

C/Calatrava 21 (91 221 96 60). Metro Puerta de Toledo. **Open** *1-5pm, 8.30pm-midnight Mon-Fri; 1-5pm, 8.30pm-1am Sat, Sun.* **No cards.** **Map** *p69 F17* ❺

A lively and unpretentious wine bar, Gerardo is an essential part of the neighbourhood, offering excellent sausage, ham and seafood tapas, as well as a particularly good selection of cheeses.

Delic

Costanilla de San Andrés 14, Plaza de la Paja (91 364 54 50, www.delic.es). Metro La Latina. **Open** *11am-2am Tue-Thur, Sun; 11am-2.30am Fri, Sat.* **Map** *p69 F16* ❻

A perennial favourite with seemingly everybody, from those looking for a morning coffee on the leafy Plaza de la Paja to those meeting up for a few bolstering cocktails before a big night out. In fact, it gets so busy at certain times that they've employed a bouncer and a one-in/one-out policy. A globetrotting menu includes tabbouleh, Japanese dumplings and filled ciabattas, and the Chilean chocolate cake is utterly irresistible.

El Ventorillo

C/Bailén 14 (91 366 35 78). Metro Ópera. **Open** *11am-1am daily.* **Map** *p69 E16* ❼

Just down from the Palacio Real, this *terraza* offers the finest sunsets in Madrid, looking out over the Casa del Campo and all the way to the Guadarrama.

Sol & Gran Vía

The **Gran Vía** was created in 1910 by slicing through the Old City so that traffic could easily reach Cibeles from C/ Princesa. Intended to be a broad modern boulevard, it got grander still when World War I made neutral Madrid a clearing house for international money. With the economy booming, developers and architects set out to embrace modernity as hard as they could to show that if you wanted something impressive, they could provide it. In the following decades, each generation added its own stamp, and the result is certainly eclectic. At the heart of this area is the **Puerta del Sol**, spiritually and geographically the very centre of Madrid, and a place where *madrileños* gather to celebrate victories and mourn losses.

Best convents

The opulent Real Monasterio de las Descalzas Reales (*p86*) and the peaceful Real Monasterio de la Encarnación (*p84*).

Best traditional cooking

La Bola (*p87*) for the best *cocido*, and La Casa de las Torrijas (*p88*) for Madrid's favourite dessert.

Best cocktails

Hemingway (*p89*) for speakeasy cool, though the man himself drank at Museo Chicote (*p89*).

Best shops

Antigua Casa Talavera (*p89*) for gorgeous ceramics, and Guantes Luque (*p90*) for gloves in every colour.

Best global flavours

Casa Lafu (*p87*) for spicy Chinese hotpots.

Best coffee breaks

La Mallorquina (*p89*) to be at the heart of things, and the Círculo de Bellas Artes (*p84*) to browse the papers.

Tucked in the middle of the area between Sol, Arenal, C/Alcalá and Gran Vía is the **Real Monasterio de las Descalzas Reales** (*see p86*). At the west side of the area, just above the Plaza de Oriente, is the little-visited **Real Monasterio de la Encarnación**, also worth a look. Just north of that, occupying the site of another convent, is the old 19th-century **Palacio del Senado** (Senate).

Running almost alongside C/ Preciados up to Gran Vía is the pedestrianised and slightly shabby **C/Montera**, lined with cheap, dated shops and the main area for street prostitution in the city centre. At the top, parallel with Gran Vía, is **C/Caballero de Gracia**, with a 19th-century oratory that lays on special Masses for the working girls, many of them Latin American, who operate along the street. While seedy, this area is not generally dangerous, and is heavily policed.

The area north and east of Sol was originally the city's financial district, hence the number of grand edifices owned by banks and insurance companies. Its other great avenue is **C/Alcalá**, which follows the centuries-old main route into Madrid from the east. In the 18th century, when it was lined by aristocratic palaces, it was described as the grandest street in Europe, and will only improve in mid 2018, when it is to close to all but residential traffic. It is still pretty impressive today, with a wonderful variety of 19th- to early 20th-century buildings, from the dignified 1882 **Banesto** building (corner of C/Sevilla) to the cautiously modernist **Círculo de Bellas Artes**. There are also fine older constructions, such as the **Real Academia de Bellas Artes de San Fernando** (*see p85*).

The **Plaza de España**, at the western end of the Gran Vía, is dominated by Franco's bombastic architecture. It is flanked by two classic buildings of the type sponsored by the regime when out to impress: the '50s-modern **Torre Madrid** (1957) and the enormous **Edificio España** of 1948-53, currently being developed into a vast hotel.

➜ Getting around

Sol, at the very centre of this area, is crisscrossed by various metro, rail and bus lines, but within the neighbourhood, walking is just as fast, and most streets are pedestrianised.

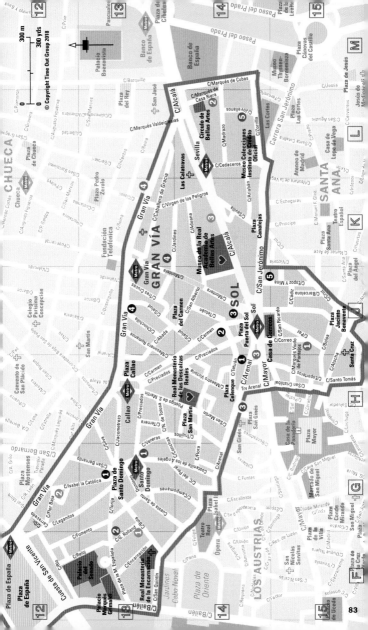

Real Monasterio de la Encarnación

Sights & museums

♥ Círculo de Bellas Artes

C/Alcalá 42 & C/Marqués de Casa Riera 2 (91 360 54 00, www. circulobellasartes.com). Metro Banco de España. **Open** *Café 8am-1am Mon-Thur; 9am-3am Fri, Sat; 9am-midnight Sun. Exhibitions 11am-2pm, 5-9pm Tue-Sun. Roof terrace 9am-2am Mon-Thur; 9am-3am Fri; 10am-3am Sat; 11am-2am Sun.* **Admission** *exhibitions €4 (€5 including access to roof terrace); €3 reductions.* **Map** *p83 L14.*

The Círculo de Bellas Artes occupies a superb building, designed by Antonio Palacios and completed in 1926. It is a key player in every aspect of the Madrid arts scene: as well as a beautifully airy main floor café, with a gracious pavement terrace, the Círculo offers a plethora of classes, exhibitions, lectures and concerts in its theatre and concert hall, as well as an annual masked ball for carnival.

♥ Real Monasterio de la Encarnación

Plaza de la Encarnación 1 (91 547 05 10, information 91 454 88 00, www.patrimonionacional. es/real-sitio). Metro Ópera or Santo Domingo. **Open** *10am-2pm, 4-6.30pm Tue-Sat; 10am-3pm Sun.* **Admission** *(incl guided tour) €6; free under-5s. Free to EU citizens Wed, Thur from 4pm.* **Map** *p83 F13.*

Before the Alcázar burned down, this understated convent was its treasury, connected by a concealed passageway. In 1611, it was inaugurated as a convent but much of the original building, including the church, was damaged by fire in 1734 and rebuilt in a classical-Baroque style in the 1760s by Ventura Rodríguez. It still contains a community of around 20 nuns, but most of the building is open to the public. Although not as lavishly endowed as the Descalzas Reales, it contains a great many pieces of 17th-century religious art, the most impressive of which is Jusepe Ribera's shimmering *chiaroscuro* portrait of John the Baptist. The Encarnación's most memorable room, however, is the *reliquiario* (relics room). In its glass casements are displayed some 1,500 saintly remains, bone fragments and former possessions of saints and martyrs, in extravagantly bejewelled copper, bronze, glass, gold and silver reliquaries. Its prize possession is what purports to be the solidified blood of San Pantaleón, kept inside a glass orb. The blood reportedly liquefies each year from midnight on the eve of his feast day, 27 July. Note that visits are by guided tour only.

💜 Museo de la Real Academia de Bellas Artes de San Fernando

*C/Alcalá 13 (91 524 08 64, www. realacademiabellasartessanfer nando.com). Metro Sevilla or Sol. **Open** 10am-3pm Tue-Sun. Closed Aug. **Admission** €8; €4 reductions; free under-18s, over-65s. Free to all Wed. Calcografía Nacional free. No cards. **Map** p83 K14.*

This under-visited museum is in fact one of Madrid's most important and oldest permanent artistic institutions (founded in 1794). The eclectic collection is partly made up of works of varying quality donated by aspiring members in order to gain admission to the academy. The museum's greatest possessions, though, are its 13 works by Goya. They include two major self-portraits; a portrait of his friend, the playwright Moratín; a portrait of Charles IV's hated minister Godoy; and the *Burial of the Sardine*, a carnival scene that foreshadows his later, darker works. Another of the academy's

most prized possessions is the Italian mannerist Giuseppe Arcimboldo's *Spring*, a playful, surrealistic portrait of a man made up entirely of flowers. It was one of a series on the four seasons painted for Ferdinand I of Austria in 1563. There are also important portraits by Velázquez and Rubens, and several paintings by Zurbarán. Among the later works, the best known are some Picasso engravings and a Juan Gris; the most surprising are the colourful fantasies of Múñoz Degrain and the De Chirico-esque work of Julio Romero de Torres. Look out, too, for Leandro Bassano's superb *La Riva degli Schiavoni*.

The academy also has a valuable collection of plans and drawings, including those of Prado architect Juan de Villanueva, and rare books. In the same building is the Museo de Calcografía Nacional, a similarly priceless collection of engraving and fine printing, which has many of the original plates for Goya's etchings.

❤ Real Monasterio de las Descalzas Reales

*Plaza de las Descalzas 3 (information 91 454 88 00). Metro Callao or Sol. **Open** 10am-2pm, 4-6.30pm Tue-Sat; 10am-3pm Sun. **Admission** (by guided tour only) €6; free under-5s. Free to EU citizens Wed & Thur from 4pm. **Map** p83 H14.*

The convent of the Descalzas Reales ('Royal Barefoot Nuns') is the most complete 16th-century building in Madrid and still houses a cloistered community. It was originally built as a palace for the treasurer of Charles V, but was converted into a convent in 1556-64 after Philip II's widowed sister Joanna of Austria became a nun. Founded with royal patronage, the Descalzas became the preferred destination of the many widows, younger daughters and other women of the royal family and high aristocracy of Spain who entered religious orders. Hence it also acquired an extraordinary collection of paintings, sculptures, tapestries and objets d'art given as bequests by the novices' families. Equally lavish is the Baroque decoration of the building itself,

belying its sternly austere façade, with a grand painted staircase, frescoed ceilings and 32 chapels.

Much of its art collection is Italian, including works by Titian, Bernardino Luini, Angelo Nardi and Sebastiano del Piombo, and Flemish, with Breughel (an *Adoration of the Magi*), Joos Van Cleve and Rubens. The Descalzas is also an exceptional showcase of Spanish Baroque religious art, with works by Gaspar Becerra, Zurbarán, Claudio Coello and even a tiny painting attributed to Goya.

As you walk around you can catch glimpses of the nuns' courtyard vegetable garden, which has remained virtually unchanged since the 16th-century and is closed to the public.

Tours leave every 20 minutes and last around 50 minutes. Frustratingly, the guides rarely speak English, there is no printed information about the convent and the paintings are not labelled. Note also that only a limited number of tickets are sold every day, so it's worth arriving early or booking tickets online in advance.

Puerta del Sol

Restaurants

❤ La Bola Taberna €€

C/Bola 5 (91 547 69 30, www. labola.es). Metro Ópera or Santo Domingo. **Open** *1-4pm, 8.30-11pm Mon-Sat; 1-4pm Sun. Closed Aug.* **Map** *p83 G13* ❶ *Spanish*

Holding court on a quiet backstreet, this dignified, classic Madrid restaurant is considered by many to be the home of *cocido*, the huge and hearty stew beloved of *madrileños*, and here still cooked in traditional earthenware pots on a wood fire. La Bola Taberna is still run by the same family that founded it in

the 19th century, but this hugely impressive pedigree has led to a certain complacency among some of the waiting staff.

❤ Casa Lafu €€

C/Flor Baja 1 (91 548 70 96, www. casalafu.com). Metro Santo Domingo. **Open** *noon-midnight Mon-Thur; noon-12.30am Fri-Sun.* **Map** *p83 G12* ❷ *Chinese*

Superb *huo guo* (Chinese hot pot) restaurant, with queues out of the door. The dim sum are also excellent, as are the dumplings and wok dishes (you can specify how spicy you'd like them), but don't expect too much by way of charm from the waiting staff.

La Terraza del Casino €€€€

C/Alcalá 15 (91 532 12 75, www. casinodemadrid.es). Metro Sevilla. **Open** *1.30-3.30pm, 9-11.30pm Mon-Sat. Closed Aug.* **Map** *p83 K14* ❸ *Modern European*

The sumptuous environs of this gentlemen's club provide the setting for a restaurant inspired by gourmet god Ferran Adrià. Paco Roncero, a former disciple, is at the helm in the kitchen, and has put his own stamp on the cooking, winning Michelin stars along the way. The menu changes seasonally, but might include such delights as lobster sashimi and crunchy black algae.

Gran Vía

Tapas bars

Casa Labra

*C/Tetuán 12 (91 531 00 81, www.
casalabra.es). Metro Sol.* **Open**
11am-3.30pm, 6-11pm daily. **Map**
p83 H14 ❶
Famously the birthplace of the
Spanish Socialist Party back in 1879,
this legendary bar, with its brown
1950s paintwork and luggage racks,
is worth a visit for its history alone.
Speciality of the house is the cod
croquetas served up by dour white-
jacketed waiters.

Cafés & bars

❤ La Casa de las Torrijas

*C/Paz 4 (91 025 29 02). Metro
Sol.* **Open** *11am-5pm Mon, Sun,
11am-11.30pm Tue-Sat. Closed Aug.*
No cards. *Map p83 J15* ❶
Formerly known as the As de
los Vinos, this is a charmingly
unkempt bar, tiled and mirrored,
with table-tops constructed from
old enamel adverts. Since 1907, it
has served little more than *torrijas*
– bread soaked in wine and spices,
coated in sugar and deep-fried –

and house wine. If that doesn't appeal, there are a handful of other, simple tapas, along with a basic set lunch.

💜 Hemingway
C/Marqués de Casa Riera (91 200 05 70, www.nh-hotels.com/hotel/ nh-collection-madrid-suecia/ restaurants). Metro Banco de España. **Open** *8pm-2am daily.* **Map** *p83 L14* ②
The *dernier cri* in bar culture is the speakeasy, but none does it better than Hemingway, entered from the street down some stairs and through the toilets. The art deco doors open on to a subterranean film set – a long old-school cocktail bar with a romantic nook of leopard-skin sofas. The DJs who play most nights make this a place that will only really appeal to a youngish crowd, however.

💜 La Mallorquina
Puerta del Sol 8 (91 521 12 01, www. pasteleriamallorquina.es). Metro Sol. **Open** *8.15am-9.15pm daily. Closed 1wk Aug.* **Map** *p83 J14* ③
While the atmospheric bakery downstairs supplies box after ribbon-tied box of flaky pastries, croissants and *napolitanas* to what seems like half of Madrid, the upstairs *salón* crackles with the animated chat of *madrileña* blue-rinses and savvier tourists. Windows overlooking the Puerta del Sol make this an unbeatable central spot for breakfast. The coffee is cheap and very good.

💜 Museo Chicote
Gran Vía 12 (91 532 67 37, grupomercado delareina.com/es/ museo-chicote). Metro Gran Vía. **Open** *7pm-3am Mon-Thur, Sun; 7pm-3.30am Fri, Sat. Closed Aug.* **Map** *p83 K13* ④
Its art deco interior is starting to look a bit shabby around the edges, but Chicote is still the doyen of Madrid cocktail bars. This was

famously where Hemingway and other international press hacks would spend their days sheltering from the artillery shells flying down the Gran Vía during the Civil War. Grace Kelly and Ava Gardner, along with just about every Spanish writer, actor or artist of the last 60 years, have passed through too. There are various resident DJs, playing electro-soul, funk, hip hop and anything with a groove.

Shops & services

💜 Antigua Casa Talavera
C/Isabel la Católica 2 (91 547 34 17, www.antiguacasatalavera. com). Metro Santo Domingo. **Open** *10am-1.30pm, 5-8pm Mon-Fri; 10am-1.30pm Sat.* **Map** *p83 G13* ①
Gifts & souvenirs
This long-standing family business specialises in traditional blue-and-white Spanish ceramics. Every available space is crammed with hand-painted designs, all sourced from small Spanish producers. The charming owner speaks good English.

Área Real Madrid
C/Carmen 3 (91 521 79 50). Metro Sol. **Open** *10am-9pm Mon-Sat; 11am-8pm Sun.* **Map** *p83 J14* ②
Gifts & souvenirs
A true emporium for the Real Madrid-inclined. On sale are, naturally, replica shirts and all manner of other stuff bearing the club's logo, from ashtrays to mouse mats, bath towels to undies.

Casa de Diego
Puerta del Sol 12 (91 522 66 43, www.casadediego.info). Metro Sol. **Open** *9.30am-8pm Mon-Sat.* **Map** *p83 J14* ③ *Gifts & souvenirs*
This much-loved shop specialises in hand-painted fans, umbrellas and classy walking sticks. **Other locations** C/Mesoneros Romanos 4 (91 531 02 23).

La Casa del Libro

Gran Vía 29 (902 026 402, www. casadellibro.com). Metro Gran Vía. **Open** *9.30am-9.30pm Mon-Sat; 11am-9pm Sun.* **Map** *p83 J13* ❹
Books & music

La Casa del Libro covers just about every subject imaginable in Spanish, but also has good sections of literature, reference and teaching material in English and other languages.

♥ Guantes Luque

C/Espoz y Mina 3 (91 522 32 87). Metro Sol. **Open** *10am-1.30pm, 5-8pm Mon-Fri; 10.30am-1.30pm Sat. Closed Aug.* **Map** *p83 J14* ❺
Fashion

This old-fashioned glove shop in Santa Ana was established in 1886. Luque sells gloves in all sizes, colours and materials, covering all types of wool, silk and leather. If you can't find them here you won't find them anywhere. Prices range from €20 to €300.

Entertainment

Café Berlin

C/Costanilla de los Ángeles 20 (91 559 74 29, berlincafe.es). Metro Callao. **Open** *10pm-5.30am Tue-Sat; 9pm-3am Sun.* **Admission** *varies.* **Map** *p83 G13* ❶ *Live music*

A stalwart on the Madrid scene, the legendary Café Berlin was forced to move from its old location in 2016, but its fancy new digs (just round the corner) are bigger and plusher. Gigs usually get going around 10pm, with salsa on Tuesdays and flamenco on Wednesdays. The concerts are followed by club sessions from 1am (Tue-Sun).

Café de Chinitas

C/Torija 7, Sol & Gran Vía (91 559 51 35/91 547 15 02, www.chinitas. com). Metro Santo Domingo. **Open** *7pm-midnight Mon-Sat.* **Performances** *8.15pm, 10.30pm Mon-Sat.* **Admission** *€36, or €67 (incl dinner).* **Map** *p83 G13* ❷
Flamenco

Joy Eslava

Squaring Up

The reinvention of Plaza de España

For an illustrative example of the changes Mayor Manuela Carmena is introducing to the city, head to Plaza de España. In February 2017 she gave *madrileños* their first-ever vote on a city planning proposal when she asked them to pick the design to polish up the *plaza*. The winner – whittled down from close to 70 projects – was architects Lorenzo Fernández-Ordóñez and Fernando Porras-Isla's 'Welcome Mother Nature, Goodbye Mr Ford', which will spruce up the square with 1,000 new trees and further cover surrounding roads to create pedestrianised green 'corridors' linking the *plaza* with the Palacio Real's Sabatini Gardens and the Parque Oeste. A new esplanade will connect the square to Gran Vía, while a central clearing will provide a space for activities.

The enormous 117-metre (384-foot) Edificio España, which looms over the *plaza*, will also be getting a long-awaited makeover after a decade lying derelict. Built as a showpiece for the Franco regime in 1948-53 it has recently been bought by Mallorcan hotel chain Riu, which plans to spend €400 million turning it into a 650-room hotel.

Scheduled to open in 2019, it won't be the only new hotel on the block. The boutique Dear Madrid on the corner with Gran Vía was the first new arrival in 2015, followed two years later by the five-star Barceló Torre Madrid in the plaza's other skyscraper, the Torre de Madrid. With the similarly exclusive VP Plaza de España adding to the square's luxury accommodation options in autumn 2017, Plaza de España is scrubbing up well.

Edificio España

An indulgent evening's entertainment for those who like to play at being 19th-century aristocrats – and don't mind paying 21st-century prices. At least this self-styled 'Cathedral of Flamenco' makes an effort, with sumptuous decor that contributes to the experience. The food and floorshow are expensive, yes, but at least it means the owners can afford to pay top euro for flamenco stars, who will send you reeling into the night.

Joy Eslava

C/Arenal 11 (91 366 37 33, joy-eslava.com). Metro Ópera or Sol. **Open** *Club nights midnight-6am daily.* **Admission** *€20 (incl 2 drinks).* **Map** *p83 H14* ❸ *Club*
Unusual in that it retains some original trappings of its former incarnation as a 19th-century theatre, in every other respect this is an ordinary high-street club, where the vast dancefloor is crammed with a young and dressed-up set,

Teatro de la Zarzuela

enjoying staple disco house. As a live music venue, Joy Eslava hosts some of the best Spanish names, from flamenco supremo Tomasito and beloved crooner Raphael to Catalan popsters Manel.

El Sol

*C/Jardines 3 (91 532 64 90, www. salaelsol.com). Metro Gran Vía or Sol. **Open** 10pm-5.30am Tue-Sat. Concerts vary. **Admission** (incl 1 drink) €12. **Map** p83 K13 ❹ Live music*

To call this Movida remnant 'no-frills' is an understatement – as its faded yellow walls and middle-aged bar staff attest. However, as everyone knows, it's the music and crowd that make a night, and that's where El Sol is a winner. A steady flow of live acts pass through, offering a mix of rock, R&B, punk, soul and hip hop. The DJ serves up an equally eclectic selection. Before long you're lured on to the floor and there you'll stay, getting down with a varied crowd of twenty- and thirtysomethings. The venue is the city's classic climax to a big night out.

Teatro de la Zarzuela

*C/Jovellanos 4, Sol & Gran Vía (box office 98 567 96 68, 902 22 49 49 teatrodelazarzuela.mcu.es). Metro Banco de España. **Box office** noon-8pm Mon-Fri; 2.30-8pm Sat, Sun. **Main season** Sept-July. Tickets €5-€50. **Map** p83 L14 ❺ Zarzuela*

The Teatro de la Zarzuela, which served as an opera house for many years before the Teatro Real's renovation, is now principally devoted to its raison d'être – staging *zarzuela*, home-grown Spanish operetta. Despite *zarzuela*'s uncool image and lack of credibility among serious music-lovers, it retains considerable popularity, drawing decent audiences for its frequent performances. Accompanying the Teatro's packed *zarzuela* programme are dance performances (often put on by the Ballet Nacional), concerts, plays, conferences and family-orientated shows. The annual Ciclo del Lied, which pays tribute to the lesser-known 19th-century German song form, has an excellent reputation.

Huertas & Santa Ana

Spain has more bars and restaurants per capita than any other country in the world, and you can get the impression that most of Madrid's are crowded into the wedge-shaped swathe of streets between C/Alcalá and C/Atocha. This was once the haunt of Madrid's Golden Age literary set, which explains the district's rather fussy alternative name of **Barrio de las Letras** ('The District of Letters'; *see p100*). Here were the theatres that provided them with a living, along with brothels and low dives for entertainment. It is still the city's most distinctive theatre district. A tidying up of the area has brought about pedestrianisation of much of Huertas's streets, and literary quotes inlaid in bronze underfoot.

❤ **Shortlist**

Best sight
The staggering, eclectic, art collection at the Museo Thyssen-Bornemisza (p96) is one of the top draws in Madrid (and Spain).

Best literary footsteps
See how the men of letters lived at the Casa-Museo Lope de Vega (p97), or stroll as they once did around the Barrio de las Letras (p100).

Best tipple
Try a house cocktail at Salmón Guru (p103) or a fragrant glass of *fino* at La Venencia (p103).

Best historical buildings
The Palacio del Congreso de los Diputados (p97) holds the Spanish parliament, while the nearby Teatro Español (p104) is just as storied.

Best new-wave restaurants
Tandem (p99) is the even more relaxed little sister to TriCiclo (p99), and both are among the best of Madrid's recent openings.

Best for old-school dining
Lhardy (p98) is hard to beat for bygone elegance, while Casa Alberto (p99) wins for convivial atmosphere.

Lope de Vega's charming old house, the **Casa-Museo Lope de Vega**, with its tiny garden, is on the street named after his enemy, Miguel Cervantes, the author of *Don Quixote*. Cervantes lived around the corner on C/León, but was buried in the enclosed convent of the **Trinitarias Descalzas** (see p98 Cervantes' dying wish) on C/Lope de Vega, which seems deliberately confusing. Coming upon the massively plain, slab-like brick walls of the Trinitarias amid the Huertas bars is a great surprise, and gives a vivid impression of what old Madrid must have looked like before the great clear-out of religious houses in the 1830s, of which this is a rare survivor.

In the north-east corner of the neighbourhood is the world-famous **Museo Thyssen-Bornemisza** (see p96), containing one of the world's most important private collections of 20th-century (and other) art. Head up the hill in the other direction and you'll reach **Lhardy**, the classic Franco-Spanish restaurant founded in 1839. North of San Jerónimo, behind the Congreso, is the grand 1856 **Teatro de la Zarzuela**, the city's most characterfully distinguished music theatre.

The core of the district, **Plaza Santa Ana**, is lined by some of the city's most popular bars and pavement terraces, Santa Ana has long been one of Madrid's favourite places for hanging out. On the eastern side of the *plaza* is the distinguished **Teatro Español**, on a site that has been a theatre continuously since 1583.

➜ **Getting around**
Packing a big punch in a small area (around ten minutes' walk between its furthest reaches), Huertas' bars and restaurants are best accessed on foot, but Anton Martín is a convenient metro station (L1).

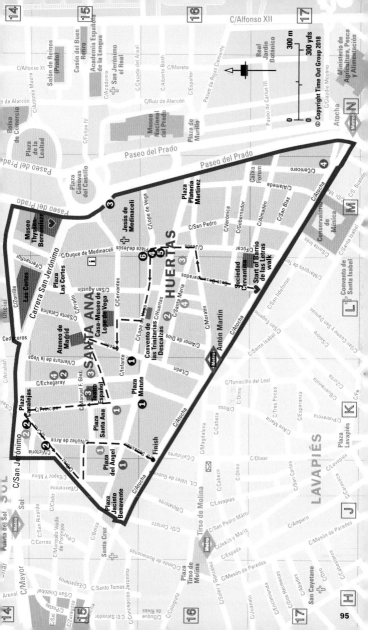

❤ Museo Thyssen-Bornemisza

Palacio de Villahermosa, Paseo del Prado 8 (91 791 13 70, www. museothyssen.org). Metro Banco de España. **Open** *Permanent collection noon-4pm Mon; 10am-7pm Tue-Sun. Temporary exhibitions 10am-7pm Tue-Fri, Sun; 10am-9pm Sat.* **Admission** *€12; €8 reductions; free under-12s. Free to all Mon. Paseo del Arte ticket €29.60. Temporary exhibitions varies.* **Map** *p95 M15.*

The formerly private collection of the late Baron Hans-Heinrich Thyssen-Bornemisza is widely considered to be the most important in the world. Consisting of some 800 paintings, from old masters to contemporary works, it is housed in the Palacio de Villahermosa, an early 19th-century edifice superbly converted by architect Rafael Moneo at fantastic cost. Thanks to this revamp, involving terracotta-pink walls, marble floors and skylights, it is possible to view the works with near-perfect illumination. A more recently added wing exhibits some 250 works from the collection of the baron's widow, Carmen 'Tita' Cervera.

The collection
Beginning on the second floor, you'll find 13th-century paintings, notably by the early Italians. You finish the tour on the ground floor, with Roy Lichtenstein's *Woman in Bath*. The collection partly complements the Prado and Reina Sofía's collections, with large holdings of 17th-century Dutch painting, plus works of Impressionism, German expressionism, Russian constructivism, geometric abstraction and pop art.

One of the Thyssen's great attractions is that, while it is extraordinarily broad in scope, it is recognisably a personal collection that reflects a distinct taste, as seen in the room dedicated to early portraits, with works by Antonello da Messina and Hans Memling. Equally quirky is the section on early North American painting, including the *Presumed Portrait of George Washington's Cook* by Gilbert Stuart.

It has its share of real masterpieces. Among the old masters, the works of Duccio, van Eyck and Petrus Christus stand out. The museum's most famous painting, however, is the great Florentine master Domenico Ghirlandaio's idealised *Portrait of Giovanna Tornabuoni* (1488) in the Portrait Room. Two rooms further on is Vittore Carpaccio's

allegorical *Young Knight in a Landscape* (1510), another gem. There are also representative works by Titian, El Greco, Rubens and Tintoretto.

Modern masters such as Braque, Mondrian, Klee, Max Ernst and Picasso (his 1911 *Man with a Clarinet*) are on the ground floor. The last few rooms focus on the USA, with works by Georgia O'Keeffe and Edward Hopper.

One wing exhibits some 250 works from the private collection of 'Tita' Cervera. It includes early Italian and Flemish works by the likes of Jan Breughel and van Dyck, and landscapes by Canaletto, Constable, Guardi and van Gogh. Two rooms are given over to Gauguin and other post-impressionists, and others to German expressionists, Fauvists and the early 20th-century avant-garde. The collection also contains four sculptures by Rodin.

Hotel Room (Edward Hopper, 1931)

♥ Casa-Museo Lope de Vega

C/Cervantes 11 (91 429 92 16). Metro Antón Martín. **Open** *(by appt only) 10am-6pm Tue-Sun. Closed Aug.* **Admission** *free.* **Map** *p95 L15.*

Spain's most prolific playwright and poet, Félix Lope de Vega Carpio (1562-1635), spent the last 25 years of his life in this simple, tranquil three-storey house. Oddly enough, the street in which it stands is now named after his arch rival Cervantes (who, confusingly, is buried in a convent on the nearby C/Lope de Vega). The house and charming garden – remarkable survivors from the Golden Age – are the most interesting things to see. The furniture and ornaments are approximations to Lope de Vega's household inventory, rather than the originals. However, even the garden contains the same fruit trees and plants he detailed in his journals. Visits are by guided tour only – call ahead to book.

♥ Palacio del Congreso de los Diputados (Las Cortes)

Carrera de San Jerónimo (91 390 65 25, www.congreso.es). Metro Banco de España or Sevilla. **Open** *Guided tours noon Mon; (by appt) noon Fri, 10.30am-12.30pm Sat. Closed Aug.* **Admission** *free.* **Map** *p95 L14.*

Spain's parliament, the Cortes, was built in 1843-50 by Narciso Pascual y Colomer on the site of a recently demolished monastery, which has led to no end of problems, as the plot is too cramped to accommodate the legislators' ancillary offices. A classical portico gives it a suitably dignified air, but the building is best distinguished by the handsome 1860 bronze lions that guard its entrance. Guided tours can be booked in advance for Fridays and Saturdays, and are available on Mondays without advance reservation; tours may be suspended, depending on parliamentary activity.

Palacio del Congreso de los Diputados

CONGRESO DE LOS DIPUTADOS

Restaurants

Ana La Santa €€

Plaza Santa Ana 14 (91 701 60 13, www.encompaniadelobos.com). Metro Sol. **Open** *noon-1am Mon-Thur, Sun; noon-2am Fri, Sat.* **Map** *p95 K15* ① *Global*

Bright, comfortable Ana La Santa functions as breakfast room and a kind of extended lobby for the ME Reina Victoria hotel, which dominates the building, but comes into its own in the evenings, when its lounge area and plant-filled gallery brim with groups of friends. Dishes range from tuna sashimi with chipotle and avocado mayonnaise to paella, and there are tapas sharing plates.

♥ Lhardy €€€€

Carrera de San Jerónimo 8 (91 521 33 85, www.lhardy.com). Metro Sol. **Open** *1-3.30pm, 8.30-11pm Mon-Sat; 1-3.30pm Sun. Closed Aug.* **Map** *p95 K14* ② *Spanish/French*

This landmark restaurant, which opened in 1839, is credited with having introduced French haute cuisine into the culinary wilderness of Madrid. Founder Emile Lhardy is said to have been enticed to the city by none other than *Carmen* author Prosper Mérimée, who told him there were no decent restaurants in the Spanish capital. These days, it's rated as much for its belle époque decor as for the food. The menu is as Frenchified as ever, although there's also a very refined *cocido*, good game and *callos* (tripe), in addition to an excellent, if pricey, wine list.

In the know
Cervantes' dying wish

Had it not been for the nuns at the Convento de Trinitarias Descalzas, the world might have been deprived of one of its all-time greatest works, *Don Quixote*. Its author, Miguel de Cervantes, was shot and injured serving in the navy, and – shortly afterwards – kidnapped by Algerian pirates. After their son had been held in slavery for five years, his parents appealed to the nuns for help. The sisters raised the ransom money and had him released, and it was Cervantes' last request that he be buried in the convent alongside those who had saved his life.

❤ Tandem €€

*C/Santa María 39 (91 138 62 98,
www.eltriciclo.es/tandem). Metro
Antón Martín.* **Open** *10am-4pm
Mon-Sat, 11am-3.30pm Sun.* **Map**
p95 L16 ❸ *Global*

Casual little sister of TriCiclo
(*see below*), Tandem is all shared
scrubbed pine tables and yelled
orders, but the food is almost as
good. Globally influenced dishes
are available as *raciones* and half-
raciones and range from excellent
mackerel tartare (not on the
menu, just ask) and pork steamed
buns to a typically Madrid squid
sandwich. Various brunch deals are
also on offer.

❤ TriCiclo €€

*C/Santa María 28 (91 024 47
98, www.eltriciclo.es). Metro
Antón Martín.* **Open** *1.30-4pm,
8.30pm-midnight Mon-Sat.* **Map**
p95 L16 ❹ *Global*

Perhaps the most exciting of Huertas'
recent raft of openings, TriCiclo
offers its dishes in three different
sizes, so it's possible to try several
without breaking the bank. Peppery
steak tartare with a crispy quail's egg
is superb, as is the marinated sardine
with fennel granita and almond milk
– finish with divine fried brioche
with ice-cream and fruits of the
forest. There's also a seven-course
tasting *menú* for €50. Book ahead.

Tapas bars

❤ Casa Alberto

*C/Huertas 18 (91 429 93 56, www.
casaalberto.es). Metro Antón
Martín.* **Open** *noon-12.30am Tue-
Sat; noon-4pm Sun. Closed Aug &
2wks Xmas.* **Map** *p95 K16* ❶

One of the city's most evocative
tabernas, hung with oil
paintings and presided over by a
septuagenarian. It still has its old
zinc bar complete with running
water trough to keep the wine cool
and a draught beer head with five

founts. Try lambs' trotters, garlicky
prawns, *morcilla* (black pudding)
with goat's cheese, or oxtail stew as
tapas, or more substantial dishes in
the restaurant at the back.

La Casa del Abuelo

*C/Victoria 12 (91 000 01 33). Metro
Sol.* **Open** *noon-midnight Mon-
Thur, Sun; noon-1am Fri, Sat.* **Map**
p95 K15 ❷

For over a century, the Casa del
Abuelo has stuck to one very
simple, and winning, formula
– prawns and small *chatos* of
slightly sweet red wine served in
bright, old-school surroundings.
The surprisingly drinkable red is
for sale by the bottle (€5.50) and
when it's over you can even buy the
T-shirt. **Other locations** C/Goya 57,
Salamanca (91 000 01 33); C/Núñez
de Arce 5, Santa Ana (91 000 01 33).

Estado Puro

*Plaza Cánovas del Castillo 4 (91 779
30 36, tapasenestadopuro.com).
Metro Antón Martín.* **Open** *noon-
1am daily.* **Map** *p95 M15* ❸

Chef Paco Roncero oversees the
kitchen at this NH Hotel initiative,
which turns out classic tapas with
a modern twist, from fancy takes
on *patatas bravas* to deconstructed
tortilla. The cool, black interior
evokes an upmarket diner while
riffing on the trad Spanish theme,
with a wave of white mantilla
combs arranged artfully overhead
and a thousand flamenco dolls in
an eruption of kitsch behind the
glass of the counter.

La Fábrica

*C/Jesús 2 (91 369 06 71). Metro
Antón Martin or Sevilla.* **Open**
10am-1am daily. **Map** *p95 M16* ❹

There are long lists of the canapés
on offer, but most are on display. Try
the *matrimonio* (preserved and fresh
anchovies – the perfect combination)
or the *divorcio* (anchovies and
mussels – no kind of match), or the
orgia (all three). Ahem.

❤ Barrio de las Letras

This 30-minute walk (marked on the map on *p95*) takes you on a tour of the cafés, theatres and churches around Plaza Santa Ana that were the centre of Spain's literary life during the 16th- and 17th-century Golden Age.

▶ *Begin at the junction of C/Atocha with Costanilla de los Desamparados.*
C/Atocha 87 was once home to the printing press where the first edition of *Don Quixote* was published. It is now the **Sociedad Cervantina**, a cultural centre with a theatre and printing press. See the bronze bas-relief of a scene from the book and, above, the head of Cervantes.

▶ *Walk up Desamparados and turn right down C/Moratín.*
At the **Plazuela de San Juan** is a plaque celebrating poet and playwright Leandro Moratín, born here in 1760.

▶ *Turn left up C/Jesús and left again on C/Lope de Vega.*
The church ahead of the junction, on the right, is the **Iglesia de Jesús de Medinaceli**, famously a 17th-century centre of rumour and gossip, especially when attended by the great actresses of the time. Up on C/Lope de Vega, on the left, is the **Convento de las Trinitarias**, where Cervantes is buried. On 22 April, the anniversary of his death, a mass is held for him and the other great Spanish writers.

▶ *Turn right up C/Quevedo.*
On the right-hand corner is a plaque marking the house where 17th-century rivals Francisco de Quevedo and Luis de Góngora lived. Quevedo, a satirist, made mincemeat of the hapless and

terminally ill poet Góngora in an exchange of verse. He also triumphed posthumously, when the council renamed the street after him, failing to mention Góngora on the plaque. At the end of the street, on C/Cervantes 11, is the **Casa-Museo Lope de Vega** (*see p97*), where Lope de Vega lived and died. No.2 on this street was built on the site of Cervantes' old house.

▶ *Turn left, and right down C/León to C/Prado.*
At no.21 is the **Ateneo** library, with an impressive marble staircase, walls lined with portraits of Spain's greatest figures and delightfully antiquated rooms. Back up C/Prado, you arrive at the **Plaza Santa Ana**, home to the **Teatro Español** and bars such as the **Cervecería Alemana** (*see p102*), where writers such as the playwright Ramón del Valle-Inclán and, later, Ernest Hemingway were regulars. The theatre itself sits on the site of one of the great open-air *corral* theatres of the Golden Age.

▶ *Facing the theatre, turn left up C/Príncipe.*
This street was home to many of the literary haunts of the day, but the only one that remains is **Las Cuevas de Sésamo** at no.7 (*C/ Príncipe 7, 91 429 65 24*), worth a visit for the quotes painted on the walls and the printed history the staff will give anyone who's interested.

▶ *At Plaza Canalejas turn left down C/Cruz.*
C/Victoria on the left has a plaque marking the site of the writers' and politicians' meeting point and

subject of Benito Pérez Galdos' eponymous novel, **La Fontana de Oro**. Further up C/Cruz is a mural depicting a reflection of the street, and asking, 'Where has the theatre gone? Or is the street the theatre?' The theatre in question is the **Corral de la Cruz**, another open-air theatre that stood on the site.

▶ *Turn left down C/Álvarez Gato, through the square and down C/San Sebastián.*

What is now a florist in the yard on the corner with C/Huertas used to be the graveyard for the adjacent **Iglesia de San Sebastián**; the ancient olive tree remains a symbol for all the literary luminaries buried there. Opposite is a plaque showing the site of the **Fonda de San Sebastián** – favoured hangout of the 18th-century writers.

Sociedad Cervantina

Plaza Santa Ana

Los Gatos

*C/Jesús 2 (91 429 30 67). Metro Antón Martin or Sevilla. **Open** 11am-1am Mon-Thur, Sun; 11am-2am Fri, Sat. **Map** p95 M16* ❺

With their reputation for staying out all night, *madrileños* are popularly known as *'los gatos'* (the cats) and there's nowhere better than here to begin a night prowling the tiles. The bar is hung with all manner of paraphernalia from gramophones to choirboy mannequins – here you can get a selection of tasty canapés and a good frothy beer.

Taberna La Dolores

*Plaza de Jesús 4 (91 429 22 43). Metro Antón Martín. **Open** 11am-1am Mon-Thur, Sun; 11am-2am Fri, Sat. **Map** p95 M16* ❻

A Madrid classic, with wonderful tiling outside and rows of dusty beer steins inside, La Dolores has been serving ice-cold frothy beer since the 1920s. There's a short list of tapas, which are good if a bit expensive. Specialities are smoked fish, anchovies and *mojama* (wind-dried tuna).

Cafés & bars

Cervecería Alemana

*Plaza Santa Ana 6 (91 429 70 33, www.cerveceriaalemana.com). Metro Sol. **Open** 11am-midnight Mon-Thur, Sun; 11am-2am Fri, Sat. **Map** p95 K15* ❶

Famous for being Ernest Hemingway's daily haunt (his table was the one in the near right-hand corner). The decor is fin de siècle German *bierkeller*, with dusty old paintings and dark wood. The tapas can be uninspired and the waiters are unfailingly gruff, but for many this will be an essential stop.

Dos Gardenias

*C/Santa María 13 (mobile 627 003 571). Metro Antón Martín. **Open** May-Oct 9.30am-2.30am Tue-Sun. Nov-Apr 9.30am-2.30am Tue-Sat; 9.30am-7pm Sun. **Map** p95 L16* ❷

There's no sign on the door – just look out for this mellow little space painted in warm yellow, orange and blue, and the emanating chilled-out vibes, soft flamenco and Brazilian jazz. Kick back on a velvet sofa with the house speciality: a mojito made with brown sugar and Angostura bitters.

Salmón Guru

Café Central p104

♥ Salmón Guru
*C/Echegaray 21 (91 000 61 85,
www.salmonguru.es). Metro Antón
Martín. Open 5pm-2am Tue-Sun.
Map p95 K15* ❸
The latest venture of mixologist
supreme Diego Cabrera is a crazily
eclectic affair, mixing tones of
gentlemen's drinking club with
colonial garden party and tossing
in some Manhattan neon and
zebra-skinned barstools for good
measure. The list of cocktails
includes 25 classics, and a list of
house specials – try the Tónico
Sprenger, with gin, lemon juice,
cardamom, cinnamon, cucumber
and ginger beer.

♥ La Venencia
*C/Echegaray 7 (91 429 73 13). Metro
Sevilla or Sol. Open 3.30-10.30pm
daily. No cards. Map p95 K15* ❹
Totally unreconstructed, La
Venencia is gloriously shabby, with
old, peeling sherry posters, barrels
behind the bar and walls burnished
gold by decades of tobacco smoke.
It serves only sherry (locals
will order a crisp, dry *fino* or
manzanilla, leaving the sweet stuff
to the occasional tourist), along
with manchego cheese, *cecina* (air-

dried beef) and chorizo by way of
tapas. Orders are still chalked up
on the bar, and an enamel sign asks
customers not to spit on the floor.

Shops & services

González
*C/León 12 (91 429 56 18). Metro
Antón Martín. Open Sept-June
9am-midnight Mon-Thur;
9.30am-1am Fri, Sat; 11am-6pm
Sun. July, Aug 6pm-midnight Mon-
Sat. Map p95 K15* ❶ *Food & drink*
Once a local grocer's, González is
now a smart delicatessen with a
fine range of cheeses, charcuterie,
preserves, fruit and nuts, olive
oils and plenty more besides. The
back room houses a pleasant, well-
stocked wine bar.

La Violeta
*Plaza Canalejas 6 (91 522 55 22,
www. lavioletaonline.es). Metro Sol.
Open 10am-8pm Mon-Sat. Closed
Aug. Map p95 K14* ❷ *Gifts*
The violet is an emblem of the city,
and La Violeta has been doling
them out in candied form since
1915, counting Alfonso XIII among
its most enthusiastic clients (it

103

is said he used to buy violets for both his wife and his lover here). Little heart-shaped tins of violet-perfumed sweets make perfect gifts, as does violet tea or honey.

Entertainment

Café Central

Plaza del Ángel 10 (91 369 41 43, www.cafecentralmadrid.com). Metro Antón Martín or Sol. **Open** *11am-2.30am Mon-Thur, Sun; 11am-3.30am Fri, Sat.* **Concerts** *9-11pm daily.* **Admission** *Concerts €15-€24.* **Map** *p95 J15* ❶ *Live music*

For many years now, this beautiful space, with high ceilings and elegant decor, has been *the* place to get your jazz fix in Madrid. The artists it attracts place it among Europe's best jazz venues. Recent acts include the Jean Toussaint Quartet, Wallace Roney, Rick Margitza Quartet, and Pia Tedesco, who is one to look out for.

Cardamomo

C/Echegaray 15 (91 429 98 75, www.cardamomo.es). Metro Sevilla. **Open** *6pm-4am daily.* **Performance** *6pm, 8pm, 10pm, 11.30pm daily.* **Admission** *(incl 1 drink) €39, set tapas and dinners €15-€65 (plus admission).* **Map** *p95 K15* ❷ *Flamenco*

A firm fixture on the scene, this frenetic flamenco bar plays a mixture of flamenco and rumba tunes, often to thundering effect.

❤ Teatro Español

C/Príncipe 25 (box office 91 360 14 84, information 91 318 47 00, www. teatroespanol.es). Metro Sevilla or Sol. **Box office** *11.30am-1.30pm, 5-7pm Tue-Sat; 11.30am-1.30pm, 5-6pm Sun (same-day tickets available until start of performance). Tickets €5-€22.* **Map** *p95 K15* ❸ *Theatre*

This grand theatre on Plaza Santa Ana dates back to 1745, but that doesn't mean it's old-fashioned – in fact, it has enjoyed some fairly radical programming in recent years. The 2017-18 season included productions of Euripides' *Trojan Women*, Nelly Arcan's *La fureur de ce que je pense*, and Luis Buñuel's *El Ángel Exterminador*.

Teatro Kapital

C/Atocha 125 (91 420 29 06, www. grupo-kapital. com). Metro Atocha. **Open** *midnight-5.30am Thur; midnight-6am Fri, Sat.* **Admission** *€10-€30.* **Map** *p95 M17* ❹ *Club*

This giant among Madrid clubs offers splendid views of the main dancefloor from many of the upper balconies. Each of the seven levels has something different to offer: the main dancefloor and bars are at ground level; the first floor has a VIP area; the second has karaoke; the third R&B and hip hop; the fourth a cosy cocktail bar; the fifth is the so-called 'Party Zone'; the sixth is all about mojitos; and at the top is a terrace with a retractable roof and smoking area. Smart casual is the order of the day.

Teatro Español

Lavapiés & the Rastro

Once the Jewish quarter, long the main working-class area and still home to a large gypsy community, Lavapiés is also the most racially mixed *barrio* in the city, though the tendrils of gentrification are spreading this way. South of Sol and the Plaza Mayor, this is the area traditionally considered the home of Madrid's *castizos* – something like London's East End cockneys. Historically these districts were known as the *barrios bajos*, in the double sense of low-lying and full of low life – the closer to the river, the shabbier the surroundings. In imperial Madrid, most of the food brought to the city came in through the Puerta de Toledo, and many of the tasks that the upper classes wanted neither to see nor smell, such as slaughtering and tanning, were concentrated here.

LAVAPIÉS & THE RASTRO

Best sights
The Museo Nacional Centro de Arte Reina Sofía (p108) for contemporary Spanish art, and the Rastro fleamarket (p111) for people-watching.

Best buildings
The art nouveau façade of the Cine Doré (p114) is a sight in itself, and the Baroque Iglesia-Catedral de San Isidro (p110) merits a detour.

Best nights out
Foot-stomping flamenco at Casa Patas (p114) or a glammed-up drag show at Medias Puri (p114).

Best views
Cultural centre La Casa Encendida (p110) has a great rooftop bar with spectacular views, but the scruffy little Casa Granada (p112) is where the cognoscenti watch the sunset.

Best nose-to-tail eating
Freiduría de Gallinejas (p110) is not for the squeamish, but Malacatín (p112) has something for anyone with a big enough appetite.

Best drinking
A glass of iced vermouth at Taberna de Antonio Sánchez (p112) or a dazzling choice of reds at La Fisna (p113).

The northernmost point of Lavapiés is just south of the Plaza Mayor, where, at the corner of C/Toledo, stand the twin baroque towers of **San Isidro**, perhaps Madrid's most important historic church. Head south of San Isidro down C/Estudios and its continuation, C/Ribera de Curtidores, to reach the **Rastro** flea market (see p111).

Plaza Tirso de Molina, with its statue of the Golden Age dramatist whose name it bears, is the main crossroads between these *barrios bajos* and the centre. From here C/Mesón de Paredes winds off down the hill. Towards the bottom is **La Corrala**, a late 19th-century courtyard tenement. The *corrala* has become a characteristic of Madrid life; this one, restored in the 1980s, is used in summer as a setting for a season of *zarzuela* comic operas. At the bottom of

this area is a dynamic cultural centre, **La Casa Encendida**.

The **Plaza de Lavapiés** has several good cafés and restaurants, as well as the Teatro Valle-Inclán. The narrow, very steep streets between the *plaza* and C/Atocha are more peaceful than those around C/Mesón de Paredes and, with geraniums on many of the balconies, often strikingly pretty. At the top of the area by C/Atocha is the Filmoteca Española film theatre, in the **Cine Doré** building.

Running away from the south-east corner of the Plaza de Lavapiés is **C/Argumosa**, with its shops and outdoor terrace bars that make a popular alternative to the more expensive and hectic places further into town. Argumosa leads towards Atocha and the **Museo Nacional Centro de Arte Reina Sofía** (see p108).

→ Getting around
The area is small enough to stroll on foot, but there are various metro stations, including La Latina (L5), Embajadores and Lavapiés (L3), and Tirso de Molina (L1).

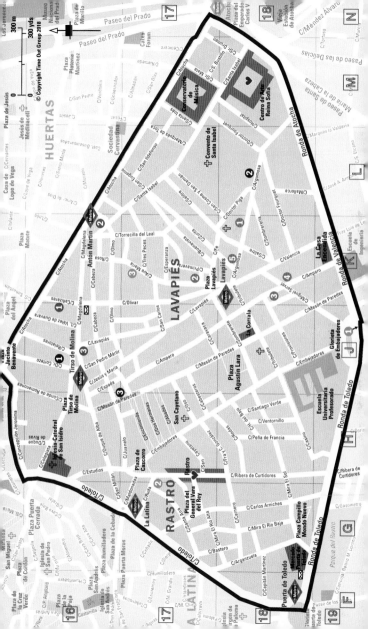

💜 Museo Nacional Centro de Arte Reina Sofía

Edificio Sabatini C/Santa Isabel 52. *Edificio Nouvel* Plaza del Emperador Carlos V s/n. *Both* 91 791 13 30, www. museoreinasofia.es. Metro Atocha. *Open* 10am-9pm Mon, Wed-Sat; 10am-7pm Sun. *Admission* €10 (€8 online); free students, under-18s, over-65s. Free to all 7-9pm Mon, Wed-Sat; 1.30-7pm Sun. Paseo del Arte ticket €29.60. *Map* p107 M18.

The Reina Sofía boasts an impressive façade with glass-and-steel lift shafts, designed by British architect Ian Ritchie. And since 2005, the museum has had just as impressive a rear, in the form of three buildings arranged round a courtyard and covered by a triangular, zinc-and-aluminium roof, the work of French architect Jean Nouvel.

The Reina Sofía's great jewel is still unquestionably *Guernica*, Picasso's impassioned denunciation of war and fascism, a painting that commemorates the destruction in 1937 of the Basque town of Guernica by German bombers that flew in support of Francoist forces in the Spanish Civil War. Picasso refused to allow the painting to be exhibited in Spain under the Franco regime, and it was only in 1981 that it was finally brought to Spain from the Museum of Modern Art in New York. *Guernica* has been in the Reina Sofía since the museum's official inauguration in 1992, when it was transferred from the Casón del Buen Retiro amid great controversy. The artist had intended the painting to be housed in the Prado – of which the Casón is at least an annexe – and his family bitterly opposed the change of location.

Edificio Nouvel

The rest of the Reina Sofía's permanent collection is a reasonable collection of Spanish modern art, with thin coverage of non-Spanish artists. It certainly contains works by practically all the major Spanish artists of the 20th century – Picasso, Dalí, Miró, Julio González, Tàpies, Alfonso Ponce de León and Antonio Saura are all present – but even here there are few major works.

The collection

The permanent collection, comprising more than 1,000 works, is spread over the first, second and fourth floors of the Sabatini building, while temporary shows are woven throughout.

The second floor is still the most important, housing Collection 1: The Irruption of the 20th Century: Utopias and Conflicts. This includes *Guernica* and the 1930s, with works by Joan Miró, Robert Capa and, of course, Picasso. Other themes and artists explored on this floor include Modernity, Progress and Decadentism, with works by Picasso and José Gutiérrez Solana; The New Culture in Spain; Dalí, Surrealism and Revolution; and Cubism's Break with Space, with more works by Picasso, as well as Georges Braque and Sonia Delaunay.

Collection 2: Is the War Over? Art in a Divided World explores themes such as European art after World War II, and 'The New Blood', with works by Kandinsky, Paul Klee and Miró. Collection 3: From Revolt to Postmodernity is in the Nouvel building and includes works by Jean Luc Godard and Sol LeWitt.

Guernica (Pablo Picasso, 1937)

Iglesia-Catedral de San Isidro

Sights & museums

♥ La Casa Encendida

*Ronda de Valencia 2 (90 243 03 22, www.lacasaencendida.es). Metro Embajadores. **Open** 10am-9.45pm Tue-Sun. **Admission** free. Cinema €3. Theatre €5. **Map** p107 K19.*
This exciting multidisciplinary centre in a large neo-Mudéjar building was conceived as a space for cultural interchange. Spread over four floors, it offers exhibitions principally by emerging artists working in all genres, but also features cutting-edge performance art and music (including short seasons of video artists) and activities for kids. It's worth a visit for the rooftop café alone, a chilled-out space with a spectacular view across the city and beyond.

♥ Iglesia-Catedral de San Isidro (La Colegiata)

*C/Toledo 37 (91 369 20 37). Metro La Latina or Tirso de Molina. **Open** Closed Aug. 7.30am-1pm, 6-9pm daily. **Map** p107 H16.*
Still popularly known as La Colegiata, this massive church, built between 1622 and 1633, once formed part of an important Jesuit college attended by many of the Golden Age playwrights. The high-Baroque design by Pedro Sánchez

was inspired by the quintessential church of the Jesuits, the Gesù in Rome; the façade was completed by Francisco Bautista in 1664.

In 1768, after Charles III expelled the Jesuits from Spain, the church was separated from the college, dedicated to San Isidro and altered by Ventura Rodríguez to house the remains of the saint and his wife, which had been brought here from the Capilla de San Isidro (*see p59*).

La Colegiata was the city's provisional cathedral for nearly a century, between 1885 and 1993, when the Catedral de la Almudena (*see p68*) was finally finished and inaugurated.

Restaurants

♥ Freiduría de Gallinejas €

*C/Embajadores 84 (91 517 59 33, www.gallinejasembajadores84. com). Metro Embajadores. **Open** 11am-11pm Mon-Sat; noon-10pm Sun. Closed 3wks Aug. **No cards**. **Map** p107 J19* ① *Spanish*
Still going strong after a century, this is the best place in the city for deep-fried lamb's intestines and other tasty titbits. Not for weak stomachs, this offal institution offers superbly prepared testicles, glands and stomach linings, all accompanied by strong red wine. Worth checking out just for the lively scene and a taste of old Madrid's innard circle.

In the know
Antiques and arcades

If you want antiques, head to the **Rastro** (*see p111*). On the main drag, C/Ribera de Curtidores, are several arcades where you'll find everything from old junk to authentic antiques. The adjoining streets, such as C/Mira el Río Alta and C/Carnero, are more downmarket and can yield real bargains.

❤ The Rastro

C/Ribera de Curtidores, between Plaza de Cascorro & Ronda de Toledo (no phone, www.elrastro. org). Metro La Latina. **Open** *9am-approx 2pm Sun.* **Map** *p107 H17.*

The city's most famous flea market dates back nearly five centuries. There are various theories on the origin of its name, which used to mean 'slaughterhouse', and might refer to the abattoir that once sat here (*'curtidores'*, from the name of the market's main drag, means 'tanners' and refers to the workshops that once lined this street). Another meaning of *rastro* is 'trace' or 'vestige', so it may refer to the cast-offs sold here, or perhaps the stolen goods that inevitably ended up here (and still do).

Stalls start setting up from around 8am, with the hardcore bargain-hunters arriving soon afterwards, though trading officially begins at 9am. In truth, there are few real deals to be had these days, but in among the piles of tat are Moroccan stalls selling lovely leather bags (though be sure to haggle hard), and antiques stalls and shops that are worth a trawl. The tributaries that run off the main street mostly specialise: some in art, some in clothes, toys or plants. There is undeniably an awful lot of junk – broken electronic equipment and knock-off toiletries – but it's still a quintessential stop on the tourist map, especially as a pre-La Latina tapas bars jaunt. Do keep an eye on your bag, though.

♥ Malacatín €€

C/Ruda 5 (91 365 52 41, www. malacatin.com). Metro La Latina. **Open** *11am-5.30pm Mon-Wed, Sat; 11am-5.30pm, 8.15-11pm Thur, Fri. Closed 5wks July-Aug.* **Map** *p107 G17* ❷ *Spanish*

Let us be clear – this is not a place for those who tag their Instagram photos with #cleanliving. This is good, old-fashioned, nose-to-tail eating for unapologetic carnivores, who come for the most traditional local dining experience – the *cocido*, a hearty, meaty chickpea stew – eaten under the dusty bullfighting posters and memorabilia of old Madrid.

Moharaj €€

C/Ave María 26 (91 527 17 87, www. moharaj.com). Metro Lavapiés. **Open** *1-5pm, 8pm-midnight daily.* **Map** *p107 K17* ❸ *Indian*

It may not look fancy, but among curry-lovers Moharaj is widely believed to serve the best Indian food in Madrid. The secret is that most dishes are made from scratch when ordered, avoiding that greasy gloop so prevalent in some establishments. If there are four of you, order the tasty Moharaj platter to start, which has samosas, bhajis and more, then maybe prawns rezala, lamb jalfrezi, beef madras and matar paneer.

Tapas bars

♥ Casa Granada

C/Doctor Cortezo 17 (91 420 08 25). Metro Tirso de Molina. **Open** *noon-midnight Mon-Thur, Sun; noon-1am Fri, Sat.* **Map** *p107 J16* ❶

A very ordinary bar serving very ordinary food, but with an extraordinary view. To get in, ring the buzzer on the street level, and then ride the lift all the way up to the sixth floor – in summer you'll have to fight tooth and nail for a seat on the terrace.

La Casa de las Tostas

C/Argumosa 29 (91 527 08 42). Metro Lavapiés. **Open** *noon-4.30pm, 7pm-midnight Mon-Thur; noon-midnight Fri-Sun.* **Map** *p107 L18* ❷

Welcome to the House of Toast. Toast with scrambled eggs, prawns and wild mushrooms; toast with salmon in white vermouth; toast with gammon and melted cheese; toast with anchovies and Roquefort; toast with cod pâté. And most importantly, toast with wine, many available by the glass.

♥ La Taberna de Antonio Sánchez

C/Mesón de Paredes 13 (91 539 78 26). Metro Tirso de Molina. **Open** *noon-4pm, 8pm-midnight Mon-Sat; noon-4.30pm Sun.* **Map** *p107 J17* ❸

Little changes at this historic bar, from the zinc bar to the bull's head hanging on the wall. Its various owners have all been involved in bullfighting, and *tertulías* of critics, *toreros* and *aficionados* are still held here. It's local and friendly, with superior tapas. Try the fried shrimp *tortillitas* and the tomato salad, followed, perhaps, by the house speciality, *torrijas* – custardy fried bread.

In the know
Local hero

The statue of a dishevelled soldier – so different from Madrid's grand equestrian statues elsewhere – that sits in the Plaza Cascorro is a tribute to Eloy Gonzalo, who grew up in a local orphanage and offered to sacrifice his life in the Cuban War of Independence. Heading over enemy lines clutching a petrol can and a rope, so that his comrades might drag his body back, he set fire to a crucial Cuban stronghold and was able to escape, though he died of disease the following year.

Los Chuchis

Cafés & bars

Bar Automático

C/Argumosa 17 (91 530 99 21).
Metro Lavapiés. **Open** *6pm-1.30am*
Mon-Fri; noon-2am Sat; noon-1am
Sun. Closed 2wks Aug. **No cards.**
Map *p107 K18* ❶

A scruffy post-Rastro classic,
Automático has been around for
over 20 years, and sees all sorts
within its turquoise walls, hung
with black-and-white photos of
the jazz greats. There is a gentle
soundtrack to match – jazz, blues
and swing – and some decent tapas,
from cod *brandade* to *salmorejo* (a
kind of thick gazpacho).

Café Barbieri

C/Ave María 45 (91 527 36 58).
Metro Lavapiés. **Open** *daily*
8am-1am. Closed 2wks Aug. **Map**
p107 K17 ❷

An airy and peaceful space, this
has recently had a facelift, but still
features high ceilings, marble-
topped tables and plush red-velvet
banquettes. A favourite haunt of
journos and wannabe travel writers,
Barbieri has plenty of newspapers
and magazines, but its ordinary
coffee comes at a premium.

Los Chuchis

C/Amparo 82 (91 127 66 06). Metro
Lavapiés. **Open** *noon-midnight*
Tue-Thur; noon-12.30am Fri, Sat;
noon-6pm Sun. Closed 2wks Aug.
Map *p107 K18* ❸

A warm and welcoming little
café, with perky teal paintwork
and chequerboard floor, just off
the main Rastro drag. The British
influence in the team behind it
is evident everywhere, from the
collection of teapots to the bowler
hat on a rack, the Penguin Classics
and the complete works of British
chefdom – Jamie, Delia, Nigella et
al – that influences the kitchen.

❤ La Fisna

C/Amparo 91 (91 539 56 15, www.
lafisna.com). Metro Lavapiés.
Open *7pm-midnight Mon-Fri;*
1-5pm, 8pm-1am Sat. **Map** *p107*
K18 ❹

A superb little wine boutique,
in a cosy bare-bricked space,
with a truly impressive range of
wines, spanning many countries
and vintages. In the evenings
it functions as a bar, where you
might occasionally catch a *cata*
(wine-tasting). There is a short list
of tapas and *conservas* – tinned
shellfish, highly prized in Spain.

La Heladería

C/Argumosa 7 (91 528 80 09). Metro
Lavapiés. **Open** *10am-11pm daily.*
Closed Nov-mid Feb. **No cards.**
Map *p107 K18* ❺

Peruvian owner Yoli is unfailingly
charming, and happy to let you
try her excellent ice-creams before
you buy – blackberry (*mora*) and
lemon come recommended. Try
the *blanco y negro*, a delicious café-
frappé with ice-cream, or one of her
milkshakes.

Entertainment

♥ Casa Patas

C/Cañizares 10, Lavapiés (91 369 04 96, www.casapatas.com). Metro Antón Martín. Open Sept-July 1-4.30pm, 8pm-midnight Mon-Thur; 1-4.30pm, 7.30pm-1am Fri; 7.30pm-1am Sat. Aug 8pm-midnight Mon-Thur; 7.30pm-1am Fri, Sat. Performances 10.30pm Mon-Thur; 9pm, midnight Fri, Sat. Admission (incl 1 drink) €34. Map p107 J16 ❶ *Flamenco*

This is a plush and somewhat pricey place to savour traditional or *nuevo* flamenco. Recent headliners have included Chaquetón, Remedios Amaya and Niña Pastori. Casa Patas is deservedly proud of its reputation and treats its loyal, knowledgeable and sometimes intimidating audience with respect. The same owners have a bar, Pata Chico, alongside for pre-flamenco drinks.

♥ Cine Doré (Filmoteca Española)

C/Santa Isabel 3, Lavapiés (box office 91 369 11 25, information 91 369 21 18, bookshop 91 369 46 73, www.mecd.gob.es/cultura-mecd/areas-cultura/cine/mc/fe/cine-dore). Metro Antón Martín. Open Bar-cafés 4-11pm Tue-Sun. Bookshop 5-10pm Tue-Sun. Tickets €2.50; €2 reductions. 10 films €20; €15 reductions. No cards. Map p107 K16 ❷ *Cinema*

Known affectionately as 'la filmo' and featured in films by Almodóvar, this chic art nouveau national film theatre was founded more than 50 years ago. The neon-lit foyer/café is a lively meeting place and the tiny bookshop is always full of browsers. A free, expansive, fold-out monthly programme guide features details of its eclectic seasons of films from the Spanish National Archive and world cinema. The grand auditorium is an especially marvellous place to see silent movies, sometimes accompanied by live music. The outdoor rooftop cinema and bar are open – and unsurprisingly very popular – during the summer months. Note that the box office opens at 4.15pm and stays open until 15 minutes after the start of the last performance of the night. Advance tickets can only be bought for the following day's performance and then only until a third of the capacity has been booked. Note also that you can only buy three tickets per person for each performance.

♥ Medias Puri

Plaza Tirso de Molino 1 (91 521 69 11, mediaspuri.com). Metro Tirso de Molina. Open 10.30pm-5.30am Thur (Karate Kid Sessions); 11.30pm-6am Fri, Sat. Admission €18 (incl 1 drink) 1st visit, when you're given a key card; thereafter €15 (incl 1 drink). Map p107 J16 ❸ *Club*

The hottest address in town, Medias Puri plays on all the best speakeasy traditions and was designed by the creators of *The Hole*, a risqué show which combines burlesque and Cirque du Soleil-style showmanship. First of all, the entrance is through what appears to be an old-fashioned haberdashery. Once inside, you'll find three dancefloors, one with spectacular dance and acrobatic shows, and a fabulous cocktail bar decked out like an old apothecary. There's a complicated key system: you're given one on your first visit, and it gets you a discounted admission price on subsequent visits.

Chueca & Malasaña

Madrid has undergone rapid change in the last few years but nowhere more than around Malasaña and, particularly, Chueca. These two neighbourhoods, roughly divided by C/Fuencarral, have always been lively, but many of the area's old *tabernas* and family-run *casas de comida* have been replaced with industrial-themed gin bars, vintage-style cupcake shops and the like. There's still plenty keeping it real, however, particularly in Malasaña, which has retained some of its grungy, studenty feel. Chueca, gay capital of Madrid (and probably Spain), has been spruced up of late, and you can now find boutique hotels and gluten-free bakeries among its leather bars.

Best museums
Museo de Historia (p120)
gives a great introduction to
the city, while the Museo del
Romanticismo (p116) shows how
its other half once lived.

Best LGBT
Escape (p123) is Madrid's principal
haunt for Sapphic sisters, while
Gymage (p129) is where boy meets
boy.

Best historical tabernas
Sit where Lorca sat at La
Carmencita (p117) or among the
bullfighters' portraits at Casa
Salvador (p117).

Best platters
Meat (p121) for unapologetic
carnivores, while seafood fans
might prefer Ribeira do Miño
(p121).

Best cafés
Try elegant little Café de Ruiz
(p129) for hot chocolate, or sip a
morning coffee at Café Comercial
(p129).

Best of Spanish modern art
Wander upstairs to the little
gallery at the Centro Cultural
de Conde Duque (p126) or find
bigger names at the Fundación
Telefónica (p126).

Chueca

The epicentre of the gay scene
is **Plaza de Chueca**; its terraces
are packed with crowds on hot
summer nights, and the only
limitation on the scene is whether
the *plaza* can actually hold any
more people. On the back of the
scene, many more restaurants,
trendy shops, cafés and clubs have
opened up, and **C/Fuencarral**,
the borderline between Chueca
and Malasaña, is now the heart of
Madrid's club-fashion scene.

The north side of the district,
above C/Fernando VI, is not
really Chueca proper and is often
known as **Alonso Martínez**,
after the metro station. It, too,
has many new restaurants and
bars. This is one of the foremost
preserves of Madrid's teen scene,
with streets lined with bars and

clubs catering to a young crowd.
Just west of here is the city's
history museum, the **Museo de
Historia** (*see* p120) and the **Museo
del Romanticismo**. Towards
Recoletos, Chueca also becomes
more commercial and more
upmarket by day.

Sights & museums

❤ Museo del Romanticismo
*C/San Mateo 13 (91 448 10 45,
museoromanticismo.mcu.
es). Metro Tribunal.* **Open**
*May-Oct 9.30am-8.30pm
Tue-Sat; 10am-3pm Sun. Nov-
Apr 9.30am-6.30pm Tue-Sat;
10am-3pm Sun.* **Admission** *€3;
€1.50 reductions. Free to all from
2pm Sat. No cards.* **Map** *p118 K11.*
The Museo del Romanticismo is
essentially a reconstruction of a
typical aristocratic house of the

➜ Getting around
The area is bisected by C/Fuencarral, along which various buses run and
where you'll also find the Tribunal metro station (L1 and L10); Malasaña is
also served by Noviciado (L2), and Chueca station is useful for L5.

Spanish Romantic period (early to mid 19th century); a charming collection of furniture, paintings, ornaments, early pianos and other pieces that evoke the time. As well as these objets d'art, there are paintings from the likes of Francisco Goya and Vicente López Portaña, thousands of prints and lithographs and a substantial number of antique photographs. There's also a tearoom with a pretty garden (you don't need a museum ticket to enter).

Restaurants

♥ La Carmencita €€
C/Libertad 16 (91 531 09 11, www. tabernalacarmencita.es/en). Metro Chueca. **Open** *1pm-1am daily.* **Map** *p118 L13* ❶ *Spanish*
Originally opened in 1854, Carmencita has an illustrious past, and was once a favourite of Pablo Neruda and Federico García Lorca (who lived upstairs). It lay empty for many years but its glorious wall tiles and bronze luggage racks have been sensitively restored, as have some of the original recipes. The emphasis is on slow food, happy cows and chickens, and local produce – try the chicken *en pepitoria* or the oxtail stew.

♥ Casa Salvador €€
C/Barbieri 12 (91 521 45 24, www. casasalvadormadrid.com). Metro Chueca. **Open** *1.30-4pm, 9-11.30pm Mon-Sat. Closed Aug.* **Map** *p118 L13* ❷ *Spanish*
Every inch of this old classic is crammed with bullfighting memorabilia. You'll find good traditional fare – lentil soup, *revueltos* (concoctions with scrambled egg, often with seafood or asparagus), hake, *solomillo* (sirloin steak) with French fries – but the real treat is the atmosphere.

Museo del Romanticismo

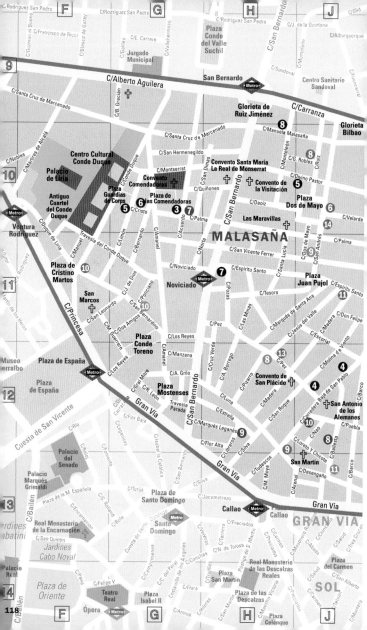

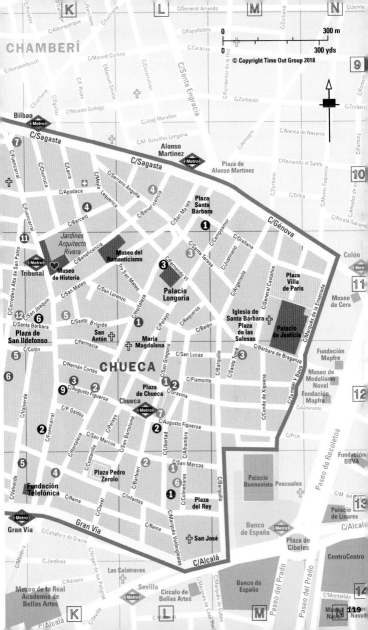

❤ Museo de Historia

*C/Fuencarral 78 (91 701 18 63, www. munimadrid.es/museodehistoria). Metro Tribunal. **Open** Sept-July 9.30am-8pm Tue-Fri; 10am-2pm Sat, Sun. Aug 10am-7pm Tue-Sun. **Admission** free. **Map** p118 K11.*

Previously known as the Museo Municipal, the Museo de Historia has been given a complete makeover and is now one of the most interesting of the city-run museums. Located in an old hospice, it has an exuberantly ornate entrance by Pedro de Ribera, one of the finest examples of Baroque architecture in Madrid, and worth seeing in itself. The collection picks up from where the **Museo de San Isidro** (*see p78*) leaves off – telling the story of the history of Madrid from around the reign of Philip II, in the 16th-century.

Apart from one space filled with antique maps and a scale model of Madrid from 1830, the exhibits are arranged in chronological order and include paintings, sculpture, guns, fans, ceramics and a host of other fascinating objects, such as a beautifully decorated 17th-century litter used to transport the sick to hospital. Perhaps most interesting, however, are the photographs of old Madrid on the top floor, since so many of its squares and landmarks are instantly recognisable today.

Children with a grasp of Spanish (or possibly without), will enjoy the free guided tours tailored to six- to 12-year-olds at noon on Sundays.

❤ Meat €€

*C/Santa Teresa 4 (91 029 60
41, www.meatmadrid.com).
Metro Alonso Martínez.* **Open**
*1pm-midnight Mon-Wed, Sun;
1pm-2am Thur; 1pm-2.30am Fri,
Sat.* **Map** *p118 L11* ❸ *American*

Come for the brunch – pancakes
with maple syrup; egg and bacon
sandwich; avocado toast – and stay
for the burgers, made with local
beef and available in three sizes,
and the triple-cooked fries. The
decor is very on point, with its bare
bricks, open kitchen, scrubbed pine
tables and retro American feel, but
there's a lot of heart and soul here.

Media Ración €€

*C/Beneficiencia 15 (91 447 51 11,
www.mediaracion.es). Metro
Alonso Martínez.* **Open** *1.30-4pm,
8.30-11pm Tue-Thur; 1.30-4pm,
8.30-11.30pm Fri, Sat.* **Map** *p118
L10* ❹ *Spanish*

Recent years have seen many new
openings in Chueca, but this is
one of the best. A cosy, pale-wood
dining room is the setting for some
supremely tasty dishes, like skate
escabeche and a crunchy pig's
trotter with smoked eel. The mixed
vegetables served with a velouté is
a great accompaniment, and even
the bread is superb – but don't eat
too much of it because you'll want
to leave space for the chocolate
ganache with salt and olive oil.

❤ Ribeira do Miño €€

*C/Santa Brígida 1 (91 521 98 54,
www.marisqueriaribeiradomino.
com). Metro Tribunal.* **Open**
*1-4pm, 8pm-midnight Tue-Sun.
Closed Aug.* **No cards**. **Map** *p118
K11* ❺ *Seafood*

Galician in origin, this one's for
seafood lovers. Heaped platters
of prawns, crab, goose-necked
barnacles, lobster and other sea
creatures make it the ideal place
to roll up your sleeves and get
cracking shells. Other typical
gallego dishes that add a little

heat to the fun are pancakes
doused in *orujo* (a fiery spirit very
similar to grappa) and set aflame,
and the *queimada* – a bowl of
orujo set on fire and then cooled
with black coffee. Reservations
are recommended, particularly
at weekends.

Thai Orchid €€

*C/Colmenares 5 (91 531 85 37,
www.thaiorchid.es). Metro Banco
de España.* **Open** *1-4.30pm Mon;
1-4.30pm, 8pm-midnight Tue-
Thur; 1-4.30pm, 8pm-1am Fri, Sat;
1.30-5pm Sun. Closed 1wk Aug.*
Map *p118 L13* ❻ *Thai*

A tiny, simple little Thai restaurant
that doesn't look much from
outside but is a bit of a gem. The
fixed *menú*, available day (€12.50)
and night (€14.50), is amazing
value, with three properly spicy
and generously portioned courses
and a drink. As a bonus, the Orchid
eschews trickling fountains and
garlanded Buddhas for some
monochrome Thai prints and a
gentle piano soundtrack.

Tienda de Vinos
(El Comunista) €

*C/Augusto Figueroa 35 (91 521 70
12). Metro Chueca.* **Open** *noon-
4pm, 8pm-midnight Mon-Sat.
Closed mid Aug-mid Sept.* **No
cards**. **Map** *p118 L12* ❼ *Spanish*

This restaurant's popular name
comes from its role as a leftie
meeting point years ago under
Franco (but Tienda de Vinos is all
you'll see above the door). It's one
of the city's real classics and a visit
is essential, but no one makes any
grand claims about its unchanging
and unchallenging menu. To start,
there are soups: gazpacho, lentil or
own-made broth, followed by liver
and onions, lamb cutlets, kidneys
in sherry and plenty of fish. Service
is known for being deadpan, but if
you're lucky, you'll get one of the
two charming great-grandsons of
the original owner.

Tapas bars

El Bocaíto

C/Libertad 4-6 (91 532 12 19, www. bocaito.com). Metro Chueca. **Open** *12.30-4pm, 8pm-midnight Mon-Sat; 12.30pm-4pm Sun. Closed Aug.* **Map** *p118 L13* ❶

El Bocaíto is film-set traditional, from the bullfight posters and Andalucían ceramics to the old-school tapas and unsmiling, white-jacketed waiters. If you're famous, though, they'll grin for the camera, just as they did with Pedro, Hugh and, goddammit, Mark Knopfler.

Mercado de San Antón

C/Augusto Figueroa 24 (91 330 07 30, www.mercadosananton. com). Metro Chueca. **Open** *Shops 10am-10pm Mon-Sat. Bars/ restaurants 10am-midnight Mon-Thur; 10am-1.30am Fri, Sat.* **Map** *p118 L12* ❷

Part gastro market, part tapas village, the covered Mercado de San Antón opened in 2011 and has been rammed with appreciative customers ever since. Stalls selling immaculate produce are on the ground floor; tapas bars specialising in all manner of things, from topped blinis to sushi, are on the next floor; and at the top is a bar-restaurant with a great view over the rooftops.

Cafés & bars

Ángel Sierra

C/Gravina 11 (91 531 01 26). Metro Chueca. **Open** *11am-2.30am Mon-Thur, Sun; 11am-3am Fri, Sat.* **Map** *p118 L12* ❶

This battered old bar with its tiled walls, zinc bar top, overflowing sink and glasses stacked on wooden slats has become the Chueca meeting place par excellence, thanks to its position overlooking the main square. A newer room to the back of the bar, however, has

a faux pub look enhanced with amplified MOR radio and a rule that only doubles and pints are served after midnight.

Café Figueroa

C/Augusto Figueroa 17 (91 521 16 73). Metro Chueca. **Open** *Oct-May noon-1am Mon-Thur; noon-2.30am Fri, Sat; 4pm-1am Sun. June-Sept 4.30-11.30pm daily.* **No cards.** **Map** *p118 K12* ❷

Madrid's original gay café is a sedate place. The lace curtains and 19th-century chandeliers have gone in a smart revamp, but it's still a cosy destination for those who want gay in an old Spain way. It's a popular place for a late breakfast.

Olivera

C/Santo Tomé 8 (mobile 697 198 543). Metro Chueca. **Open** *7pm-2am Mon-Thur, Sun; 7pm-2.30am Fri, Sat.* **Map** *p118 M12* ❸

A relaxed lounge bar, presided over by a portrait of the owner's mother, Yugoslav film star Olivera Markovic. The musical mood is nu jazz and funk, and the mismatched armchairs and sofas make it easy to stay up all night.

Stop Madrid

C/Hortaleza 11 (91 521 88 87, www. stopmadrid.es). Metro Chueca or Gran Vía. **Open** *noon-1am Mon-Wed; noon-2am Thur; noon-2.30am Fri, Sat; noon-12.30am Sun.* **Map** *p118 K13* ❹

When it opened in 1929, this was the first ham and charcuterie shop in Madrid. It's undergone a few changes since then, but many of the original fittings have been retained, and great pride is taken in sourcing the best ingredients for tapas. Of the 50-strong wine list, all are available by the glass. **Other locations** C/León 10, Huertas, 91 429 56 95; C/Hortaleza 11, 91 521 88 87; C/Atocha 73, Huertas, 91 504 78 43.

Cacao Sampaka

*C/Orellana 4 (91 319 58 40, www.
cacaosampaka.com). Metro Alonso
Martínez. **Open** 10am-9.30pm
Mon-Sat. **Map** p118 L10* **❶** *Food
& drink*

Handmade choccies are arrayed
in dazzling displays and for sale
singly or in themed boxes, such
as 'Spices of the Americas' or
'Flowers and herbs'. There are also
chocolate jams, chocolate sauces
and chocolate ice-creams.

Custo Barcelona

*C/Fuencarral 29 (91 360 46 36,
www.custo-barcelona.com).
Metro Gran Vía or Chueca.
Open 10am-9pm Mon-Sat;
11.30am-8.30pm Sun. **Map** p118
K12* **❷** *Fashion*

This Catalan designer is famous for
his funky patterned T-shirts, but
has expanded the range to include
creative and flattering dresses,
skirts and coats. Custo was all the
rage a few years back, but a host
of copycat stores have led to the
closure of all but this one.

La Duquesita

*C/Fernando VI 2 (91 308 02 31).
Metro Alonso Martínez. **Open**
8.30am-8.30pm daily. Closed Aug.
Map p118 L11* **❸** *Food & drink*

This traditional *pastelería*, dating
from 1914, has featured in lots of
period-piece movies. Gorgeous
chocolates and cakes are offered,
along with *turrón* in the run-up to
Christmas.

Areia

*C/Hortaleza 92 (91 310 03 07, www.
areiachillout.com). Metro Chueca.
Open 4pm-3am Mon-Fri; 2pm-3am
Fri, Sat. **Admission** free. **Map** p118
L11* **❶** *Club*

Areia is a chill-out space that has
all the angles covered: by day it's
somewhere to get lunch or a snack,
in the afternoon it becomes a place
to chill, and by the evening the
vibe has hotted up enough for a
cool crowd that passes through on
their nightly tour of the city (there
are DJ sessions from Wednesday
to Saturday nights). The seductive
eastern decor, along with sofas and
cushions for lounging, can make it
difficult to leave.

❤ Escape

*C/Gravina 13 (91 532 52 06). Metro
Chueca. **Open** midnight-6am Fri-
Sun. **Admission** (incl 1 drink) €10.
Map p118 L12* **❷** *Gay club*

This cavernous dance hall draped
in bullfighter red is one of the
most popular destinations for
lesbians and is filled to the brim
with the sexiest *chicas* in the city
at weekends. In fact, its popularity
has spiralled to the extent that it's
now one of the more boisterous
clubs around Plaza de Chueca.

El Intruso

*C/Augusto Figueroa 3 (91 531 89
96, www.intrusobar.com). Metro
Chueca. **Open** 9pm-5.30am
Mon-Thur, Sun; 9pm-6am Fri,
Sat. **Admission** varies. **Map** p118
K12* **❸** *Live music*

The name means 'the intruder',
and that's what you may feel like
as you slip into this new venue,
which is housed in what looks like
an office block and lies behind a
large, intimidating wood-panelled
door. But you're on safe ground
once inside, where you can get
comfy at the tables or perch on
the diner-style bar stools. The
small stage plays host to a variety
of local acts, including bigger
names such as Gecko Turner,
as well as international visitors
such as Bob Stroger. Late opening
makes it perfect if you're on a
midweek bender.

Pride Without Prejudice

LGBT Madrid marches on

Spain's Socialist government of the noughties made history when it became one of the first to legalise gay marriage and to allow transsexuals to choose whichever gender they wished on their identity cards. These were milestone achievements that were celebrated with leather, rubber, bears, tanned toned flesh and non-stop hedonism in the LGBT Pride parade.

Organised by COGAM and FELGBT (see p179), the parade has continued to grow since then, despite continued threats to the event by some Chueca residents, who want the week-long June party to be moved to the outskirts of the city. The parade runs from the Puerta de Alcalá to Plaza España, and attracts some two million people. For an entire week, the city is invaded by visitors from all over the world, partying hard by night and sporting an array of ludicrously coloured banana hammocks at the swimming pools by day, with the rooftop terrace of the Room Mate Oscar hotel (see p169) a big hotspot. In 2017, Madrid hosted World Pride, a spectacular city-wide event that was attended by three million people.

As well as the parties and the parades, the week boasts some 300 cultural, artistic and sporting events – kicking off with the Carrera en Tacones (a race where contestants run in stilettos) – as well as off-site parties at the end of the week.

Despite such leaps, bounds and high-heeled trotting towards an equal Spain, there is much still to be done, according to Madrid's numerous gay rights associations. Madrid may be one of the most tolerant cities in the world, but this is still a deeply conservative country in many ways and there is still plenty to march for.

Ocho y Medio

Sala But, C/Barceló 11 (no phone, www.ochoymedioclub.com). Metro Tribunal. **Open** *midnight-6am Fri, Sat.* **Admission** *€15 (incl 1 drink).* **Concerts** *€10-€25.* **Map** *p118 K10* ❹ *Club*

This popular club night has been running since the late 1990s, and relies on an alcohol-fuelled mass of party energy that's driven by the eclectic mix of indie, electro-clash, electro-pop, new wave and New York rock spun by the resident DJs. Located practically in the basement of Teatro Barceló (*see below*), this is the place to head to if the glammed-up crowds jostling to get in via the VIP queue of that club fill you with dread.

Teatro Barceló

C/Barceló 11 (91 447 01 28, teatrobarcelo.com). Metro Alonso Martínez. **Open** *midnight-6am Thur-Sat.* **Admission** *€15 (incl 1 drink).* **Map** *p118 K10* ❹ *Club*

This club (formerly Pachá) calls itself the 'best in Madrid', and it does a good job of living up to its own hype with its roster of top national and international DJs and a glamorous crowd. Thursday nights are student nights, while Friday and Saturday nights are for the over-25s (bring ID). There are

two dancefloors, with reggaeton in the smaller of the two and house and electro pop in the larger one.

Ya'sta

C/Valverde 10 (no phone, www. facebook.com/YastaClub). Metro Gran Vía. **Open** *8pm-5am Mon; 9pm-5am Tue; midnight-5am Wed; midnight-6am Thur-Sat; 5pm-5am Sun.* **Admission** *€9-15 (incl 1 or 2 drinks).* **No cards.** **Map** *p118 J13* ❺ *Club*

There's perhaps only one place in Madrid where you'll find funk, breaks, reggae, techno, dubstep, salsa, swing, country and boogie all under one roof – and Ya'sta is it. The club itself is industrial-style, with psychedelic projections on the walls and graffiti in the corridors. Depending on the night, the venue attracts anyone from young techno-heads and breakdancers to a more grown-up rock crowd.

Malasaña & Conde Duque

Malasaña, between C/Fuencarral and San Bernardo, still has a laid-back neighbourhood feel, with old ladies watering their geraniums on wrought-iron balconies and idiosyncratic corner shops. Less showy than Chueca, this is the city's hipster *barrio*, albeit with a grungy edge. Malasaña is still associated with chilled-out cafés, rock bars and cheap, studenty socialising – although the tentacles of gentrification are taking hold. The streets between Fuencarral and San Bernardo brim with great cafés, bars and restaurants. One of the most rewarding streets is **C/San Vicente Ferrer**, with jewellery shops and a delightful 1920s tile display advertising the long-defunct pharmacy Laboratorios Juanse. Other old ceramic signs on the **C/San Andrés** feature a little boy signalling that his chamber pot is full and a dramatic, reclining vamp.

Fundación Telefónica

Sights & museums

❤ Centro Cultural Conde Duque

C/Conde Duque 11 (91 480 04 01, www.condeduquemadrid.es). Metro Noviciado or Ventura Rodríguez. **Open** *10am-2pm, 5.30-8pm Tue-Sat; 10.30am-2pm Sun.* **Admission** *varies.* **Map** *p118 F10.*
Housed in a former barracks, built in the 18th century for Philip V's guard by Pedro de Ribera, the magnificently restored Conde Duque is a multipurpose cultural centre. Around a dozen shows, both artistic and historical, are held annually in the two exhibition spaces and on the two vast patios. Open-air concerts in summer bring in a range of performers. Also housed here are the city's newspaper and video libraries, as well as the Museo de Arte Contemporáneo, which opened in 2001, and slightly hidden next to it the **Palacio de Liria**.

❤ Fundación Telefónica

C/Gran Vía 28, entrance at C/ Valverde 2 (91 580 87 00, www. espacio.fundaciontelefonica.com). Metro Gran Vía. **Open** *10am-8pm Tue-Sun.* **Admission** *free.* **Map** *p118 K13.*
Run by Telefónica, the national telephone company, this foundation functions on several levels. The Museo de las Telecomunicaciones is a permanent exhibition illustrating the history of telecommunications. Another large space is used to display selections from Telefónica's permanent collection of Spanish art, including various works by

Eduardo Chillida, Luis Fernández, Miró, Picasso and Tàpies, and it also has a permanent show based around post-Civil War Spanish artists of the so-called Madrid and Paris schools, the latter in exile. Temporary exhibitions feature both the arts and technology.

Restaurants

Gumbo €€

*C/Pez 15 (91 532 63 61, www.gumbo. es). Metro Noviciado. **Open** 2-4pm, 9pm-midnight Tue-Sat; 2-4pm Sun. Closed 2wks Aug. **Map** p118 H12* **8** *North American*

Bona fide N'Awlins chef Matthew Scott has some good Creole spices simmering in his gumbo pot. In a simple locale tastefully decorated (with a poster of *Gone with the Wind*), you can sample scrumptious New Orleans classics: fried green tomatoes, seafood gumbo, black steak. For festive group dinners, ask Matthew to bring out a parade of tapas-like dishes to share. And only a fool would make any attempt to resist the desserts.

Centro Cultural Conde Duque

Ojalá €€

*C/San Andrés 1 (91 523 27 47, www. grupolamusa.com/restaurante-ojala). Metro Noviciado or Tribunal. **Open** 10am-1am Mon-Wed; 10am-1.30am Thur; 10am-2am Fri; 11am-2am Sat; 11am-midnight Sun. **Map** p118 J11* **9** *Global*

A 2014 makeover gave Ojalá a hipster vibe, with dozens of plants hanging from the ceiling amid strings of fairy lights. The food is a cosmopolitan hotchpotch of designer salads, sandwiches, burgers, tacos and wraps. Waiters are friendly, the food is well presented and the seating comfortable. Below the main dining room is a bar (open at 6pm) that resembles a beach cove with an industrial twist: sand coats the floor and harsh craggy bricks are framed by steel pipes on the walls, on to which old black-and-white movies are occasionally projected.

Siam €€

*C/San Bernardino 6 (91 559 83 15). Metro Noviciado or Plaza de España. **Open** noon-4pm, 8pm-midnight daily. **Map** p118 G11* **10** *Thai*

Siam was originally set up by a Texan, who poured his heart and the experience of years spent in Thailand into this restaurant, and the investment paid off. Authenticity is key (please don't ask for bread). The new owner imports vegetables and spices that he can't get hold of in the city. Try the spicy Thai green curry, or just ask for a recommendation. Set lunch €12. There is also a fabulous range of cocktails and special teas.

La Tasquita de Enfrente €€€

*C/Ballesta 6 (91 532 54 49). Metro Gran Vía or Callao. **Open** 1.30-3.30pm, 8.30-11.30pm Mon-Sat. Closed Aug. **Map** p118 J13* **11** *Spanish*

One of Madrid's best restaurants, La Tasquita de Enfrente is run by Juanjo López Bedmar, a former executive who chucked it all in to devote himself to cooking. There are only half a dozen tables, so you need to book well ahead. The menu changes according to what is best at any given time, but don't miss the *pochas* (white beans) with clams, if they're available. Also fabulous are the squid gnocchi and the slow-cooked acorn-fed Iberian pork cheeks. But the best idea is to go for the special menu of the day.

Tapas bars

El Maño
C/Palma 64 (91 521 50 57). Metro Noviciado. **Open** *7.30pm-12.30am Mon-Thur; 12.30-4.30pm, 7.30pm-1.30am Fri, Sat; 12.30-4.30pm Sun.* **Map** *p118 G10* ❸
A relaxed place, with French windows opening on to the street in summer, marble-topped tables and bar, faded yellow paintwork and

In the know
Eating on the run

It's a phenomenon often noted by visitors that Madrid lacks the sandwich bars found on every corner of most European capitals. The Spanish have always been appalled by the idea of lunch as refuelling, let alone – horror of horrors – eating at one's desk. No, lunch here is a leisurely affair. However, if time is short or if you're eating alone and don't fancy a drawn-out affair, then head to Chueca's C/San Marcos for café/takeaway hotspot **Diurno** (no.37) or grab a quesadilla at **La Chelinda** (no.8). Another street to note is Malasaña's C/Espíritu Santo, which among other places, has the popular **Home** (C/Espíritu Santo 12, 91 522 97 28, www.homeburgerbar.com) for gourmet beef in a bun.

art deco touches. A good selection of wine is chalked up on the walls, some of it poured from ancient barrels, and there are tortillas served with *pisto*, ragu or squid, brochettes of chicken and lamb and a small selection of canapés.

Pez Gordo
C/Pez 6 (91 522 32 08, www. elpezgordo.es). Metro Noviciado. **Open** *7.30pm-2am daily.* **Map** *p118 J12* ❹
Popular with audiences and actors from the nearby Teatro Alfil, the Fat Fish (the Spanish equivalent to 'Big Cheese') buzzes at night and is fabulously mellow earlier in the evening. The main attraction (aside from the photos of the owner's hideous bulldog) comes in the shape of the creative tapas. Try fried plantain with guacamole, goose confit with red fruit compôte, or the *patatas* Pez Gordo, with alioli, anchovies and hot peppers.

La Taberna de Corps
Plaza Guardia de Corps 1 (mobile 690 177 301). Metro Ventura Rodríguez. **Open** *1-6pm Tue-Thur; 1pm-midnight Fri-Sun.* **No cards.** **Map** *p118 G10* ❺
The *surtido* (mixed plate) of canapés and excellent selection of wines aside, the main attraction in this tiny bar is the location – on a quiet leafy plaza. Grab a Rioja or a draught *vermut* and settle down with the papers.

La Tabernilla del Gato Amadeus
C/Cristo 2 (91 541 41 12). Metro Noviciado. **Open** *1pm-1am daily.* **Map** *p118 G10* ❻
Named after a late, great, Persian cat, this is a tiny, welcoming bar, whose *croquetas* are the stuff of legend. The other favourite is the *patatas con mojo picón* (baked new potatoes with a spicy sauce). Although there's not much seating inside the premises (the sister bar

nearby is bigger), in summer there are tables outside. **Other location** C/Limón 32, Malasaña & Conde Duque (91 542 54 23).

Cafés & bars

La Ardosa

C/Colón 13 (91 521 49 79, www. laardosa.com). Metro Tribunal. **Open** *8am-2am Mon-Thur; 8am-2.30am Fri; 11am-2.30m Sat; noon-2am Sun.* **No cards.** **Map** *p118 J12* ⑤
Having an affair? Then simply duck under the counter to find the most intimate bar room you could wish for. Out front, meanwhile, this is a lovely old tiled *taberna* lined with dusty bottles, old black-and-white lithographs and beer posters. A range of canapés has just been added, and the speciality of the house is its draught beer – Bombardier, Budvar and, especially, Guinness.

Bar El 2D

C/Velarde 24 (91 448 64 72). Metro Tribunal. **Open** *noon-2am Mon-Thur; 11.30am-2.30am Fri, Sat; 11.30am-2am Sun.* **Map** *p118 J10* ⑥
The emblematic Malasaña hangout, packed at weekends and drowsily mellow in the afternoons, with a tiled bar and engraved mirrors, nicotine-stained walls and lazily circling ceiling fans. To drink, there's vermouth, lager and Beamish on tap, plus plenty of bottled beers and a small selection of wines, served (if you dare) in *porrones*, which are long-spouted drinking jars.

❤ Café Comercial

Glorieta de Bilbao 7 (91 521 56 55). Metro Bilbao. **Open** *7.30am-midnight Mon-Thur, Sun; 7.30am-2am Fri, Sat.* **Map** *p118 J10* ⑦
There was city-wide mourning when this scruffy but classic Madrid bar closed down, but it

reopened in 2017 with a brand new look. Some of its original fittings remain – brown leather seats, revolving doors and marbled walls – but it's an altogether glitzier proposition nowadays, and you'll no longer be able to observe old men playing chess as you sip your beer. For one thing, you're more likely to be drinking a vodka martini.

❤ Café de Ruiz

C/Ruiz 11 (91 446 12 32). Metro Bilbao. **Open** *4pm-2am Mon-Thur; 4pm-2.30am Fri; 3.30pm-2.30am Sat.* **Map** *p118 J10* ⑧
A quiet favourite with the smarter denizens of the neighbourhood, Café de Ruiz is an elegant place, with comfortable sofas and dramatic flower arrangements. A big draw is its own-made ice-cream and other tempting sweet treats, such as milkshakes and homemade cakes.

❤ Gymage

C/Luna 2 (91 532 09 74, www. gymage.es). Metro Gran Vía. **Open** *7am-1.30am Mon-Thur, Sun; 10am-2.30am Fri, Sat.* **Map** *p118 H12* ⑨
Located on top of the old Luna cinema, Gymage describes itself as an 'urban resort', which is really just a fancy way of saying it's a (gay-friendly) gym with a restaurant. The gym is great, the restaurant decent, but the real draw here is the spectacular rooftop terrace, where Madrid's glitterati like to lounge about on the white-on-white furnishings and sip cocktails.

El Jardín Secreto

C/Conde Duque 2 (91 541 80 23, www.eljardinsecretomadrid.com). Metro Plaza de España or Ventura Rodríguez. **Open** *6pm-1am Mon-Thur; 6.30pm-2.30am Fri, Sat; 5.30pm-2.30am Sun.* **Map** *p118 F11* ⑩

Although it also functions as a restaurant, El Jardín Secreto – decked out with mismatched furniture and arty knick-knacks – is most popular as a *merienda* (afternoon tea) spot. The crowds tend to show up when the place opens. Its cakes and desserts – in particular the chocolate orgasm – are much talked about, and there's a large selection of chocolate drinks, teas and coffees on the menu. Open late, it's also popular as a cocktail spot.

Lolina Vintage Café

C/Espíritu Santo 9 (91 523 58 59, www.lolinacafe.com). Metro Tribunal. **Open** *10am-midnight Mon-Thur, Sun; 10am-2.30am Fri, Sat.* **Map** *p118 J11* **⑪**
Now a few years old, Lolina was among the new wave of openings on Calle Espíritu Santo. The cute, retro space – with its 1970s wallpaper and vintage floor lamps – is a popular hangout for arty types and young expats, drawn by its pan-European vibe, brunch-style menu and large selection of teas, coffees and juices. The good-value breakfasts start from €3; and if you visit in the evening, be sure to order a mojito or caipirinha – the house specialities.

Naif

C/San Joaquín 16 (91 007 20 71). Metro Tribunal. **Open** *1pm-12.30am Mon-Wed; 1pm-2am Thur-Sat; 1pm-1am Sun.* **Map** *p118 J11* **⑫**
Naif is very much of its time; a high-ceilinged post-industrial space with Banksy-inspired murals, exposed ventilation ducts, recycled furniture and a bit of attitude behind the bar. It's sympathetically lit, though, does a great burger, and is one of very few places to serve BLTs or pastrami with mustard.

Passenger

C/Pez 16 (91 169 49 76). Metro Noviciado. **Open** *8pm-3am Mon-Thur; 4pm-3.30am Fri-Sun. Closed Aug.* **Map** *p118 H12* **⑬**
Party like it's 1939 in this supremely elegant Orient Express lookalike bar. Long and narrow, with wood panelling, an art deco bar, leather banquettes and screens showing footage of scenery in mocked-up windows – sure, it's a gimmick, but it's one hell of a gimmick. Cocktails are the speciality and there's a long list of tequilas and organic whiskies.

Pepe Botella

C/San Andrés 12 (91 522 43 09, www.pepebotella.com). Metro Tribunal. **Open** *10am-2am Mon-Thur, Sun; 10am-2.30am Fri, Sat.* **Map** *p118 J10* **⑭**
The name ('Joe Bottle') was the nickname of Joseph Bonaparte, who slashed taxes on alcohol when he was put on the Spanish throne during the French occupation of Spain. A cineaste's delight, the colourful Pepe Botella is frequented by the likes of director Alejandro Amenábar and actor Eduardo Noriega. For all that, it's wonderfully unpretentious, and attracts an intelligent bunch of mainly thirty- and fortysomethings, engaged in lively debate.

Shops & services

La Antigua
C/Corredera Baja de San Pablo 45 (91 142 54 99, www.laantiguadepez. blogspot.com.es). Metro Tribunal. **Open** *11am-9pm Mon-Sat.* **Map** *p118 J12* ❹ *Fashion*
Run by three designers, this kooky little boutique sums up all that is good about Malasaña, with a playful selection of clothes, jewellery and accessories. You might also pick up a *Royal Tenenbaums* tote, a *Fantastic Mr Fox* enamel mug or a pair of socks in a sea-horse pattern.

Antigua Casa Crespo
C/Divino Pastor 29 (91 521 56 54, www.alpargateriacrespo.com). Metro Bilbao. **Open** *10am-1.30pm, 5-8.15pm Mon-Sat. Closed last 2wks Aug.* **No cards.** **Map** *p118 J10* ❺ *Fashion*
This perfectly preserved, old-fashioned, family-run store, founded in 1863, is dedicated to espadrilles of all sizes and colours.

Bunkha
C/Santa Bárbara 6 (91 522 09 50, www.bunkha.com). Metro Tribunal or Gran Vía. **Open** *11am-3pm, 5-9pm Mon-Sat.* **Map** *p118 K11* ❻ *Fashion*
The stylish boutique stocks a host of upmarket yet hip labels, such as Swedish brand Uniforms for the Dedicated, Spanish brand Broken Porcelain and Italian label Camo. Menswear is in the front space, while womenswear is in the mezzanine area.

J&J Books & Coffee
C/Espíritu Santo 47 (91 521 85 76, www.jandjbooksandcoffee.com). Metro Noviciado. **Open** *4-11.30pm Mon-Thur; 4pm-1.30am Fri; noon-11.30pm Sat; noon-6pm Sun.* **Map** *p118 H11* ❼ *Books & music*
J&J is at once a relaxing little café (at ground-floor level) and a well-stocked second-hand bookshop (in the basement). Activities include language exchanges (Wednesdays, Thursdays and Saturdays from 8pm) and quizzes (Fridays from 11pm).

Popland
C/Manuela Malasaña 24 (91 591 21 20, www.popland.es). Metro Bilbao. **Open** *11am-9pm Mon-Sat.* **Map** *p118 H10* ❽ *Gifts & souvenirs*
For times when only a Jesus action figure will do, Popland saves the day. The shop is packed with all things pop culture and plastic, but also film posters, shower curtains and T-shirts. There's also a good range of greetings cards – quite a rarity in Madrid.

Vialis
C/Fuencarral 40 (91 199 74 84, www.vialis.es). Metro Chueca. **Open** *10.30am-8.30pm Mon-Sat.* **Map** *p118 K12* ❾ *Fashion*
Madrid's only branch of the stylish Spanish footwear brand is located on Malasaña's main shopping drag. Expect chunky but hip shoes and boots, and a small selection of high-quality leather bags.

Entertainment

BarCo
C/Barco 34 (91 531 77 54 www. barcobar.com). Metro Tribunal or Gran Vía. **Open** *10pm-5.30am daily.* **Concerts** *times vary.* **Admission** *Concerts free to €12 (incl 1 drink). Club €8 (incl 1 drink).* **Map** *p118 J12* ❻ *Live music*
The lines snaking up Calle del Barco will give away the location of this excellent venue, which hosts concerts in the early evening and then DJs into the wee small hours. Everything from funk and soul to rap-metal goes on the turntables, letting the near pitch-black ground floor and basement areas. A classic in the 'hood.

Café la Palma

*C/Palma 62 (91 522 50 31, www.
cafelapalma.com). Metro
Noviciado. Open 5pm-3am Mon-
Thur, Sun; 5pm-3.30am Fri,
Sat. Concerts 10pm; DJs from
midnight. Admission Concerts
€5-€10 (incl 1 drink). DJ sets free.
Map p118 G10* ➐ *Live music*
This is a longstanding favourite
with the Malasaña crowd and has
been going for more than two
decades. Choose from an area
with tables; a chill-out zone where
everyone lazes around on cushions
on the floor; or the main room,
where you can catch concerts from
big local names such as La Bien
Querida or Vetusta Morla from
Thursday to Saturday.

Démodé

*C/Ballesta 7 (mobile 680 202
576). Metro Gran Vía. Open
11pm-3.30am Thur-Sat. Admission
free. Map p118 J12* ➑ *Club*
A juxtaposition of the über-trendy
and the super-cheesy, this hugely
popular pre-club joint is housed in
an old brothel. Faux oil paintings
still adorn the walls, but red
lighting, sofas and an ample sound
system have transformed it into
one of the coolest nightspots in
town. DJs spin everything from nu
disco and tech-house to deep house
and disco for an appreciative mixed
gay/straight crowd.

El Fabuloso

*C/Estrella 3 (mobile 651 829
373). Metro Noviciado or Callao.
Open 8.30pm-3.30am Wed-Sat.
Admission free. Map p118
H12* ➒ *Club*
The glamorous Silvia Superstar
is behind this neighbourhood
favourite, which is tucked away
in a corner off one of the seedier
squares in the capital. The former
frontwoman of the splendidly
monikered Killer Barbies rock
group, Silvia is often to be found

behind the decks, either in the
kitsch upstairs lounge or on the
heaving basement dancefloor.
Along with the other Fabuloso DJs,
she plays a heady mix of northern
soul, swing, rock 'n' roll and 1960s
and '70s classics. A magnet for
gorgeous Malasaña hipsters.

El Perro de la Parte Atrás del Coche

*C/Puebla 15 (mobile 618 783
054). Metro Gran Vía or Callao.
Open 10pm-3.30am Thur-Sat.
Admission €10 (incl 1 drink) Fri,
Sat; free Tue, Thur & before 1am.
Concerts €3-€10. No cards. Map
p118 J12* ➓ *Club*
You're guaranteed a top night at El
Perro, a quirky basement club with
a vaulted ceiling whose full name
translates as 'the nodding dog'.
After the early live gigs, resident
DJ and owner Jamie Steel mixes
up everything from pop and rock
to early electro on Friday and
Saturday nights, while there are all
kinds of weird and wonderful live
acts on Thursdays, followed by DJ
sessions.

Tupperware

*C/Corredera Alta de San Pablo 26
(91 446 42 04). Metro Tribunal.
Open 8pm-3am Mon, Tues, Sun;
9pm-3am Wed, Thur; 9pm-3.30am
Fri, Sat. Admission free. No
cards. Map p118 J11* ⓫ *Club*
Truly postmodern, this popular
bar is outrageously kitsch but
with a pop art sensibility that
saves it from crossing over too
far into tackiness. The fake fur,
Star Wars pictures, 1970s toys
and faux-cool psychedelia hang
together surprisingly well, and
there's a pleasant anything-goes
music policy that brings all kinds
of sounds, from rock and indie
to funk and soul, to a sociable,
slightly older crowd. Something
of a neighbourhood nightlife
institution.

The Retiro & Salamanca

Most visitors encounter the area around the Retiro park within the first few days, when they visit Madrid's star attraction, the Museo del Prado. The world-famous art museum is often referred to in relation to the 'Paseo del Arte' it forms with the nearby Thyssen-Bornemisza and the Reina Sofía. This 'art stroll' nowadays also includes the post-modern CaixaForum arts centre. North of the Retiro area is the *barrio* of Salamanca, a district known for its designer shopping, expensive restaurants and futuristic architecture.

Best art museum
Museo Nacional del Prado (p142) is one of Spain's most visited sites, a vast palace of Spanish art spanning several centuries.

Best quirky museums
You'll have the wonderfully eclectic Museo Lázaro Galdiano (p148) almost to yourself, and the Museo Naval (p140) is good fun for the nautically minded.

Best temporary exhibitions
The CaixaForum (p139) and the Fundación Mapfre (p146) have some of the most interesting programming in the city for art and photography exhibitions.

Best green spaces
The verdant Jardín Botánico (p140) is a place to rest post-Prado, but for the full park experience, the Retiro (p136) is unbeatable.

Best statues
The Ángel Caído (p137) in the Retiro is said to be the only monument to the devil in the world. The goddess Cybele, however, in the Plaza de Cibeles (p136), brings only good fortune to the city.

Best tapas
You can't go wrong in either Hevia (p150) or Jose Luís (p150), both beloved of Salamanca's denizens.

Retiro & around

The most attractive section of Madrid's north–south avenue is the oldest: the Paseo del Prado, from Atocha up to Plaza de Cibeles. Despite the traffic, the tree-lined boulevard still has many attractions on and around it, most notably Madrid's 'big three' art museums, joined in recent years by the **CaixaForum** art and cultural centre (see p139). The knot of elegant streets in between the Paseo and the **Retiro** (see p136) make up Madrid's most concentrated museum district, with, as well as the **Museo del Prado** (see p142), the **Museo Naval** and the **Museo Nacional de Artes Decorativas**.

Heading south from here, other highlights include the **Real Jardín Botánico**, on the Paseo del Prado itself; the rows of second-hand bookstalls on the pedestrianised **Cuesta de Moyano**, which runs along the southern side of the botanical garden; the magnificently grandiose 1880s **Ministerio de Agricultura**, right on Glorieta de Atocha and designed by Ricardo Velázquez, the same architect who created the delicate exhibition halls inside the Retiro itself; and the landmark 19th-century **Atocha** station. A few blocks east from here along the (traffic-filled) Paseo Reina Cristina, a turn right down C/Julián Gayarre leads to the **Real Fábrica de Tapices**. On

→ **Getting around**
Many buses run up and down the paseos – Prado, Recoletos and Castellana – but the area is also well served by the metro. Banco de España station (L2) is useful for the Prado and Retiro, and Colón (L4) is a good hopping-off point for Salamanca, but there are many more.

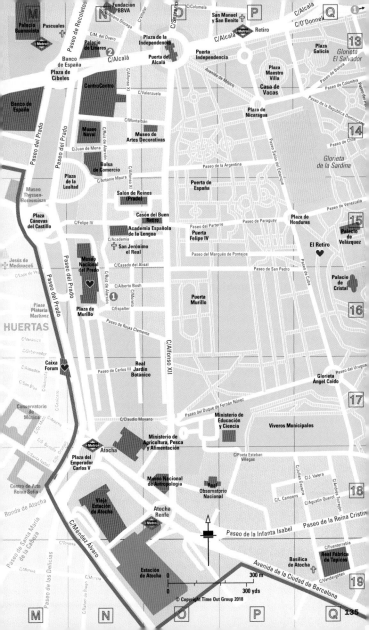

Julián Gayarre there is also the much rebuilt **Basílica de Atocha** and the odd, often deserted, **Panteón de Hombres Ilustres** containing the elaborate tombs of Spanish politicians of the 19th century.

Midway between the Puerta del Sol and the Retiro, the **Plaza de Cibeles** and its statue signify Madrid to Spaniards as much as the Eiffel Tower or the Empire State Building identify their particular cities. The four-way intersection is surrounded by some of the capital's most prominent buildings: the **Palacio de Cibeles** (which has been turned into a stunning information centre and exhibition space, **CentroCentro**), the **Banco de España**, the **Palacio Buenavista** (now the Army headquarters) and the Palacio de Linares, which houses the **Casa de América**. The Ventura Rodríguez statue in the middle is of Cybele, Roman goddess of fertility and symbol of natural abundance, on a chariot drawn by lions.

Sights & museums

CentroCentro
Plaza de Cibeles 1 (91 480 00 08, www.centrocentro.org). Metro Banco de España. **Open** *10am-8pm Tue-Sun. Mirador 10.30am-1.30pm, 4-7pm Tue-Sun.* **Admission** *free. Mirador €2; 50¢ under-12s. Free to all 1st Wed of mth.* **Map** *p135 N14.*
This extraordinary construction, which dwarfs the Plaza de Cibeles and is regularly compared to a sandcastle or a wedding cake, was until recently the world's most spectacular post office. It was designed in 1904 by Antonio Palacios and Joaquín Otamendi and completed in 1918, and is the best example of the extravagant style favoured by Madrid's elite

❤ The Retiro

When Philip II ruled Madrid, this whole area was just open country, apart from the church of **San Jerónimo** and a few other royal properties. In the 1630s, it was made into gardens – unprecedented in size for the era, at nearly 122 hectares (300 acres) – that became part of the **Palacio del Buen Retiro**, built by the Conde Duque de Olivares for Philip IV to impress the world. Gardeners were brought in from across Europe to create the park and its lake, and to ensure that it would feature shade and flowers throughout a Madrid summer. Charles III first opened sections of the park to the public in 1767, but it was only after the fall of Isabel II in 1868 that the gardens became entirely free to the public. After it became a park, the Retiro acquired most of its many statues, most notably the giant 1902 monument to King Alfonso XII presiding over the lake.

Since it was made open to all, the Retiro has found a very special place in the hearts and habits of the people of Madrid. On a Sunday morning stroll, especially before lunch, you will see multigenerational families watching puppet shows, dog-owners and their hounds, children playing on climbing frames, vendors hawking everything from *barquillos* (traditional wafers) to etchings, palm and tarot readers, buskers from around the world, couples on the lake in hired boats, kids playing football, elderly men involved in leisurely games of *petanca* (boules), cyclists, runners, and a good many bench-sitters who want nothing more than to read the paper. During the week it's much emptier, and it's easier to take a look at some of the 15,000 trees, the rose garden and the park's fine exhibition spaces: the **Palacio de Cristal**, the **Palacio de Velázquez** and the **Casa de Vacas**. Built in the 19th century, they were extensively renovated during the 1980s.

At the southern end of the park is the **Real Observatorio Nacional**, a fine neoclassical building. However, the greatest curiosity of the park is Madrid's monument to Lucifer, in the moment of his fall from heaven. Known as the **Ángel Caído** (Fallen Angel), this bizarrely unique statue on the avenue south of the Palacio de Cristal is thought to be the only monument to the Devil in the world.

After the death of Philip IV in 1665, little use was made of the Retiro, although the palace gained a new lease of life when the Alcázar burned down in 1734, as it became the primary royal residence in Madrid until the Palacio Real was completed in 1764. However, in 1808 Napoleon's troops made it a barracks, and when the British army arrived in 1812 to fight over Madrid, much of the palace was destroyed.

On the north side of the park, forming a bridge between it and Salamanca, is the grand **Puerta de Alcalá**, still imposing despite being surrounded by the hectic traffic of the Plaza de la Independencia. The districts around and south of the Retiro are in some ways similar to Salamanca, but less emphatically affluent and more mixed.

at its most expansive. The design was influenced by Viennese art nouveau, but it also features many traditional Spanish touches, with a grand entrance (complete with an oversized revolving door), a Hollywood film-set staircase, soaring ceilings, stunning columns and grand marble floors. In 2011, the building was transformed into a five-storey exhibition space, with a cultural information centre in the main entrance hall. There's a colourful and comfortable reading area, with sofas, beanbags, newspapers and iPads, and a café, while upstairs are various exhibition halls and the *mirador* – a lookout point with a panoramic view of the city.

Estación de Atocha

Glorieta del Emperador Carlos V. Metro Atocha. **Map** *p135 N18/O19.* Madrid's classic wrought-iron and glass main rail station was completed in 1892, to a design by Alberto del Palacio. It remained much the same, gathering a coating of soot, until the 1980s, when Rafael Moneo – he of the Museo Thyssen and Prado extension – gave it a complete renovation in preparation for Spain's golden year of 1992. Entirely new sections were added for the AVE high-speed train to Andalucia and Barcelona, and for the *cercanías* local rail network; an indoor tropical garden was installed in an imaginative blend of old and new. To the front of the station you can visit the monument to the victims of the horrific terrorist bombings of March 2004, a large glass cylinder inside which thousands of messages to the victims are written and displayed on a type of 'membrane', although in recent years the monument has fallen into disrepair.

Museo Nacional de Antropología

C/Alfonso XII 68 (91 539 59 95, mnantropologia.mcu.es). Metro Atocha. **Open** *9.30am-8pm Tue-Sat; 10am-3pm Sun.* **Admission** *€3; €1.50 reductions; free under-18s, over-65s.* **Map** *p135 O18.*
This three-storey building between the Retiro and Atocha station houses several levels, each devoted to a specific region or country. The first level has an extensive collection from the Philippines (a former Spanish colony), dominated by 6m (19ft 8in) dugout canoe. Among the bizarre highlights are a 19th-century Philippine helmet made from a blowfish, shrunken human heads from Peru, and the skeleton of Don Agustín Luengo y Capilla, an Extremaduran who stood 2.25m (7ft 4in) tall. Even more enticing is a shrivelled tobacco leaf-skinned mummy, said to have once been in Charles III's royal library. Both are in the annexe to the first level.

Museo Nacional de Artes Decorativas

C/Montalbán 12 (91 532 64 99, www.mecd.gob.es/ mnartesdecorativas). Metro Banco de España. **Open** *Sept-June 9.30am-3pm Tue, Wed, Fri, Sat; 9.30am-3pm, 5-8pm Thur; 10am-3pm Sun. July, Aug 9.30am-3pm Tue-Sat; 10am-3pm Sun.* **Admission** *€3; €1.50 reductions; free under-18s, over-65s. Free to all Thur pm, Sat 2-3pm & all day Sun.* **Map** *p135 O14.*
The Decorative Arts Museum houses more than 15,000 objets d'art, furniture and tapestries from all over Spain, plus many from China. One of the most prized rooms is the fifth-floor tiled kitchen, painstakingly transferred from an 18th-century Valencian palace, whose 1,604 painted tiles depict a domestic scene, with a huddle of servants making hot

🖤 CaixaForum Madrid

Paseo del Prado 36 (91 330 73 00, obrasocial.lacaixa.es). Metro Atocha. **Open** *10am-8pm daily.* **Admission** *€4.* **Map** *p135 M17.*

Already one of the city's landmarks, the CaixaForum is Madrid's stunning avant-garde cultural centre on the Paseo del Prado, designed by Herzog & de Meuron and completed in 2008. The building was the result of a six-year conversion of the 1899 Mediodía Electrical Power Station, one of the few examples of industrial architecture in central Madrid. By virtue of its location, CaixaForum can be considered a new addition to the 'Paseo del Arte', sitting as it does between the Prado, Reina Sofía and Thyssen, the museums on the Paseo del Prado.

The centre holds a wide range of art exhibitions, film screenings, concerts and educational programmes, and has become one of Madrid's most-visited attractions – as much for its awe-inspiring appearance as for the cultural attractions within. The arts centre's name comes from sponsorship by Catalan savings bank 'La Caixa', whose Obra Social Fundacíon 'La Caixa' operates community and welfare projects in Spain and abroad.

The building is striking for its rusted metal appearance and its apparent defiance of the laws of gravity, with the front part of the structure appearing to float off the ground. Its adjacent 24-metre (79-foot) 'vertical garden', designed in conjunction with French botanist Patrick Blanc, complements the building's intense red, and is now one of Madrid's most photographed spots. Herzog has stated that the aim of the garden is to provide a connection with the botanical gardens opposite, and the leafy landscape of the Paseo del Prado.

The only material from the original Mediodía power station that the architects were able to use was the building's brick shell, which needed to be fully restored and secured with cast iron. The extraneous parts of the building were removed with surgical precision – including the stone base, the removal of which opened up the new public square in front of the building, while simultaneously providing a sheltered space where summertime visitors can cool off.

chocolate. Also of great interest is the second floor, where the Spanish Baroque pieces are concentrated, among them ceramics from Talavera and Teruel, textiles, gold and silver work and jewellery cases from the Tesoro del Delfín (Treasure of the Grand Dauphin), the rest of which is in the Prado. Elsewhere are 19th-century doll's houses, antique fans, an ornate 16th-century four-poster bedstead and a Sèvres porcelain gift given to Queen Isabel II by Napoleon III.

♥ Museo Naval
Paseo del Prado 5 (91 523 87 89, www.armada.mde.es/museonaval). Metro Banco de España. **Open** *Sept-July 10am-7pm Tue-Sun. Aug 10am-3pm Tue-Sun.* **Admission** *free.* **Map** *p135 N14.*
Madrid's naval museum contains examples of the booty accumulated by Columbus and other mariners during Spain's period of maritime expansion, and an array of navigational instruments, muskets, guns and naval war paintings. Glass display cases enclose primitive weapons, some of which, like the swords lined with sharks' teeth from the Gilbert Islands, promise greater damage than their Western counterparts. The most impressive room is dominated by a huge mural map that traces the routes taken by Spain's intrepid explorers; in front of it are two equally impressive 17th-century giant globes. This same room also holds the museum's most valuable possession: the first known map of the Americas by a European – a parchment paper drawing by royal cartographer Juan de la Cosa, believed to have been made for Ferdinand and Isabella in 1500. Also worth a look is the room occupied by items salvaged between 1991 and 1993 from the *Nao San Diego*, which sank in the China Seas in 1600. You'll need to show a passport or other form of ID to gain entry.

Real Fábrica de Tapices
C/Fuenterrabía 2 (91 434 05 50, www.realfabricadetapices.com). Metro Menéndez Pelayo. **Open** *Guided tours only 10am-2pm Mon-Fri (last tour 1pm; tour in English noon). Closed Aug.* **Admission** *€5; €3.50 reductions; free under-6s. No cards.* **Map** *p135 Q19.*
Goya created some of his freshest images as designs for Madrid's royal tapestry factory, founded in 1721. Originally it was in Chueca, but has been here since 1889. The hand-working skills and techniques used haven't changed, and are evident from the intricate, painstaking work carried out in its two sections – the carpet room and the tapestry room. Goya designs are a mainstay of the work that's done here today (the factory also maintains carpets for royal palaces and the Ritz, as well as private clients).

♥ Real Jardín Botánico
Plaza de Murillo 2 (91 420 30 17, www.rjb.csic.es). Metro Atocha. **Open** *Nov-Feb 10am-6pm daily. Mar, Oct 10am-7pm daily. Apr, Sept 10am-8pm daily. May-Aug 10am-9pm daily.* **Admission** *€4; reductions 50¢-€2; free under-10s. No cards.* **Map** *p135 N17.*
Madrid's luscious botanical gardens were created for Charles III by Juan de Villanueva and the botanist Gómez Ortega in 1781. They sit alongside the Paseo del Prado, just south of the Prado museum, but inside this deep-green glade, with over 30,000 plants from around the world, it's easy to feel that city life has been put on hold. A sign at the entrance asks that you treat the gardens as if they were a museum, but don't feel bad about getting comfortable with a book for a while. The building in the middle of the gardens is used as a gallery space.

Real Jardín Botánico

Real Observatorio Nacional

*C/Alfonso XII 3 (91 527 01 07, www.
ign.es/rom/visitas/index.html).
Metro Atocha.* **Open** *Guided tours
(by appt only) Oct-May 4.30pm
Fri; noon, 4.30pm Sat; noon Sun.
June-Sept 5.30pm Fri; noon Sat
(also 5.30pm in June); noon Sun.*
Admission *€5; €3 reductions; free
under-3s.* **Map** *p135 O18.*
One of Charles III's scientific
institutions, the Observatorio
was completed after his death in
1790. Beautifully proportioned,
it is Madrid's finest neoclassical
building, designed by Juan de
Villanueva. It still contains a
working telescope, which can only
be seen by prior request. One room
is also open to the public, as part of
a guided tour.

Restaurants

La Castela €€

*C/Doctor Castelo 22 (91 574 00 15,
www.restaurantelacastela.com).
Metro Ibiza.* **Open** *noon-4.30pm,
9pm-midnight Mon-Sat; noon-
4.30pm Sun. Closed Aug.* **Map** *p135
Q13.* ❶ *Spanish*

The neighbourhood just east of
the Retiro has recently become
something of a gastro hunting
ground, but La Castela was ahead
of the curve, and has been around
for decades. Smart but thoroughly
authentic, with a zinc bar, pillars
and marble tables, it serves top-
notch tapas at a noisy bar area,
or you can sit in a quieter dining
room for dishes such as sirloin with
sweet sherry and foie, or bream
baked in salt.

Cafés & bars

El Botánico

*C/Ruiz de Alarcón 27 (91 420 23
42). Metro Banco de España.* **Open**
8am-2am daily. **Map** *p135 N16* ❶
Confusingly, this quiet bar-
restaurant actually sits on C/
Espalter, overlooking the
botanical gardens. Tucked away
from the tourist drag, it's very
quiet considering its proximity
to the Prado, and has a peaceful,
shaded terrace. It's a good spot for
breakfast, and there are tapas later
in the day.

❤ Museo Nacional del Prado

C/Ruiz de Alarcón 23, off Paseo del Prado (91 330 28 00, 91 330 29 00, www.museodelprado.es). Metro Atocha or Banco de España. **Open** *10am-8pm Mon-Sat; 10am-7pm Sun.* **Admission** *€15; €7.50 reductions; free under-18s, students aged 18-25. Free to all 6-8pm Tue-Sat, 5-7pm Sun. Paseo del Arte ticket €29.60.* **Map** *p135 N16.*

Housed in a vast neoclassical building begun by Juan de Villanueva for King Charles III in 1785, the Prado is Madrid's best-known attraction. Finally opened in 1819, the Prado was one of the world's first art museums, displaying the royal art collection.

In 2007, a new extension opened, on the site of the San Jerónimo cloisters behind the main building. The highly controversial cube-shaped edifice, designed by Rafael Moneo, houses the museum's temporary galleries, as well as a huge foyer containing the café-restaurant, information points, and a book and gift shop.

In the latest of several recent expansions, in 2010, a further seven new rooms opened, containing newly restored works. Dedicated to medieval and Renaissance Spanish art, they complete the ground floor collections of the Villanueva building, and significantly expand the museum's displays of 12th- to 16th-century Spanish painting.

The next major extension is the Salón de Reinos, which was once a wing of the Buen Retiro palace. It was purchased by the museum in order to create more exhibition space and stitch the various buildings of the Museo del Prado together. Norman Foster is behind the new design and building work will begin in 2018.

The collection

The Prado embraces art from the 12th to the 20th centuries, and contains the world's largest collection of Spanish works. Its core is still the royal holdings, so it reflects royal tastes from the 15th to the 17th centuries: court painters Diego Velázquez and Francisco Goya are well represented. Political ties with France, Italy and the southern, Catholic Netherlands also assure the presence of works by Titian, Rubens and Hieronymous Bosch.

But Spanish monarchs had begun collecting long before this time. By the 1500s, Queen Isabella already had a substantial collection of works by Flemish artists. During the reigns of Emperor Charles V (1519-56) and Philip II (1556-98), Italian and Flemish works continued to dominate. Titian was a favourite of both kings, and the eclectic Philip II also purchased several works by Bosch, among them the triptych *Garden of Earthly Delights* (*see p144* Visions of Hell), which he had hanging on his bedroom wall in El Escorial.

Philip IV (1621-65), a major patron of Rubens, is seen as the greatest Habsburg art collector. He was contemptuous of Spanish painters until he saw the work of the young Velázquez, who served him as court painter for nearly 40 years (1623-60).

Spain's first Bourbon King, Philip V (1700-46), brought with him one of the museum's most extraordinary possessions, displayed in the basement: the Tesoro del Delfín ('Treasures of the Grand Dauphin') – mostly 16th- and 17th-century Italian objets d'art. The last monarch to add significantly to the royal collection was Charles IV (1788-1808), the employer of Goya, who was possibly the least respectful court painter who ever lived, as shown by his portraits of Charles IV's family.

Highlights

When you arrive, pick up a floor plan (or download one from the website) to help you track down the don't-misses.

The ground floor contains Flemish works from the 17th century and Italian paintings from the 15th to the 18th centuries, such as Breughel the Elder's *Triumph of Death* and Bosch's *Garden of Earthly Delights* (Room 56A, *see p144*), as well as Spanish art from the 16th to the 19th centuries, including some of Goya's major works, and in particular his masterpiece *The Third of May* (Rooms 64-65). There's also a room dedicated to Joaquín Sorolla (Room 60A).

The highlight of the first floor is the Velázquez rooms. Here you'll find the Prado's most famous work, *Las Meninas* (Room 12), which is often described as the finest painting in the world because of its complex interplay of perspectives and realities. Elsewhere on this floor are Italian paintings from the 15th to 18th centuries and Spanish art from the 16th to the 19th centuries, including several works by El Greco.

Las Meninas (Diego Velázquez, 1656)

Visions of Hell

The Prado is home to two of the world's finest Last Judgement paintings

In Room 56A of the Prado are two of the greatest paintings ever done of the Last Judgement: Pieter Breughel the Elder's *The Triumph of Death,* painted in 1562; and The *Garden of Earthly Delights*, the triptych by Hieronymous Bosch (El Bosco to the Spanish), thought to have been completed around 1501. The latter is one of the greatest canvases of all time. And *The Triumph of Death* is no lightweight effort either; even if Breughel had not also been Flemish and an unabashed admirer of Bosch's painting, it would still be a good choice to display near *Earthly Delights*. It is smaller, a single canvas, but imagined in hallucinatory detail that is every bit a counterweight to the Bosch. In it, hundreds of skeletons herd the living into a huge coffin. The humans are terrified, helpless, shoved, pushed and prodded along by the skeletons. There is a huge bony horse and astride it is a skeletal general in death's army, huge scythe in one hand, reaping as he tramples through the waves of fearful human beings. A dog feeds on a dead woman's body. The horizon is high on the painting; the whole shocking scene in the foreground fades into dark spectral colours punctuated by pockets of leaping flames.

On the facing wall is Bosch's triptych, two metres high, the centre panel twice the width of the wings, which fold in over it. Painted on the back of the wings, forming another scene when they are covering the centre panel, is the third day of creation as described in Genesis. The main triptych depicts our peopled world in its implacable fullness and flesh, its joys and sufferings, all in amazingly modern detail.

The left panel shows the Garden of Eden in its innocence, but even here all is not peace and light, as beasts swallow other beasts, hinting at the savage brute world on which ours is built. In the centre panel is the antediluvian world of the senses – the world as we know it, a variety of human pleasure as modern as television or Hollywood's latest scandal. Sensual romps we have no trouble recognising as our own – the pleasures of the flesh in trysts, threesomes, group gropes, everyone indulging. Beside it, in the last panel, is hell itself, Judgement Day, when the former revellers are tied and tortured by ghouls and animals: miserable, dominated, impaled, ensnared and enslaved, their cities burning in the relentless darkness of the last days.

The *Garden of Earthly Delights* is full of the most modern of physical forms, from a round earth to airships. The power of its images is undimmed across the centuries, and they still resonate to this day.

Garden of Earthly Delights (detail)

James Joyce

*C/Alcalá 59 (91 575 49 01, www.
jamesjoycemadrid.com). Metro
Banco de España.* **Open** *noon-
2am Mon-Thur; noon-2.30am Fri;
11am-2.30am Sat; 11am-2am Sun.*
Map *p135 N13*

This is the Madrid outpost of what
is now a global chain of Oirish
theme pubs. With both Guinness
and Murphy's on tap, pub grub,
chatty staff and plenty of rugby and
Premier League matches showing
on two big screens and three TVs,
it's all much as you'd expect. Of
more interest, perhaps, is the fact
that the pub sits on the site of the
historic Café Lion, a haunt of post-
Civil War literati.

Salamanca & around

While other cities have rivers
cutting through them as
navigational points of reference,
Madrid has two great avenues: the
Gran Vía and its continuation, C/
Alcalá, running east–west, and
the **Paseo del Prado** – which
becomes the **Paseo de Recoletos**
and the **Paseo de la Castellana** as
it runs north.

The stretch north of Cibeles,
Paseo de Recoletos, was mostly
added in the 1830s and '40s. The
curiously grand marble palace a
little further north on the right,
which is now the **Fundación
BBVA** (a cultural foundation),
was built in the 1840s to be the
residence of the Marqués de
Salamanca, 19th-century Madrid's
huckster-in-chief. At the north
end of Recoletos, on the right,
stands the huge building that
houses the **Biblioteca Nacional**
and, behind it, the **Museo
Arqueológico Nacional**. The
most ambitious project of the
reign of Isabel II, the building was
commissioned in 1865, but only
completed in 1892. It overlooks
the **Plaza de Colón**, which has a
statue of Columbus in the central

Plaza de Toros de Las Ventas p149

roundabout. The square houses
the **Fernán Gómez** theatre and
arts centre.

The **Paseo de la Castellana**
snakes away freely northwards,
through thickets of office blocks
(*see p158* Changing the Skyline).
It also contains, near the junction
with C/Juan Bravo (location of the
Museo Arte Público de Madrid),
Madrid's 'beach' of upmarket
terrace bars, at the height of
fashion in the mid 1990s and
still thronged with *pijos* (akin to
London's Sloanes). To the east is
the Salamanca district, the heart
of affluent Madrid and the city's
most upscale shopping area.

Madrid's smartest *barrio*, a
19th-century expansion of the
city north and east in a grid
pattern, was named after a
banker, politician and speculator
notorious for his dubious
business practices, the Marqués
de Salamanca. The marquis had
previously built his own vast
residence on Paseo de Recoletos,
and spent one of the several
fortunes he made and lost in
his lifetime building a first line
of rectangular blocks along C/
Serrano, from C/Goya up to
Ramón de la Cruz.

It was only after the Restoration
of 1874 that Madrid's wealthier
citizens really began to appreciate
the benefits of wider streets and

residences with more class than the musty old neighbourhoods could supply. The wealthiest families of all built individual palaces along the lower stretch of the Paseo de la Castellana, in a wild variety of styles: French imperial, Italian Renaissance, neo-Mudéjar. Those who couldn't quite afford their own mansion moved into giant apartments in the streets behind. The area has been the centre of conservative, affluent Madrid ever since, home to some of the city's most exclusive shops and restaurants.

Sights & museums

Fundación Juan March

C/Castelló 77 (91 435 42 40, www.march.es). Metro Núñez de Balboa. *Open* Mid Sept-June 11am-8pm Mon-Sat; 10am-2pm Sun. Guided tours in English (by appointment only) 11am-1pm Wed. *Admission* free. *Map* p147 Q9.
This cultural foundation, set up by the wealthy financier Juan March in 1955, is one of the most important in Europe. Each year, a couple of major exhibitions are held here, and a decent selection of the foundation's 1,300 works of contemporary Spanish art is also on permanent display.

❤ Fundación Mapfre – Sala Bárbara de Braganza

C/Bárbara de Braganza 13 (91 581 46 09, www.fundacionmapfre.org/fundacion/en/exhibitions/barbara-braganza-hall). Metro Colón or Banco de España. *Open* 2pm-8pm Mon; 10am-8pm Tue-Sat; 11am-7pm Sun. Closed June-Sept. *Admission* €3; €2 reductions; €5 combined admission with the Sala Recoletos; free under-16s. Free to all 2-8pm Mon. *Map* p147 N12.
This striking space hosts four photography exhibitions every year, showing works by celebrated artists such as Cartier-Bresson and Paul Strand, as well as contemporary photographers such as Fazak Sheikh and Lynne Cohen.

Fundación Mapfre – Sala Recoletos

Paseo de Recoletos 23 (91 581 61 00, www.fundacionmapfre.org/fundacion/en/exhibitions/recoletos-hall). Metro Colón or Banco de España. *Open* 2pm-8pm Mon; 10am-8pm Tue-Sat; 11am-7pm Sun. *Admission* €3; €2 reductions; €5 combined admission with the Sala Bárbara de Braganza; free under-16s. *Map* p147 N12.
Set in the Palacio de la Duquesa de Medina de las Torres, the Mapfre shows some of the city's most interesting exhibitions – in various media. Until 2021, however, its greatest attraction is the 'Espacio Miró', a stunning collection of over 60 paintings ceded by the artist's family, which also includes wire sculptures by Miró's great friend Alexander Calder.

Museo Arqueológico Nacional

C/Serrano 13 (91 577 79 12, man.mcu.es). Metro Serrano. *Open* 9.30am-8pm Tue-Sat; 9.30am-3pm Sun. *Admission* €3. Free after 2pm Sat & all day Sun. *Map* p147 O12.
One of Madrid's oldest museums, dating back to 1867, the Museo Arqueológico Nacional shares the same building as the Biblioteca Nacional and Museo del Libro. It traces the evolution of human cultures, from prehistoric times up to the 15th century, and the collection of artefacts includes finds from the Iberian, Celtic, Greek, Egyptian, Punic, Roman, Paleochristian, Visigothic and Muslim cultures. Remarkably, the great majority of pieces came from excavations carried out within Spain, illustrating the extraordinary continuity and diversity of human settlement

❤ Museo Lázaro Galdiano

*C/Serrano 122 (91 561 60 84, www. flg.es). Metro Gregorio Marañón. **Open** 10am-4.30pm Tue-Sat; 10am-3pm Sun. **Admission** €6; €3 reductions; free under-12s. Free to all 3.30-4.30pm Tue-Sat, 2-3pm Sun. **Map** p147 P6.*

This unjustifiably little-known museum holds the extraordinarily eclectic collection of 15,000 paintings and objets d'art, covering 24 centuries, that was accumulated over 70 years by the financier and bibliophile José Lázaro Galdiano (1862-1947). Its holdings include paintings by Goya and Bosch, an important collection of work from the Dutch and English schools, with paintings by Jan Breughel and Constable, and some wonderful Renaissance ornamental metalwork, as well as suits of armour, weaponry, jewellery and illuminated manuscripts.

The four-storey mansion and its gardens are a sight in themselves. Be sure to take the creaky antique lift – with its original red velvet banquette – up to the first floor, where you can see the carefully restored ceiling frescoes and some of the original furniture in what were once the dining and billiard rooms.

Within the museum, temporary exhibitions – in various mediums and across a wide range of subjects –are included in the ticket price, and in the grounds is a further exhibition space, free to enter. It's worth exploring the website for more detail on some of the paintings, most notably an interactive look at the secrets hidden within Hieronymus Bosch's *St John the Baptist in Meditation*.

in the Iberian peninsula. Begin in the basement, which holds palaeontological material such as skulls, tombs and a mammoth's tusks, still attached to its skull. Some of the most interesting relics are from the area around Madrid itself, such as the many 4,000-year-old neolithic bell-shaped pottery bowls. The first floor holds the museum's most famous possession, the *Dama de Elche*, the stone bust of an Iberian priestess, believed to date from 500BC. In the garden, steps lead underground to a reproduction of the renowned Altamira prehistoric cave paintings in Cantabria.

Museo Arte Público de Madrid

Paseo de la Castellana 41. Metro Rubén Darío. **Admission** *free.* **Map** *p147 P8.*

An unconventional museum, this 1970s outdoor space at the junction of the Castellana with C/ Juan Bravo contains donated works from all the major names in late 20th-century Spanish sculpture – including Pablo Serrano, Miró and Chillida – and much of their work is spectacular, especially the dynamic stainless-steel *Món per a infants* ('A world for children') by Andreu Alfaro and the cascade by Sempere that forms the museum's centrepiece.

Museo de Cera

Paseo de Recoletos 41 (91 319 26 49, www.museoceramadrid. com). Metro Colón. **Open** *10am-2.30pm, 4.30-8.30pm Mon-Fri; 10am-8.30pm Sat, Sun.* **Admission** *€12-€19. No cards.* **Map** *p147 N11.*

Madame Tussauds it isn't (there's no queueing for starters), yet this waxwork museum still has a certain tacky charm. The usual collection of rogues, celebrities and politicians includes the Beatles, Clark Gable and Melania Trump – but doesn't include Donald. Sad.

Plaza de Toros de Las Ventas

C/Alcalá 237 (91 356 22 00, museum 91 725 18 57, www.las-ventas.com). Metro Ventas. **Open** *Museum 10am-6pm daily (until 4pm on fight days).* **Admission** *Museum free.*

More than 22,000 spectators can catch a bullfight in this, Spain's largest arena, completed in 1929 and sitting on the eastern edge of the Salamanca district. Like most early 20th-century bullrings, it is in neo-Mudéjar style, with often playful use of ceramic tiling. Around it there is ample open space to accommodate the crowds and food vendors, so it's easy to get a good look at the exterior. It's not necessary to go to a *corrida* to see the ring from within. When the bulls are back on the ranch, concerts are often held here, and alongside the ring there is the small Museo Taurino. The museum holds portraits of famous matadors, as well as *trajes de luces* (suits of lights), including the pink-and-gold outfit worn by the legendary Manolete on the afternoon of his death in the ring in 1947. Among the 18th-century paintings is a portrait of *torero* Joaquín Rodriguez Costillares.

Restaurants

Salón Cascabel €€

C/Serrano 52 (in El Corte Inglés), (91 432 54 90, www.saloncascabel. com). Metro Serrano. **Open** *1.15pm-midnight Mon-Wed, Sun; 1.15pm-2am Fri, Sat.* **Map** *p147 O10* ❷ *Mexican*

A groundbreaking haute Mexican restaurant/tapas bar, sitting in a former ironmonger's on the top floor of El Corte Inglés (the view is spectacular). The vibe is glam disco food-truck, but the food is impeccable, from the humble guacamole to the Flintstones-style femur out of which you scoop creamy roast bone marrow, the house speciality. Ingredients are mostly grown and smoked on their own land – pick up a jar of the fab chipotle sauce when you leave.

Tepic €€

Ayalá 14 (91 522 08 50, www. tepic.es). Metro Serrano. **Open** *1pm-1.15am Mon-Thur; 1pm-2.15am Fri, Sat; 1pm-5pm Sun.* **Map** *p147 O10* ❸ *Mexican*

The name comes from the capital of Nayarit state in Mexico, and a huge photo of a typical Mexican city takes up one wall of this chic restaurant. There is no doubt about what you're going to eat here: quesadillas, guacamole, tacos, enchiladas, enmoladas... all of a much higher standard than at most Mexican joints in Madrid, plus the margaritas are so good, there's no way you're going to have just one.

Tapas bars

Estay

C/Hermosilla 46 (91 578 04 70, www.estayrestaurante.com). Metro Velázquez. **Open** *8am-12.30am Mon-Thur; 1-4.30pm, 8pm-1.30am Fri, Sat.* **Map** *p147 Q11* ❶

The bright, air-conditioned interior, usually filled with baying young mothers heavily laden with shopping bags, does not immediately suggest gastronomic promise. Stick with the place, however, and you'll enjoy scrumptious and sophisticated tapas and cheap wines by the glass.

❤ Hevia

C/Serrano 118 (91 562 30 75, www. heviamadrid.com). Metro Gregorio Marañón. **Open** *10am-midnight Mon-Sat. Closed 1wk Aug.* **Map** *p147 P7* ❷

A quiet, well-heeled crowd frequents this smart bar. Tapas are correspondingly sophisticated – foie gras, caviar, crab and duck liver pâté – and pricey. In summer, the tables outside can prove irresistible.

❤ José Luis

C/Serrano 89 (91 563 09 58, www. joseluis.es). Metro Núñez de Balboa. **Open** *9am-1am Mon-Sat; noon-1am Sun.* **Map** *p147 P7* ❸

Despite its rather anodyne interior, this is probably one of Madrid's most famous tapas bars and namechecked in a song by the Catalan folk singer Serrat. The food here is little changed since the 1950s and of a high standard. If your appetite is up to it, try the superb *brascada* (sirloin with ham and onions). **Other locations** throughout the city.

Cafés & bars

Café Gijón

Paseo de Recoletos 21 (91 521 54 25, www.cafegijon.com). Metro Banco de España or Colón. **Open** *7.30am-1.30am daily.* **Map** *p147 N12* ❸

Still charming after all these years, this is Madrid's definitive literary café, open since 1888. It still holds poetry *tertulias* on Monday nights, and publishes a magazine filled with doodles and thoughts from visiting writers. A pianist tinkles the ivories to a packed terrace in summer.

El Pavellón del Espejo

Paseo de Recoletos 31 (91 308 23 47,). Metro Colón. **Open** *8am-midnight daily.* **Map** *p147 N12* ④

Not nearly as historic as the neighbouring Gijón, although it may look it: when it opened in 1978, 'The Mirror' set out to be the art nouveau bar Madrid never had, with positively Parisian 1900s decor. Its terrace bar out on the Paseo de Recoletos occupies a splendid glass pavilion reminiscent of a giant Tiffany lamp. Fashionable and comfortable, it's a good spot for breakfast, but the tapas can be mediocre.

Shops & services

Salamanca is a shopper's paradise, with several specialities. If you're all about labels, then this is the place to be, in particular C/Serrano, where on the same block you will find Loewe, Yves Saint Laurent and La Perla, as well as smaller designer boutiques throughout the area. On and around C/Claudio Coello are lots of upmarket, specialist antique dealers. A great place for cheap second-hand books, from rare editions to remainders, is the line of kiosks on Cuesta de Moyano (also known as C/Claudio Moyano), by the Jardín Botánico.

ABC Serrano

C/Serrano 61 & Paseo de la Castellana 34 (91 577 50 31, www. abcserrano.com). Metro Rubén Darío. **Open** *10am-9pm Mon-Sat.* **Map** *p147 P8* ① *Shopping centre*

Occupying the building that once housed the ABC newspaper, this upmarket and perfectly located shopping mall has eight floors. Four of them are dedicated to designer and high street fashion, as well as sportswear, jewellery, crafts and electronics. There are three restaurants on the upper floors, a

Agatha Ruiz de la Prada

café on the ground floor and a lively summer *terraza* on the fourth, plus a gym at the top.

Adolfo Domínguez

C/Serrano 96 (91 576 70 53, www. adolfodominguez.es). Metro Rubén Dario. **Open** *10am-8.30pm Mon-Sat.* **Map** *p147 P8* ② *Fashion*

Simple, classic pieces from the well-known Galician designer. The suits are well cut and long-lasting, while the accessories and shoes are also some of the brand's strong points. **Other locations** throughout the city.

Agatha Ruiz de la Prada

C/Serrano 27 (91 319 05 01, www. agatharuizdelaprada.com). Metro Serrano. **Open** *Sept-July 10am-8.30pm Mon-Sat. Aug 10am-2pm, 5-8pm Mon-Fri, 10am-2pm Sat.* **Map** *p147 P10* ③ *Fashion*

Loud, colourful patterns characterise this designer's work, with many pieces emblazoned with her trademark hearts and flowers. The childrenswear range is hugely popular, as are the homewares.

La Boulette

*Stands 63-68, Mercado de La Paz, C/Ayala 28 (91 431 77 25, www.laboulette.com). Metro Serrano. **Open** 9am-8pm Mon-Fri; 9am-2.30pm Sat. **Map** p147 P10* ❹ *Food & drink*

La Boulette probably has the largest selection of cheeses in Madrid and possibly the country, with over 400 varieties, both Spanish and imported, on sale. The range of goods in the charcuterie section is similarly impressive.

Camper

*C/Serrano 24 (91 578 25 60, www.camper.com). Metro Serrano. **Open** 10am-9pm Mon-Sat; noon-8pm Sun. **Map** p135 O12* ❺ *Fashion*

Branches of the Mallorcan family firm continue to spring up all over the city (and all over the world). At this one, two large plinths display the entire men's and women's collection – brightly coloured, fun shoes and sandals. **Other locations** throughout the city.

El Jardín de Serrano

*C/Goya 6-8 (91 577 00 12, www.jardindeserrano.es). Metro Serrano. **Open** 9.30am-9.30pm Mon-Sat. **Map** p147 P11* ❻ *Shopping centre*

This Salamanca mall may be small but it's a retail gem, with designer boutiques, expensive shoe shops and a classy café.

Joaquín Berao

*C/Lagasca 44 (91 577 28 28, www.joaquinberao.com). Metro Serrano. **Open** Sept-July 10am-8.30pm Mon-Sat. Aug 10am-2pm, 5-8.30pm Mon-Fri; 10am-2.30pm Sat. **Map** p147 P11* ❼ *Fashion*

Chunky, twisted and contorted, but also fluidly elegant, Joaquín Berao's solid silver bracelets,

necklaces, earrings and chokers are increasingly the choice of those in the know.

Lavinia

*C/José Ortega y Gasset 16 (91 426 06 04, www.lavinia.es). Metro Nuñez de Balboa. **Open** 10am-9pm Mon-Sat. **Map** p147 P9* ❽ *Food & drink*

No oenophile should miss visiting Lavinia, which claims to be Europe's largest wine shop. In stark contrast to many of Madrid's dusty old *bodegas*, it's bright, airy and spacious, and staff are knowledgeable and helpful.

Mantequerías Bravo

*C/Ayala 24 (91 575 80 72). Metro Serrano. **Open** 9.30am-2.30pm, 5.30-8.30pm Mon-Fri; 9.30am-2.30pm Sat. Closed Aug. **Map** p147 P10* ❾ *Food & drink*

A marvellous selection of foodstuffs is on sale in this Salamanca shop, including meats and cheeses, wines and spirits, and coffees and teas. Homesick Brits will be pleased with imports such as English mustard and cream crackers.

¡Oh, qué Luna!

*C/Ayala 32 (91 431 37 25, www.ohqueluna.com). Metro Serrano. **Open** 10am-8.30pm Mon-Fri; 11am-2pm, 5-8.30pm Sat. **Map** p147 P10* ❿ *Fashion*

Glam, sexy lingerie, negligées and dressing gowns. It also does a line in bedlinen and swimwear.

Purificación García

*C/Serrano 28 (91 435 80 13, www.purificaciongarcia.es). Metro Serrano. **Open** 10am-8.30pm Mon-Sat. **Map** p147 O11* ⓫ *Fashion*

Purificación García is where the capital's older but elegant woman heads when she wants something smart for the office. Well cut and using natural materials, the clothes are very well priced for the quality of the fabrics. **Other locations** throughout the city.

Beyond the Centre

Building restrictions over the centuries have kept even Madrid's more far-flung attractions within reasonably easy reach of the city centre. Head out of the old city and you can take in the Madrid skyline by cable car, visit an authentic Egyptian temple or inspect General Franco's old home. The more distant areas are a welcome green escape, with the woods and hills around El Pardo serving as a refuge for wildlife and humans seeking respite from the summer heat. But this is Madrid, so there's also magnificent art, from frescoes adorning Goya's tomb to Europe's finest collection of pre-Columbian American art.

Best parks
Two of the best: the vast Casa de Campo (*p155*) and the quirky little Parque El Capricho (*p157*).

Best view
Take a glass lift up the Faro de Moncloa comms tower (*p154*).

Best restaurants
Put yourself in the hands of the larger-than-life Sacha (*p161*), or check out Fismuler (*p160*), the latest foodie hotspot.

Best museums
The endearing Museo del Ferrocarril (*p164*) celebrates all things train-related, and the Museo Sorolla (*p156*) is packed with colourful, light-filled art.

Best curiosities
Visit Franco's bathroom at the Real Palacio de El Pardo (*p159*), and see a sunset at the Egyptian Templo de Debod (*p160*).

North & west

Sights & museums

Ermita de San Antonio de la Florida

Glorieta de San Antonio de la Florida 5, Moncloa (91 542 07 22). Metro Príncipe Pío. **Open** *9.30am-8pm Tue-Sun.* **Guided Tours** *1pm Sat, in Spanish and English, free.* **Admission** *free.*
This plain neoclassical chapel was completed by Felipe Fontana for Charles IV in 1798. North of Príncipe Pío station on the Paseo de la Florida, it is famous as the burial place of Goya, and for the unique frescoes of the miracles of St Anthony, incorporating scenes of Madrid life, which Goya painted here in 1798. In contrast to the staid exterior, the colour and use of light in his images are stunning. Featuring a rare mix of elements, including his unique, simultaneously ethereal and sensual 'angels', they are among his best and most complex works. On the other side of the road into the park is a near-identical second chapel, built in the 1920s to allow the original building to be left as a museum.

Estadio Santiago Bernabéu

Paseo de la Castellana 144, Chamartín (91 398 43 00, www. realmadrid.com). Metro Santiago Bernabéu. **Open** *(guided tours) 10am-7pm Mon-Sat; 10.30am-6.30pm Sun; tours stop 5hrs before kick-off on match days.* **Tickets** *Stadium tours €25; €13-18 reductions. Match tickets €40-€325.*
After a few years blighted by infighting and power struggles, the Whites are thriving under the leadership of coach Zinedine Zidane. They won four major titles for the first time in their 115-year history during the 2016-2017 season, making it their best ever year. Tickets can be purchased online or at the stadium's ticket offices, but getting hold of one can be extremely difficult as 90% of tickets are taken up by club members. For more information on stadium tours, visit the Real Madrid website.

❤ Faro de Moncloa

Avda de los Reyes Católicos, Moncloa (91 550 12 51, www. esmadrid.com/faro-de-moncloa). Metro Moncloa. **Open** *9.30am-8pm Tue-Sun.* **Admission** *€3; €1.50 reductions; free under-6s.*

❤ Casa de Campo

Once a royal hunting estate, the verdant, sprawling parkland of the **Casa de Campo**, to the west of the city in Moncloa, was only opened to the public under the Republic in 1931. Five years later, it became a key site for Franco's forces in the Civil War battle for Madrid, its high ground being used to shell the city centre and the university. Remains of trenches still exist.

Today, the Casa is home to the **Parque de Atracciones** funfair (*91 526 80 30, www. parquedeatracciones.es*) and the attractively landscaped **Zoo Aquarium** (*91 512 37 70, www.zoomadrid.com*), as well as swimming pools, tennis courts, and a large boating lake. The cafés that ring the lake are good for an outdoor lunch, and cyclists should note that most of the park's roads are closed to cars on Sunday mornings.

Once you stray away from the criss-crossing roads, much of the park is surprisingly wild, and it's possible to have a real country walk through its woods and gullies. A favourite way to visit is via the **Teleférico de Madrid** cable car, closed for major renovation at the time of writing, but which runs over the trees from the **Parque del Oeste** almost to the middle of the Casa de Campo, where there are viewpoints, an (undistinguished) bar-restaurant and picnic spots.

Couples seeking seclusion favour the park by day and night, and the area by the Teleférico has long been a gay cruising spot, although police have been cracking down on this. Prostitution used to be a major problem, but in recent years the park has mostly been closed to traffic, which has vastly improved the situation.

BEYOND THE CENTRE

This former radio and communications tower, 92m (302ft) tall, provides one of the best views of the whole of the city and the *sierras* in the distance. Diagrams along the floor point out highlights of the city. The best bit, though, is the ride up in the glass lift.

Museo de América

Avda de los Reyes Católicos 6, Moncloa (91 543 94 37, www.mecd. gob.es/museodeamerica). Metro Moncloa. **Open** *9.30am-3pm Tue, Wed, Fri, Sat; 9.30am-7pm Thur; 10am-3pm Sun.* **Admission** *€3; €1.50 reductions; free under-18s, free to all Sun.*

This finest collection of pre-Columbian American art and artefacts in Europe is a combination of articles brought back at the time of the Conquest and during the centuries of Spanish rule over Central and South America, plus later acquisitions generally donated by Latin American governments. The collection includes some near-matchless treasures: there is the *Madrid Codex*, one of only four surviving Mayan illustrated glyph manuscripts in the world; the *Tudela Codex* and illustrated manuscripts from central Mexico, which depict the Spanish Conquest; superb carvings from the Mayan city of Palenque, sent back to Charles III in 1787; and the Gold of the Quimbayas, a series of exquisite gold figures from the Quimbaya culture of Colombia, which were presented to Spain by the Colombian government. Further highlights include Aztec obsidian masks from Mexico, Inca stone sculptures and funeral offerings from Peru, and finely modelled, comical and sometimes highly sexual figurines from the Chibcha culture of Colombia. There are also exhibits from the Spanish colonial period, such as the *Entry of the Viceroy Morcillo into Potosí* (1716) by the early Bolivian painter Melchor Pérez Holguín; a series of paintings showing in obsessive detail the range of racial mixes possible in colonial Mexico; and a collection of gold and other objects from the galleons *Atocha* and *Margarita*, sunk off Florida in the 18th century and only recovered in 1988.

Museo Cerralbo

C/Ventura Rodríguez 17, Argüelles (91 547 36 46, museocerralbo. mcu.es). Metro Plaza de España. **Open** *9.30am-3pm Tue, Wed, Fri, Sat; 9.30am-3pm, 5-8pm Thur; 10am-3pm Sun.* **Admission** *€3; €1.50 reductions; free under-18s, over-65s. Free to all Thur pm, Sat from 2pm, all day Sun.*

Laid out in a sumptuous 19th-century mansion is the remarkable collection of artworks and artefacts assembled by the 17th Marqués de Cerralbo. A politician, traveller and a man of letters, he bequeathed his collection to the state with the stipulation that it should be displayed exactly how he had arranged it himself. Thus the contents are laid out in a crowded manner, with paintings in three levels up the walls, and few items labelled. Among the many paintings, though, there is El Greco's *The Ecstasy of St Francis of Assisi* – the real highlight – and works by Zurbarán, Alonso Cano and other Spanish masters. The upstairs area contains an astonishing collection of European and Japanese armour, weapons, watches, pipes, leather-bound books, clocks and other curiosities.

♥ Museo Sorolla

Paseo del General Martínez Campos 37, Chamberí (91 310 15 84, museosorolla.mcu.es). Metro Gregorio Marañón or Iglesia. **Open** *9.30am-8pm Tue-Sat; 10am-3pm Sun.* **Admission** *€3; €1.50 reductions; free under-18s & over-65s. Free to all 2-8pm Sat, all day Sun.*

💜 Parque El Capricho de la Alameda de Osuna

*Paseo de la Alameda de Osuna 25, northern suburbs (91 588 01 14). Metro El Capricho. **Open** Oct-Mar 9am-6.30pm Sat, Sun. Apr-Sept 9am-9pm Sat, Sun. **Admission** free.*

Now surrounded by Madrid's eastern sprawl, the Parque El Capricho is a remarkably preserved monument to 18th-century taste. Within its 14 hectares (2.5 acres) is an artificial river that meanders between lakes, woods, rose gardens and replica Greek and Egyptian temples. The gardens were begun in the 1780s for the Duke and Duchess of Osuna, who were enthusiastic promoters of the ideas of the Enlightenment and great patrons of the artists, writers and musicians of their day. In the 1790s, an invitation to spend a day there was the hottest ticket in Madrid, for both the aristocracy and the intelligentsia.

The Duchess's main architect was Jean-Baptiste Mulot, a French gardener who had previously worked for Marie Antoinette, although much of the Capricho is in the English style, with simulated natural landscapes between smaller formal gardens. An Italian theatre designer, Angelo Maria Borghini, was brought in to construct many of the Capricho's fanciful buildings.

The liberal informality between aristocrats and artists and intellectuals, encouraged by the duchess – already deeply suspect for her 'French' ideas – soon led to unstoppable rumours that far more illicit activities were going on among the Capricho's intimate arbours than just chat. The Duke and Duchess were also among the first important patrons of Goya, and their support played a major part in winning him acceptance among high society. The Capricho is also famous as the place where Goya, then aged 40, met the 23-year-old Duchess of Alba in 1786, and where his obsession with her began. Scandalous and impulsive, known for breaking whichever social conventions suited her, the Duchess of Alba was nevertheless a good friend of the high-minded Duchess of Osuna, and a frequent visitor to El Capricho.

Changing the Skyline

The buildings that jostle for attention at the top of the Paseo de la Castellana

▶ *Sights along the upper Castellana are listed here from bottom to top, south to north. The metro system partly avoids the avenue, but the 27 bus runs up and down the whole stretch.*

In the 1970s and '80s, banks and insurance companies vied with each other to commission trendy architects to create corporate showcases along the upper Castellana; see the **Bankinter** building at No.29 and **Bankunión** at No.46. Beyond the latter, the **Museo de Ciencias Naturales** is set back from the road on a grassy hill; further still, on the left, is the Kafka-esque grey bulk of the enormous **Nuevos Ministerios** government complex. Begun in 1932, it contains many government ministries, and is one of the largest projects bequeathed by the Spanish Republic to Madrid. It was designed in a monolithic '30s rationalist style; then, after the victory of General Franco, some curving, traditionalist details more to the taste of the new regime were added. Inside it has a garden, open to the public.

Beyond that, a huge branch of El Corte Inglés signals your arrival at the **AZCA** complex. The Asociación Zona Comercial A, known to some as 'Little Manhattan', is a glitzy skyscraper development first projected during the Franco regime's industrial heyday in the '60s, which gained extra vigour in democratic Spain's 1980s boom to become a symbol of Madrid yuppiedom. At its centre is the **Plaza Picasso**, a small park, and amid the office blocks is a chic shopping mall, restaurants and other facilities to make it a self-contained 'workers' city'. At its north end is the **Torre Picasso**, designed by Japanese architect Minoru Yamasaki in 1988 and, at 157 metres (515 feet), one of Madrid's tallest buildings. Beyond it is the circular **Torre Europa**.

A little further up again, opposite each other, is the Real Madrid stadium, **Estadio Bernabéu** (see p154), and the **Palacio de Congresos** conference centre. By this time, the view up the Paseo de la Castellana is dominated by the two leaning towers officially known as the **Puerta de Europa** at Plaza Castilla. These remarkable smoked-glass blocks, leaning in at 15 degrees off the perpendicular, are perhaps the greatest monument to Spain's 1980s boom.

Often regarded as a neo-Impressionist, Valencia-born Joaquín Sorolla was really an exponent of 'luminism', the celebration of light. He was renowned for his iridescent, sun-drenched paintings, including portraits and family scenes at the beach and in gardens. Sorolla's leisured themes and greetings card-style aesthetic (and indeed his paintings are often used as such) are easy to dismiss, but most find his luminous world at least a little seductive. This delightful little museum, housed in the mansion built for the artist in 1910 to spend his latter years, holds 250 works. The salon, dining room and breakfast room are furnished in their original state and the garden, Moorish-inspired but with an Italianate pergola, is a delightful, peaceful oasis of calm, seemingly miles away from the roaring traffic outside.

Museo Tiflológico

C/La Coruña 18, Tetuán (91 589 42 19, museo.once.es). Metro Estrecho. **Open** *10am-2pm, 5-8pm Tue-Fri; 10am-2pm Sat. Closed Aug.* **Admission** *free.*
Owned and run by ONCE, the organisation for blind and partially sighted people, this special museum presents exhibitions of work by visually impaired artists (the name comes from the Greek *tiflos*, sightless). Work here is intended to be touched, and is generally sculptural, three-dimensional, rich in texture and highly tactile. There is a collection of instruments devised to help the blind and a series of scale models of monuments from Spain and around the world.

Museo del Traje (Museum of Clothing)

Avda Juan de Herrera 2, Moncloa (91 550 47 00, museodeltraje. mcu.es). Metro Moncloa. **Open** *9.30am-7pm Tue-Sat; 10am-3pm Sun.* **Admission** *€3; free under-18s, over-65s. Free to all 2.30-7pm Sat, all day Sun.*
The collections comprise around 21,000 garments covering six centuries of Spanish fashion, although there are some much older items, among them fragments of Coptic cloth and Hispano-Muslim pieces. The rotating exhibition shows up to 600 items at any one time and is arranged chronologically. There are two outstanding monographic rooms, one covering regional costume, the other containing pieces by Mariano Fortuny y Madrazo, son of the painter, whose creations were worn by the likes of Isadora Duncan. Other rooms cover costume from the Enlightenment to the *castizos* (Madrid's working classes), early 19th-century French influences, Romanticism, belle époque, the avant-garde, post-Civil War fashion and the modern era. A room is dedicated to the great couturier Balenciaga and another to Spanish haute couture.

♥ Real Palacio de El Pardo

C/Manuel Alonso, El Pardo (91 376 15 00, www.patrimonionacional. es). Bus 601 from Moncloa. **Open** *Apr-Sept 10am-8pm daily. Oct-Mar 10am-6pm daily.* **Admission** *€9; €4 reductions; free under-5s. Free to EU citizens 5-8pm (3-6pm Apr-Sept) Wed, Thur pm.*
In 1405, Henry III constructed a hunting lodge here, but the first monarch to take a really serious interest in El Pardo's excellent deer and game hunting estate was Charles I of Spain (Charles V of the Holy Roman Empire), who built a sizeable palace here. His successor, Philip II, added many important works of art but most of these were lost in a fire in 1604, and after various architectural changes the building was finally reconstructed on Charles III's orders by 18th-century architect Francesco Sabatini; superb murals by Bayeu and Maella were added at this time. The current furnishings, paintings and tapestries were added during the 19th and 20th centuries.

Nowadays the palace is partially open to the public and there are tours of its ornate and gaudy interior with ornamental frescoes, gilt mouldings and some fine tapestries, many of which were woven in the Real Fábrica de Tapices to Goya designs. There's an ornate theatre, built for Charles IV's Italian wife María Luisa of Parma, where censorious film fan Franco used to view films with his cronies before deciding on their suitability for the great unwashed but, in truth, the only rooms of real fascination are the Generalísimo's bedroom, dressing room and '70s bathroom – decorated according to his own exacting specifications.

Sala del Canal de Isabel II

C/Santa Engracia 125, Chamberí (91 545 10 00, www.madrid.org). Metro Ríos Rosas. **Open** *11am-2pm, 5-8.30pm Tue-Sat; 11am-2pm Sun.* **Admission** *free.*

This water tower, built in elaborate neo-Mudéjar style between 1907 and 1911, is considered to be a gem of Madrid's industrial architecture. It is now home to a stylish exhibition space that specialises in photography, ranging in quality from good to world-class. Two kilometres north of here, just off the Plaza de Castilla, is the Fundación Canal (www.fundacioncanal.com), another arts and education centre run by the Canal de Isabel II.

❤ Templo de Debod

Paseo de Pintor Rosales s/n, Argüelles (91 366 74 15, templodedebod.memoriademadrid. es). Metro Plaza de España or Ventura Rodríguez. **Open** *10am-8pm Sun.* **Admission** *free.*

This Egyptian structure, which sits on the outskirts of the Parque del Oeste, dates back 2,200 years and is dedicated to the gods Amun and Isis. It was sent, block by block, by the Egyptian government in 1968 in thanks for Spain's help in preserving monuments threatened by the Aswan Dam.

Restaurants

Asador Donostiarra €€€

C/Infanta Mercedes 79, Tetuán (91 579 08 71, www.asadordonostiarra. com). Metro Tetuán. **Open** *1.30-4pm, 8.30pm-midnight Mon-Sat; 1.30-4pm Sun.* Steakhouse

The once-preferred *asador* (steakhouse) of David Beckham and the rest of the team, located near the Bernabéu stadium. The celeb crowd is as legendary as the *solomillo*, and they often give away signed photos and other goodies from the team. Dissenting voices

say that all the press has had an adverse effect, and the run-of-the-mill salad, steak and potato offerings are not commensurate with the hefty prices; others still claim it's the best *asador* in Madrid.

Bar Tomate €€

C/Fernando El Santo 26, Chamberí (91 702 38 70, www.grupotragaluz. com). Metro Colón. **Open** *8am-2am daily.* Mediterranean

Great for breakfast, a snack, lunch or dinner. Part of the wildly successful Tragaluz group, which has several restaurants in Barcelona, Bar Tomate specialises in light and tasty Mediterranean cuisine, such as gorgonzola croquettes, anchovies and red piquillo peppers on toast, rice cooked in squid ink with clams, and carpaccios.

Casa Mingo €

Paseo de la Florida 34, Casa de Campo (91 547 79 18, www. casamingo.es). Metro Príncipe Pío. **Open** *11am-midnight daily.* **No cards.** Spanish

A vast and noisy Asturian cider house, open since 1888. This is a great opportunity to rub elbows with *madrileños* really enjoying themselves at one of the long wooden tables. The restaurant specialises in roast chicken and cider, and also serves classic *cocido* on weekday lunchtimes. Turn up early for a terrace seat, or take out a chicken and a bottle of cider and head for the River Manzanares for a picnic.

❤ Fismuler €€€

C/Sagasta 29, Chamberí (91 827 75 81, www.fismuler.es). Metro Alonso Martínez. **Open** *1.30-4pm, 8.30-11.30pm Mon-Thur; 1.30-4pm, 8.30pm-12.30am Fri, Sat.* Spanish

Nino Redruello is of good Madrid restaurant stock, and draws on old family recipes, adding his own distinctive stamp and drawing praise from the likes of Anthony Bourdain. Fismuler is his latest venture, a sociable, welcoming place with long wooden shared tables. Dishes change daily depending what looks good in the market, but don't miss the sea anemone tortilla, if it's on offer.

❤ Sacha €€€
C/Juan de Hurtado de Mendoza 11, Chamartín (91 345 59 52). Metro Cuzco. **Open** *1.30-4pm, 8.30pm-midnight Mon-Sat.*
Spanish/French
Larger-than-life chef Sacha Hormachea is such a Madrid institution that local foodie types refer to 'sachismo' – the concept of flavour and enjoyment of simple food made with great produce but without the frills and furbelows employed by most of Madrid's top restaurants. His parents set the place up in 1972 and he has remained faithful to their philosophy ever since: signature dishes include crab lasagne with sea urchin, battered hake and sole meunière.

Sudestada €€
C/Ponzano 85, Chamberí (91 533 41 54, www.sudestada.eu). Metro Ríos Rosas or Cuatro Caminos. **Open** *1-4pm, 9pm-midnight Mon-Sat.*
Asian
Run by young Argentines with a passion for Asian food, Sudestada is the Madrid branch of a Buenos Aires favourite. It can get very booked up, and given the authentic spiciness of its curries – from all over south-east Asia – this gives the lie to the idea that Spanish diners prefer their food bland. Less *picante* options include Vietnamese rolls and dim sum from Singapore.

Tapas bars

Bodegas la Ardosa
C/Santa Engracia 70, Chamberí (91 446 58 94). Metro Iglesia. **Open** *11am-3pm, 7-11pm Mon, Tue, Thur-Sun. Closed mid July-mid Aug.* **No cards**.
A tiny bar with a lovely old tiled exterior (marked no.58) and walls lined with bottles. There are especially good *patatas bravas* and fried pigs' ears, as well as sardines and beer. Not to be confused with the Malasaña bar of the same name.

Entertainment

Clamores
C/Alburquerque 14, Chamberí (91 445 79 38, 91 445 54 80, www. salaclamores.com). Metro Bilbao. **Open** *6pm-2am Mon-Thur, Sun; 6pm-6am Fri, Sat.* **Admission** *varies. Jazz club*
This legendary jazz club opened in 1979, and for eight years served as the set for TV show *Jazz Entre Amigos*. It has a hugely varied programme these days, with tango, pop, rock, bossa, samba and folk all on the bill, as well as the jazz that made its name. The live acts sprawl into late-night DJ sessions on Friday and Saturday nights, helped along by the exotic list of cocktails

Galileo Galilei
C/Galileo 100, Chamberí (91 534 75 57, www.salagalileogalilei. com). Metro Islas Filipinas or Quevedo. **Open** *5pm-2am Mon-Wed; 5pm-5.30am Thur-Sun.* **Admission** *varies.* **No cards.** *Live music*
Galileo Galilei presents possibly the widest range of artists in Madrid. There's Latin jazz, flamenco, salsa, singer-songwriters and myriad types of fusion. There are also occasional comedy nights. It's a former cinema, and as such is very spacious, though the mock-Hellenic decor can be a bit over the top.

Moby Dick

Avda del Brasil 5, Tetuán (91 555 76 71, www.mobydickclub.com). Metro Cuzco or Santiago Bernabéu. **Open** *9pm-3am Wed; 9pm-5am Thur; 9pm-5am Fri, Sat.* **Admission** *€5-€20. Live music*

With music on two different levels, Moby Dick caters for a range of tastes. It's mainly a venue for local tribute bands and touring Spanish bands, but it can still pull a few surprises. Start the evening off with a pint of Guinness in its sister bar, the Irish Rover, next door.

La Riviera

Paseo Bajo de la Virgen del Puerto s/n (91 365 24 15, www.salariviera. com). Metro Puerto del Ángel. **Open** *Concerts times vary. Club midnight-6am Fri, Sat.* **Admission** *varies. Live music*

On the banks of the Manzanares river, La Riviera is ranked by many as the city's best medium-sized live-music venue. It's certainly popular, and comes equipped with an excellent sound system. All sorts of acts have passed through in recent times, among them Lana del Rey, Eels and Mogwai.

South of the centre

Sights & museums

Planetario de Madrid

Avenida del Planetario 16, Parque Tierno Galván, Legazpi (91 467 34 61, www.planetmad.es). Metro Arganzuela-Planetario. **Open** *5-7.45pm Tue-Fri; 11am-1.45pm, 5-8pm Sat, Sun.* **Admission** *€3.60; €1.65 2-14s, over-65s.*

The Planetarium has three exhibition spaces, with shows on the solar system (though the narration is only in Spanish and may test your kids' interest in the heavens if they don't speak it) and an observation tower.

Restaurants

Bodegas Rosell €€

C/General Lacy 14 (91 467 84 58, www.bodegasrosell.es). Metro Atocha. **Open** *noon-4pm, 7pm-midnight Tue-Sat; noon-4pm Sun. Spanish*

A great pit-stop if you're coming in or out of Atocha station, or even for the Reina Sofía museum, Bodegas Rosell is a fabulous old tavern that has been around since 1920. It serves *raciones* of shellfish and cheese alongside more substantial dishes such as lamb cutlets or duck magret.

Entertainment

Fabrik

Avda de la Industria 82, Ctra Fuenlabrada–Moralejos de Enmedio (902 930 322, www. grupo-kapital.com/fabrik). Metro Fuenlabrada then bus 496, 497. **Open** *11.30pm-6am Sat; 3pm-3am occasional Sun.* **Admission** *varies. Club*

A converted warehouse kitted out with a dazzling array of disco surprises: there's a huge outdoor terrace complete with a fake river and two covered dance floors; and, in the main area, a vertical and horizontal megatron to shoot freezing bursts of nitrogen gas into the crowd. The nighttime sessions attract a young, up-for-it crowd seeking hard techno or electronica.

💙 Matadero Madrid

*Plaza de Legazpi 8 (91 517 73 09, www. mataderomadrid.org). Metro Legazpi. **Open** Site 9am-10pm Mon-Fri; 11am-10pm Sat, Sun. Cineteca 5-10pm Mon. Exhibitions 4-9pm Tue-Fri; 11am-9pm Sat, Sun. **Admission** free; Cineteca €3.50.*

An innovative and multidisciplinary arts centre, the **Matadero** has become a key socio-cultural symbol for the city.

The vast, ambitious space consists of ten impressive neo-Mudéjar buildings strung along the bank of the Manzanares. These once formed the city's slaughterhouse (*matadero*), and the painted tiles at the entrance to each announce *'deguello de ganado'* (throat cutting of cattle), *'deguello de cerdos'* (throat cutting of pigs), and so on, which can create a slightly melancholy air, though the architecture itself is far too ornate to be gloomy.

Each building is dedicated to a different discipline, with the exception of the offices and the Cantina, a great café-restaurant in the former boilerhouse.

The Nave de la Música contains rehearsal rooms, a recording studio and a performance space, while the Nave del Español is all about theatre, with auditoria and exhibition spaces. The foyer comprises a café with a small stage for theatre groups to showcase work, but the loveliest space is the *plaza*. Mobile platforms carry, variously, speaker stacks or small trees to provide shade for daytime performances.

Other buildings include the Casa del Lector (Reader's House), which has a children's library, literature exhibitions and a Kindle-lending service; the Cineteca, which focuses mainly on documentaries (€3.50); and the Central de Diseño, which holds design-related workshops, conferences and exhibitions. There are reading rooms with newspapers and Wi-Fi, and even a seed bank.

Unusually, the Matadero has been created with Madrid's citizens in mind, rather than its visitors, but there's plenty here to see and be inspired by, all just a short ride south of Atocha station.

BEYOND THE CENTRE

💜 Museo del Ferrocarril de Madrid

Paseo de las Delicias 61, Delicias (91 506 83 33, www. museodelferrocarril.org). Metro Delicias. **Open** *Oct-Mar 9.30am-3pm Mon-Thur; 10am-8pm Fri-Sun (until 6pm every second Fri); June-Sept 10am-3pm daily.* **Admission** *€6 Mon-Thur, €2.50 Fri from 2pm, Sat, Sun; €4-1.50 reductions; free under-4s. No cards.*

Housed in the elegant but disused Delicias station, with ironwork by Gustave Eiffel, Madrid's railway museum has an evocative collection of models, old locomotives, railway equipment and memorabilia. There is also a room dedicated to clocks, including the one that marked time when Spain's first-ever train chugged from Barcelona to Mataró in 1948, and displays of antique stationmasters' caps, old tickets, Bakelite telephones, punching machines and the like.

The real attraction, however, for both kids and adults, are the trains themselves, including the sleek 1954 American electric locomotive, 'Marilyn', named after Monroe. You can climb aboard a steam engine, have a drink in an elegant 1928 restaurant car and watch surprisingly absorbing (even – or especially – for children) film footage of Spanish railways. Another hit with the kids is the section of model railways, including engines puffing actual smoke running through miniature landscapes. Real fans won't want to miss the second-hand market for all things railway-related, which takes place here on the first Sunday of every month.

BEYOND THE CENTRE

Madrid
Essentials

Accommodation

For a compact city, Madrid has an unusually large number of hotels. In fact, so many new properties have opened in the past few years that some locals believe there are too many, in the centre at least. For visitors, of course, this can only be a good thing. Intense competition means higher standards of accommodation and service, even in lower-priced places. In particular, the difference between budget and mid-range hotels is becoming increasingly marginal, with the newer *pensiones* now offering en suite bathrooms in most rooms. And, across all price brackets, staff are friendlier and keener to help than ever before.

Stars, prices and discounts

Star ratings are somewhat arbitrary in Spain, and the difference between four- and five-star hotels can be hard to spot. Moderate hotels have not been the city's strong point, but this is beginning to change thanks to chains such as **Room Mate** and **Petit Palace**.

Due to trade fairs and conferences, prices tend to be highest in January, when some hotels require minimum stays of two to three nights. Conversely, there are great deals to be had in the summer months. Note that the cheapest online rate is often non-refundable.

Where to stay

Although Madrid is pretty small for a capital city, its accommodation is spread over a wide area, so it's good to have an idea of what you want before you book.

Sol and **Gran Vía** are the best areas for mid-range accommodation right in the thick of things and, though undoubtedly touristy, are home to a clutch of decent bars and restaurants, and are great for shopping. Heading north from here, **Malasaña** has a choice of good budget *pensiones*, particularly along C/ Palma, and an increasing number of boutique hotels. Bordering Malasaña to the east, gay-friendly **Chueca** is home to some fine one-off properties. Both areas, especially Malasaña, offer a real neighbourhood vibe.

South of Chueca, lively **Huertas** and **Santa Ana** are great districts for cheap *pensiones* and boutique hotels. On the edge of here, the Paseo del Prado has a variety of budget accommodation right on the doorstep of the big three art museums. Upmarket areas include **Retiro** and **Los Austrias**. Although on opposite sides of town (Retiro, with its famous park, is in the east, while history-imbued Los Austrias is in the west), both

---

In the know
Price categories

We have included a selection of the best hotels in the city in each pricing category. Categories are based on the cost of a double room in spring.

Luxury	over €200
Expensive	€150-€200
Moderate	€100-€150
Budget	up to €100

are home to Madrid's old money, and are peaceful – though bars and restaurants can be expensive.

Just north of the Parque del Retiro, around the chic shopping street C/ Serrano, is **Salamanca**. If you feel at home among the smart, wealthy set, you'll blend in well here. Business travellers should head for **Chamberí**, north of the centre, and, further north still, to **Chamartín**, both of which are convenient for the airport.

Luxury
Gran Meliá Palacio de los Duques
Cuesta de Santo Domingo 5-7, Sol & Gran Vía (91 541 67 00, www.melia.com). Metro Ópera or Santo Domingo. **Map** *p83 G13.*
One of Madrid's most glamorous hotels was built on the site of a convent and 19th-century palace and designed in homage to Velázquez. There are two excellent restaurants – the Montmartre bistro and the upmarket Dos Cielos, which overlooks a pretty garden – and a spa with sauna, but the hotel's crowning glory is the rooftop sundeck, with small pool, jacuzzi and panoramic views.

Hotel Orfila
C/Orfila 6, Chamberí (91 702 77 70, www. hotelorfila.com). Metro Alonso Martínez or Colón.
This small mansion in a tranquil residential area has been transformed into an elegant five-star hotel. Built in the 1880s as a private home for an artistic family, the Orfila also contained a theatre and a literary salon during the 1920s. Thankfully, the hotel has held on to its 19th-century decor, not to mention its façade, carriage entrance and dramatic main stairway. Bedrooms are wonderfully quiet. The elegant restaurant looks on to the lovely garden patio.

Hotel Único
C/Claudio Coello 67, Salamanca (91 781 01 73, www.unicohotelmadrid.com). Metro Serrano. **Map** *p147 P10.*

The Hotel Único achieves the perfect blend of modern and classic. It's housed in a graceful 19th-century Salamanca building with slick black-and-white chequered tiles and upholstered chairs in the public areas, impressive staircases that are perfect for making a grand entrance, and mod cons throughout. The 44 spacious rooms and suites are comfortable and well designed, with huge comfy beds, wooden floors, muted tones and patterns and slick bathrooms. The Michelin-starred restaurant is another plus.

ME Madrid Reina Victoria
Plaza Santa Ana 14, Santa Ana (91 701 60 00, www.melia.com). Metro Antón Martín. **Map** *p95 K15.*
This grand old hotel has had a spectacular revamp and caters to a glamorous set. Rooms are smallish, with unimaginably comfortable beds, lighting systems that require a manual but are great once you figure them out, good-quality Apivita toiletries and complimentary tea and coffee. Get a room overlooking the lovely Plaza Santa Ana if you can. The rooftop restaurant has amazing views of the city, but has recently been enclosed by glass panels thanks to the volume favoured by the DJs who play here nightly.

Only You Boutique Madrid
C/Barquillo 21, Chueca (91 005 22 22, www.onlyyouhotels.com). Metro Chueca. **Map** *p118 M12.*
Spain's best-loved designer, Lázaro Rosa-Violán, was behind the maximalist interiors at the Only You, where you'll find a riot of styles in the eclectic decor. The lifts alone have launched a thousand Instagram shots with their Chinese-tiled façade and faux bookshelves inside. Rooms, too, are luxuriously kitted out with studded navy blue leather headboards, plush carpets and animal-print bathrobes. The restaurants serves excellent food but you may need to book (it's small), particularly for a table out on the terrace.

The Principal Madrid Hotel

C/Marqués de Valdeiglesias 1, Chueca (91 521 87 43, www.theprincipalmadridhotel.com). Metro Banco de España or Sevilla. **Map** *p118 L13.*

The cognoscenti love The Principal for its speakeasy feel (from an almost anonymous street entrance, a lift whisks you up to the top-floor reception), buzzy rooftop cocktail bar and sundeck, and luxurious touches from Gilbert & Soames toiletries to the complimentary pastries available all day in the bar. Ask for a room overlooking the stunning Metropolis building.

Other upmarket places include **Hotel Urban** (www.hotelurban.com), with ancient figurines and artworks in the rooms and in the painfully hip public spaces, and **Hotel Wellington** (www.hotel-wellington.com), a graceful place with chandeliers and marble just a stone's throw from Salamanca, the city's most expensive shopping area.

Expensive
Círculo Gran Vía Hotel

Gran Vía 24 (91 521 03 00, www.marriott.com). Metro Gran Vía. **Map** *p83 K13.*

From the hotel's common areas, it's easy to stray into the frenetic and glitzy world of Madrid's casino, with which the Círculo shares a building, but the calm zen room interiors are a world apart. The feel is Scandinavian, with modern beechwood furniture and sinuously curved wing chairs and headboards. On the corner of Gran Vía and C/Hortaleza, the hotel is right in the heart of things, but the soundproofing is such that a good night's sleep is guaranteed.

Dear Hotel

Gran Vía 80 (91 412 32 00, www.dearhotelmadrid.com). Metro Plaza de España. **Map** *p83 G12.*

The Dear was ahead of the curve when it opened in what was then the unloved area at the end of Gran Vía, which is now undergoing an ambitious facelift, with a raft of new openings. The hotel is chic, minimalist and excellent value, not least for the view from its small rooftop pool and restaurant/breakfast room. This takes in the whole of the city, but most spectacularly the vast Casa de Campo park, which stretches out to the west.

Hotel Casual Madrid del Teatro

C/Echegaray 1, Santa Ana (91 429 95 51, casualhoteles.com). Metro Sevilla. **Map** *p95 K15.*

It's rare to find somewhere this much fun at this price level. Rooms carry a theatrical theme, along with complementary fittings (ruched satin curtains, fringed lampshades) that predate this incarnation of the hotel but fit right in. If you can, get the corner room with terrace and a bathtub. Breakfast and other facilities are sparse, but the Mi-Fi gadget (free to use for guests) is useful for getting online around town.

Hotel Emperador

Gran Vía 53 (91 547 28 00, www.emperadorhotel.com). Metro Santo Domingo. **Map** *p83 G12.*

While the traffic speeds by on the Gran Vía outside, the Emperador has to deal with a flow of student groups and tourists that is almost as unrelenting. Decor is rather dreary, and it's not the most exciting hotel, but it does have as its USP a wonderful rooftop swimming pool (which is also open to non-residents for a hefty €45), four times the size of most hotel pools.

NH Collection Madrid Suecia

C/Marqués de Casa Riera 4, Gran Vía (91 200 05 70, www.nh-hotels.com). Metro Banco de España. **Map** *p83 L14.*

In common with most NH hotels, the Suecia is done up in simple pastel tones, without too many frills, but is smart, comfortable and well thought out. Tea- and coffee-making facilities in the rooms come as standard, and staff are particularly attentive to any requests you might have. The rooftop bar is one of Madrid's loveliest, and in the basement is the seductive speakeasy-style cocktail bar, aptly named Hemingway.

Urso Hotel

C/Mejía Lequerica 8, chueca (91 444 44 58, www.hotelurso.com). Metro Alonso Martinez or Tribunal. **Map** *p118 L10.*

A luxury boutique with smart but understated rooms, the better to showcase the glorious lobby – a cleverly designed space of mirrors and Chinois wallpaper. There is a spa and indoor pool, and downstairs, behind another wall of mirrors, is the wonderful Media Ración restaurant. Breakfast is a sumptuous affair served in a beautifully designed space on the first floor, and the price of a room includes two tickets to the Prado museum.

Other options include the **Hotel Villa Real** (www.hotelvillareal.com), offering elegant rooms, marble bathrooms and Roman mosaics, and **Iberostar Las Letras Gran Vía** (www.hoteldelasletras. com), with literary quotations strewn across its colourful walls.

Moderate
Hotel Abalu

C/Pez 19, Malasaña (91 521 44 92, www.hotelabalu.com). Metro Noviciado. **Map** *p118 H12.*

The Abalu is near the Gran Vía and metro, but its extravagant interior design pulls in as many visitors as its location does. Rooms range from restrained to gloriously over the top; the staff are generally friendly although sometimes hard to pin down.

Hotel Sercotel Gran Conde Duque

Plaza Conde del Valle Suchil 5, Chamberí (91 447 70 00, www. sercotelhoteles.com). Metro San Bernardo.

A quiet, out-of-the-way hotel with front rooms facing a pretty, leafy *plaza*. Rooms are tastefully kitted out with yellow and green upholstery, while the belle époque salon downstairs serves afternoon tea. Beds are king-size and one room, 315, has a waterbed. Previous guests have included Celia Cruz and Marcel Marceau, and Pedro Almodóvar has been spotted in the bar. Guests can use the gym on the other side of the square.

Palacio de Tepa

C/San Sebastian 2, Santa Ana (91 389 64 90, www.nh-collection.com). Metro Sol. **Map** *p95 K15.*

The NH group prides itself on comfort and customer service, and the five-star Palacio de Tepa is no exception. A sombre palette of creams and browns guides the modern decor, and won't frighten the horses, but it's the little touches that make the place, such as the ground-floor sitting room with complimentary tea, coffee, mineral water and newspapers. Original features of the 1808 building, with a façade by Juan de Villanueva, have been respected, and superior rooms are under the eaves, with wooden ceilings. Like the suites, these have Nespresso machines.

Petit Palace Ópera

C/Arenal 16, Los Austrias (91 564 43 55, www.petitpalaceopera.com). Metro Sol. **Map** *p69 H14.*

Fans of chintz should steer well clear, but the good-value Petit Palace chain of hotels is perfect for techno fiends on a budget. The Ópera's compact but sleekly designed rooms come with iPads and Mi-Fi devices free for guests to borrow, with Mi-Fi giving you online access around town. Bikes are also offered and the hotel is particularly family-friendly, with gifts for the little ones.

Posada del León de Oro

C/Cava Baja 12, La Latina (91 119 14 94, www.posadadelleondeoro.com). Metro La Latina or Tirso de Molino. **Map** *p69 G16.*

A converted 19th-century coaching inn, the León de Oro has a somewhat stark approach to modern design, but is comfortable and friendly, with decent-sized beds and underfloor heating. Its 17 rooms sit around a central atrium, their minimal lines softened by wooden beams and bold splashes of colour.

Room Mate Oscar

Plaza Pedro Zerolo 12, Chueca (91 701 11 73, room-matehotels.com). Metro Chueca or Gran Vía. **Map** *p118 K13.*

Room Mate Oscar oozes affordable chic, from the ergonomic white plastic chairs to the smart bathrooms. The staff are as welcoming and easy on the eye as the spacious rooms, and the location in one of Chueca's main squares is unbeatable. The huge roof terrace – which comes complete with a bar and swimming pool – is a big plus, and a prime hangout on the city's gay scene.

Other mid-range hotels include **Room Mate Alicia** (room-matehotels. com), another hit from this classy but reasonably priced chain (*see above*) and **The Hat** (thehatmadrid.com), which is right in the heart of things in Los Austrias and has a rooftop bar.

Budget

Hostal Benamar

C/San Mateo 20, 2ª, Chueca (91 308 00 92, www.hostalbenamar.es). Metro Alonso Martínez or Tribunal. **Map** *p118 K11.*
Well situated between Chueca and Alonso Martínez, this *hostal* can be divided into two different parts. The friendly owners promote the renovated section, which has marble floors, modern en suite bathrooms and computers in every room. The other section is older but clean, with shared bathrooms.

Hostal Gala

C/Costanilla de los Ángeles 15, Sol (91 541 96 92, www.hostalgala.com). Metro Santo Domingo. **Map** *p83 G13.*
This well-located boutique *hostal* on a quiet but central street is run by a very friendly couple. Rooms are comfortable and tasteful, with wooden floors, air-conditioning, retro-modern wallpaper and spacious bathrooms with power showers. Some rooms have balconies, while the superior double has a lounge area.

Hostal Oriente

C/Arenal 23, Sol (91 548 03 14, www.hostaloriente.es). Metro Ópera. **Map** *p83 G14.*

Right on the doorstep of the opera house, and just a short walk from Sol, the comfortable Oriente is in an excellent location. The rooms are stylish – particularly for this price range – and pristine, and have compact bathrooms and TVs. The friendly staff are a further draw.

Hostal Riesco

C/Correo 2, 3ª, Sol (91 522 26 92, www. hostal-riesco.com). Metro Sol. **No cards**. **Map** *p83 J15.*
The Riesco is a *hostal* that feels more like a hotel, with its balconied façade, stucco ceilings and chintzy curtains. All rooms come with en suite bathrooms, and the location is hard to beat – it's rare to find such good-value accommodation so close to Sol and the Plaza Mayor.

Hostal Sil & Serranos

C/Fuencarral 95, Malasaña (91 448 89 72, www.silserranos. com). Metro Bilbao. **Map** *p118 J10.*
Clean and smartly decorated, these *hostales* are well located for night-time revelling – indeed, rooms looking out on to C/Fuencarral will bear witness to the *madrileño* enthusiasm for partying. Although interior rooms are a little darker, the noise is minimal and the price slightly lower. All rooms have air-conditioning, small bathrooms and digital TV, and the properties are run by a fun couple.

Lapepa Chic B&B

Plaza de las Cortes 4, 7ª, Huertas (mobile 648 474 742, lapepa-bnb.com). Metro Banco de España. **Map** *p95 M15.*
A cheerful B&B with an unbeatable location between the major art museums and the bars of Santa Ana. All 14 rooms are pristine, en suite, and decorated in red and white. Breakfast is included and available until noon.

Other affordable options include **Hostal Triana** (www.hostaltriana. com), a traditional, good-value *hostal* with sparklingly clean rooms, and **Hostal Atocha Almudena Martín** (hostalatocha.es), a very friendly *hostal* offering air-conditioned rooms with en suite bathrooms and decent showers.

Getting Around

ARRIVING & LEAVING

By air
Barajas Airport
91 321 10 00, 902 404 704.
Madrid's airport is 14km (9 miles) north-east of the city on the A2 motorway. All airlines that are members of the Oneworld network (including BA, Iberia and American Airlines) share terminal T4, a further 6km (4 miles) away, for national and international flights. All other traffic is distributed between the 3 older terminals. All terminals are linked by shuttle buses.

There are 24hr exchange facilities in T1: those in T3 and T4 are open 6.30am-10.30pm. All terminals have ATM machines, and there are tourist offices in T1, T2 and T4.

Airport buses
The city council's **express airport bus** (no.203) runs a 24/7 service (every 16-18mins in the day and 35mins at night). The easily identifiable yellow buses – which run between T1, T2, T4 and, in town, O'Donnell, Cibeles and Atocha – take around 40mins and the journey costs €5. Note that Cibeles is the first/last stop between 11.30pm and 6am. Timetables are available at www. emtmadrid.es.

Aerocity (902 151 654, www.aerocity. com) provides shuttle services between the airport and city hotels. Handy for small groups and cheaper than taking several taxis. Prices vary (€20-€40) depending on group size.

Local buses (91 406 88 10, www. emtmadrid.es) 200 and 204 run between the public transport hub on the Avda de América and T1, T2 and T4. A single ticket costs €1.50.

Metro
The metro is another cheap way to get to central Madrid, though there is a €3

supplement for journeys to the airport, so a regular journey will cost between €4.50 and €5. Bear in mind that the Aeropuerto metro station is between T2 and T3, a 10-15min walk from T1. From T4, take the shuttle to T2 (allow 20mins in total). From the airport it's 4 stops on metro line 8 (pink) and 12mins to Nuevos Ministerios. From here it's around 15mins to the centre of Madrid. You can save money by buying a Metrobús ticket at the airport station.

Taxis
Taxi fares to central Madrid are set at €30, or €20 if the distance is less than 10km (6 miles) from the airport, including a €5.50 airport supplement (no luggage supplement). There are lots of taxis at Barajas, but ignore drivers who approach you inside the building; use ones at the ranks outside the terminal. For more on taxis, *see p173*.

Train
The RENFE *cercanías* line from the airport will take you from T4 to Atocha in 25mins (€2.60).

By bus
Almost all international and long-distance coach services to Madrid terminate at the Estación Sur de Autobuses, C/Méndez Álvaro (info 91 468 42 00, 5.30am-1am, www. estacionautobusesmadrid.com). It's next to metro (line 6) and *cercanía* (local train lines C5, C7 and C10) stations, both also called Méndez Álvaro. Bus 148 also runs from there to the centre (Plaza del Callao and Plaza de España). Taxi fares from the bus station carry a €3 supplement.

By train
The Spanish state railway company RENFE has 2 main stations in Madrid.

Trains from France, Catalonia and northern Spain arrive at **Chamartín**, on the north side of the city, some distance from the centre. High-speed AVE trains from Andalucía, Barcelona and Valencia, express services from Lisbon and trains from southern and eastern Spain arrive at **Atocha**, at the southern end of the Paseo del Prado. There are exchange facilities at both stations, and a tourist office at Chamartín. Both have easy metro links to the rest of the city. Atocha is also the main hub of RENFE's local rail lines (*cercanías, see p173*).

A taxi fare to the centre from Chamartín should be around €14, including a €3 station supplement.
RENFE *912 32 03 20, www.renfe.com.* **Open** *24hrs daily.*

Estación de Atocha *Glorieta del Emperador Carlos V. Metro Atocha Renfe.* **Map** *pull-out N18.*

Estación de Chamartín *C/Agustín de Foxá, Chamartín. Metro Chamartín.*

PUBLIC TRANSPORT

Most of Madrid's attractions are within walking distance of one another, with Puerta del Sol at the centre. Public transport is cheap and efficient, however – both bus and metro will get you where you want to go within 30mins, although it's best to avoid the buses during rush hour. Note: transport fares are subject to revision in Jan.

For transport for disabled travellers, *see p177.*

Fares & tickets

Madrid's fare structure is based on a €1.50 minimum, valid for up to 5 stops, and then 10¢ for each stop thereafter up to a maximum of €2 (excluding Barajas Airport, which carries a €3 supplement) within the capital, no matter how long the journey. On the metro you can change any number of times as long as you don't leave a station. The exceptions are trips to the stations Rivas Urbanizaciones, Rivas Vaciamadrid, La Poveda and Arganda del Rey (all Line 9), and all stations beyond Puerta del Sur on the Metro Sur line, which circles the southern suburbs.

However, it's easier and more economical to buy a ticket for 10 journeys (*billete de diez/Metrobús*), which can be used on the bus and metro, available at all metro stations and some *estancos* and *kioskos*, but not on the bus. You can share the ticket between 2 or more people and keep it for as long as you like (or until the prices go up). The current price of a Metrobús is €12.20. Season tickets are also available.

On the metro, you simply insert the ticket into the machine at the gate that leads through to the platform, which cancels one unit for each trip – remember to collect it afterwards – and will reject expired tickets. There is no checking or collection of tickets at station exits. On buses, the Metrobús should be inserted arrow downwards into the blue and yellow machine just behind the driver.

Metro

The metro is the quickest and simplest means of travelling to most parts of the city, and open 6am-2am daily. Tickets are available at all stations from coin-operated machines and staffed ticket booths. Trains run every 3-6mins on weekdays, and every 10-15mins after 11pm and on Sun. The metro can get packed in rush hours (7.30-9.30am, 1-2.30pm, 7.30-9pm).

Metro information *Sol metro station, Sol & Gran Vía (91 779 63 99, www. metromadrid.es).* **Open** *7am-10pm Mon-Fri; 10am-10pm Sat-Sun.* This customer service point provides information and sells transport tickets, tourist passes and season tickets.

Buses

Run by **Empresa Municipal de Transportes (EMT)**. *See p172* for information about fares and tickets.

Most run about 6am-11.30pm daily, with buses every 10-15mins (more often on more popular routes). Night buses then take over. You board buses at the front, and get off via the middle or rear doors. Officially, there is a limit to how much luggage you can take on city buses, and trying to board with luggage during rush hours is almost impossible. Drivers are not obliged to give you the change for anything larger than a €20 note, nor will they allow you to travel for free. But they must write down your contact details for the bus company to send you the change later on.

Night buses

Between midnight and around 5am there are 27 night routes in operation – N1 to N27 (N27 goes out to the airport) – called Búho (Owl) buses. All begin from Plaza de Cibeles and run out to the suburbs, and are numbered in a clockwise sequence. Although the metro closes at nights, at the weekends special buses, called Metro Búho, cover the routes of the 11 central metro lines (L1-L11). The buses alight at the bus stop nearest to each metro station. The timetable for each line varies, but generally the buses run from 12.45am until 5.45am. L1-L11 buses run every 15-20mins. There are 3 buses that cover the L12 Metrosur route every 30mins, from 1.15am to 5.30am.

EMT Information *C/Cerro de la Plata 4, Retiro (91 406 88 10, www. emtmadrid.es). Metro Pacífico.* **Open** *8am-2pm Mon-Fri; telephone information line open 7am–9pm daily.*

Cercanías/local trains

The highly efficient *cercanías* or local network of railways for the Madrid area consists of 10 lines converging on Atocha, several of which connect with metro lines along their routes.

As well as the suburbs, *cercanías* trains are useful for trips to Guadarrama and towns near Madrid such as Aranjuez or El Escorial. Also, line C-7 effectively forms a circle line within Madrid that

is quicker than the metro for some journeys, and the RENFE line between Chamartín and Atocha is the fastest link between the 2 main stations. *Cercanías* lines run from 5-6am to 11pm-midnight daily, with trains on most lines about every 10-30mins. Fares vary with distance, but the lines are included in the monthly season ticket.

TAXIS

Madrid taxis are white, with a diagonal red stripe on the front doors. The city has more than 15,000 taxis, so they are rarely hard to find, except late at night at the weekend or on days when it's raining heavily. When a taxi is free there is a *'Libre'* (free) sign behind the windscreen, and a green light on the roof. If there is also a sign with the name of a district in red, it means the driver is on the way home, and is not obliged to take you anywhere that isn't near that particular route. There are taxi ranks, marked by a blue sign with a white T, throughout the centre of Madrid. To avoid being swindled by a non-official taxi, make sure the driver has their licence number visible on the front and a meter, and always ask for the approximate fare before getting in.

Fares

Official fare rates and supplements are shown inside each cab (in English and Spanish), on the right-hand sun visor and/or the rear windows. The minimum fare is €2.40-€2.90 (depending on the day/time), which is what the meter should show when you first set off. The higher rate applies at night (9pm-7am) and on Sun and public holidays, and there are extra supplements for trips starting from the bus and train stations (€3) and to and from the trade fair complex (€3). There are set fares between Madrid and the airport: €20 if travelling within 10km of the airport, or €30 between the airport and the city centre. Also, the fare rate is higher for journeys to suburban towns in the outer tariff zone (zone B). Drivers are not officially required to carry more than

€20 in change, and some accept credit cards.

Phone cabs

You can call for a cab from any of the companies listed below. Operators will rarely speak much English, so if you aren't at a specific address give the name of the street and a restaurant or bar that makes a suitable place to wait, or position yourself near a street corner and say, for example, 'San Agustín, *esquina* Prado' (San Agustín, corner of Prado). The operator will also ask you your name. Phone cabs start the meter from the point when a call is answered. Some cabs will take credit cards.

Radio-Taxi Asociación Gremial *91 447 32 32, www.radiotaxigremial.com.*
Radio-Taxi Independiente *91 405 12 13, www.radiotaxindependiente.com.*
Radioteléfono Taxi *91 547 82 00, www.radiotelefono-taxi.com.*
Teletaxi *91 371 21 31.*

CYCLING

Cycling in Madrid used to be a terrifying prospect, but things have changed considerably over the last few years. The city-run **BiciMad** (www.bicimad.com) bike-sharing scheme was introduced in 2014, and the number of bike lanes has steadily expanded since then. Cycling is still a challenge – many streets are steep, and local drivers are still learning to share the roads with cyclists – but the city is now relatively bike-friendly. Bikes are a great idea for trips to the larger city parks (Retiro, Casa de Campo) and especially the Madrid Sierras. Bikes can be taken free of charge on some *cercanías* lines and on the metro at weekends. Cycle hire shops often ask that you leave proof of identity as well as a cash deposit. There is an increasing number of companies and associations in Madrid that are dedicated to cycling, including **Pedalibre** (www.pedalibre.org) and **Ciclos Otero** (www.oterociclos.es).

DRIVING

Thanks to traffic jams, driving in the city is rarely a quick way of getting anywhere, and finding a parking space is another headache.

Signs & terms

cede el paso – give way
usted no tiene la prioridad – you don't have the right of way
único sentido – one way
cambio de sentido – indicates a junction that allows you to change direction
recuerde – remember
cinturón de seguridad – seat belt
ronda de circunnavegación – ring road.

Car & motorbike hire

Car hire can be pricey, so shop around; there are often good weekend deals. Most companies have a minimum age limit (usually 21, sometimes 25) and require you to have had a licence for over a year. You will also need a credit card (as opposed to a debit card), or leave a big cash deposit (sometimes up to €500). Check if IVA (VAT) and unlimited mileage are included. All the companies listed require you to take out a *franquicia* (excess).

Avis *Estación de Chamartín, C/Agustín de Foxa 25, Chamartín (902 090 343, www.avis.es). Metro Plaza de Castilla. Open 8am-9pm Mon-Fri; 8am-2pm Sat, Sun.*
BlaferMotos *C/Clara del Rey 17, Chamartín (91 413 00 47, www.blafermotos.com). Metro Alfonso XIII. Open 8.30am-6.30pm Mon-Fri; 10am-1.30pm Sat.*
Motorcycle specialists.
Easycar *Barajas Airport (www.easycar.com).*
Enterprise *Plaza de España car park (1st floor) (91 542 50 15, www.enterprise.es). Metro Plaza de España. Open 8.30am-7.30pm Mon-Fri; 9am-1pm Sat.*
Europcar *Paseo de la Castellana 193 (91 555 99 30, www.europcar.com). Metro Plaza de Castilla. Open 8am-7pm Mon-Fri; 9am-2pm Sat.*
PlanCar *C/Mauricio Legendre 3, Chamartín (91 530 92 69, www.*

plancar.com). Metro Chamartín.
Open *9am-2pm, 4.30-8pm Mon-Fri; 9am-2pm Sat.*

▶ *See the Avis, Enterprise and Europcar websites for other locations throughout the city.*

Breakdown services

If you are planning to take a car to Spain it's advisable to join a motoring organisation such as the AA or RAC, which have reciprocal arrangements with their Spanish equivalent, RACE.

RACE (Real Automóvil Club de España) *Assistance 900 112 222, info 900 100 992, www.race.es.*

The RACE has English-speaking staff and will send immediate 24hr breakdown assistance. Repairs are carried out on the spot when possible; if not, your vehicle will be towed to the nearest suitable garage. Members of affiliated organisations abroad are not charged for call-outs, but non-members pay around €115 (on-the-spot membership) for the basic breakdown service.

Legal requirements

For driving laws and regulations (in Spanish) see the Ministry of Interior's website (www.dgt.es).

Parking

For car-owning *madrileños* parking is a daily trauma. The city police (Policía Municipal) give out tickets readily (many locals never pay them). Be careful not to park in front of doorways with the sign '*vado permanente*', indicating an entry with 24hr right of access. The SER (Servicio de Estacionamiento Regulado) system applies (*see below*) to the whole city centre. Residents park for free if they have an annual sticker.

SER Non-residents must pay to park in zones painted in blue or green from 9am to 9pm Mon-Fri and 9am to 3pm Sat (9am-3pm Mon-Sat in Aug). These hours will be extended until midnight

from 2018. Pay-and-display machines are located on pavements. Maximum validity of tickets is 2hrs in blue zones and 1hr in green, after which a new card must be used, and the car parked in a new spot. Cars parked in the SER zone without a card can be towed away (*see right*). In the blue areas, tickets cost €2.75 for 2hrs, €8.20 for 4hrs (maximum stay of 4hrs) and in the green areas, €2.35 for 1hr, €4.70 for 2hrs (maximum stay of 2hrs). All streets in this zone that have no additional restrictions posted are SER parking areas.

Central car parks *Plaza de las Cortes, Plaza Santa Ana, C/Sevilla, Plaza Jacinto Benavente, Plaza Mayor, Plaza Descalzas, C/Tudescos, Plaza de España.* **Open** *24hrs daily.* **Rates** *€1.25 for 30mins; €3.45 for 90mins, €8.90 for 3hrs; €31.25 for 12 to 24hrs (the maximum).*

There are some 50 municipal car parks around Madrid, indicated by a white 'P'-on-blue sign. It's especially advisable to use a car park if your car has foreign plates. Car parks have disabled access. See also www.madridmovilidad.es for more details.

Towed vehicles *Information 91 406 88 10 (operator 7am-9pm Mon-Fri; other times, automated service), www.emtmadrid.es/EMTGruas.*

Main pounds *Plaza Colón. Metro Colón.* **Map** *pull-out map N11. C/ Velázquez 87. Metro Nuñez de Balboa.* **Map** *pull-out map Q8.* **Open** *24hrs daily.*

If your car seems to have been towed away, call the central number and quote your number plate to be told which pound it has gone to, or go to the website and input your licence plate number. It will cost €147.55 to recover your car. You'll have to pay €1.85 per hr for the first 10hrs, timed from the moment it was towed away. For each complete extra day in the pound it's €19.20. You can also locate your car by entering your registration plate number on the website. Bring your ID and all car papers when you pick it up.

Resources A-Z

ACCIDENT & EMERGENCY

Emergency numbers
Emergency services *112.*
Police, fire or ambulance.

A&E departments

In a medical emergency go to the casualty department (*urgencias*) of any of the city's major hospitals. All are open 24hrs daily; Clínico or Gregorio Marañón are most central. If you are an EU citizen with no EHIC (*see p178*) or insurance, you can still be seen at any casualty department (pay on the spot and get reimbursed back home by presenting the invoices and medical reports). In a non-emergency, pharmacists are very well informed. Call 112 for an ambulance.

Hospital Clínico San Carlos *C/Profesor Martín Lagos, Moncloa (91 330 30 00). Metro Moncloa.*
Hospital General Gregorio Marañón *C/ Doctor Esquerdo 44-46, Salamanca (91 586 80 00, www.hggm.es). Metro O'Donnell.*
Hospital Universitario La Paz *Paseo de la Castellana 261, Chamartín (91 727 70 00, www.madrid.org/hospitallapaz). Metro Begoña.*

AGE RESTRICTIONS

Buying/drinking alcohol 18
Driving 18
Smoking 18
Sex 16

CLIMATE

Winter in Madrid can be very cold, although there's often bright, crisp sunshine and most rain falls in autumn and spring. Spring is unpredictable – February can often be freakishly warm, while in April, rain is likely. Summer temperatures range from hot to unbearably hot. Traditionally there's a mass exodus in August. Autumn weather is usually bright and warm and it's often possible to eat and drink outside well into October.

CUSTOMS

Customs declarations are not usually necessary if you arrive from another EU country and are carrying legal goods for personal use. Guidelines for quantities accepted as being for personal use include:

Travel Advice

For up-to-date information on travel to a specific country – including the latest on safety and security, health issues, local laws and customs – contact your home country government's department of foreign affairs. Most have websites with useful advice for would-be travellers

Australia
www.smartraveller.gov.au

Canada
www.voyage.gc.ca

New Zealand
www.safetravel.govt.nz

Republic of Ireland
www.dfa.ie

UK
www.fco.gov.uk/travel

USA
www.state.gov/travel

• up to 800 cigarettes, 400 small cigars, 200 cigars or 1kg of loose tobacco
• 10 litres of spirits (more than 22% alcohol), 20 litres of fortified wine or alcoholic drinks with less than 22% of alcohol, 90 litres of wine (less than 22%) or 110 litres of beer.

Coming from a non-EU country or the Canary Islands, you can bring:

• 200 cigarettes or 100 small cigars or 50 regular cigars or 250g (8.82oz) of tobacco
• 1 litre of spirits (more than 22% alcohol), 2 litres of any other alcoholic drink with less than 22% alcohol, 4 litres of wine or 16 litres of beer
• personal goods with to a value of €430.

DISABLED

Madrid is still not a city that disabled people, especially wheelchair users, will find it very easy to get around. However, the situation is steadily improving as new buildings are constructed with accessibility in mind and old ones are gradually adapted: technically all public buildings should have been made accessible by law, although in practice a great deal still remains to be done. Access to public transport is improving: all buses are wheelchair accessible, along with all the interchange ('*intercambiador*') stations. The Madrid metro website (www.metromadrid.es) lists all the accessible stations.

Information is available from disabled association FAMMA at C/Galileo 69 (91 593 35 50, www.famma.org), and can also be accessed via the city council website (www.esmadrid.com; click on 'Plan your trip' then 'Accessibility').

Transport

Buses There are seats reserved for people with mobility problems behind the driver on most of the city's buses. All buses are

Local Weather

Average temperatures and monthly rainfall in Madrid

	High (°C/°F)	Low (°C/°F)	Rainfall (mm/in)
January	9 / 48	2 / 36	39 / 1.5
February	11 / 52	2 / 36	34/ 1.3
March	15 / 59	5 / 41	43 / 1.7
April	18 / 64	7 / 45	48 / 1.9
May	21 / 70	10 / 50	47 / 1.8
June	27 / 81	15 / 59	27 / 1.0
July	31 / 88	17 / 63	11 / 0.4
August	30 / 86	17 / 63	15 / 0.6
September	25 / 77	14 / 57	32 / 1.2
October	19 / 66	10 / 50	53 / 2.0
November	13 / 55	5 / 41	47 / 1.8
December	9 / 48	2 / 36	48 / 1.9

now the *piso bajo* (low floor) type, with low doors and spaces for wheelchairs.

Metro The metro map in this guide (*see* p190) and the free maps available at metro stations indicate stations with lifts, or you can check the Madrid Metro website (www.madridmetro.es).

RENFE & cercanías All mainline stations have good access. *Cercanías* trains have limited access but some newer stations, including all the city's interchanges (such as Puerta del Sol, Méndez Alvaro, Moncloa and Plaza Castilla), have lifts connecting metro, train and bus stations.

Taxis Special taxis adapted for wheelchairs can be called through **Eurotaxi** (91 547 82 00) and **Teletaxi** (91 371 21 31, www.tele-taxi.es). Make it clear you want an adapted model (ask for a Eurotaxi). Fares are the same as for standard cabs, but the meter is started as soon as a request is received, so the cost can be quite high.

Wheelchair-friendly museums & galleries

Most of the city's museums and cultural centres are now wheelchair-friendly – see www.esmadrid.com (click on 'Plan your trip' then 'Accessibility') for the full list.

DRUGS

Many people smoke cannabis fairly openly in Spain, but possession or consumption in public is illegal. In private the law is contradictory: smoking is OK but you can be nabbed for possession or distribution. Enforcement is often not the highest of police priorities, but you could theoretically receive a fine and, in extreme cases, get sent to prison. Smoking in bars is also prohibited. Cocaine is common in Spain as well but if you're caught in possession of this or any other Class A drug, you are looking at a hefty fine, and possibly a long prison sentence.

ELECTRICITY

The standard current in Spain is 220V. Plugs are all of the two-round-pin type. The 220V current works fine with British 240V products, with a plug adaptor. With US 110V appliances you will need a current transformer as well as an adaptor.

EMBASSIES & CONSULATES

American Embassy *C/Serrano 75, Salamanca (91 587 22 00, es.usembassy. gov). Metro Rubén Darío.*

Australian Embassy *24th floor, Torre Espacio, Paseo de la Castellana 259D, Northern suburbs (91 353 66 00/visas +44 (0)207 420 3690, www.spain. embassy.gov.au).*

British Embassy *Torre Espacio, Paseo de la Castellana 259D, Northern suburbs (91 714 63 00, www.gov.uk).*

British Consulate *Torre Espacio, Paseo de la Castellana 259D, Northern suburbs (91 714 63 00).*

Canadian Embassy *Torre Espacio, Paseo de la Castellana 259D, Northern suburbs (91 382 84 00, www. canadainternational.gc.ca/spain-espagne).* Emergency number for citizens (reverse charge calls accepted) is 00 613 996 8885.

Irish Embassy *Paseo de la Castellana 46 4º, Salamanca (91 436 40 93/visas 91 431 97 84, www.irlanda.es).*

New Zealand Embassy *C/Pinar 7 3º, Chamberí (91 523 02 26, www. nzembassy.com/spain).*

HEALTH

EU nationals are entitled to free basic medical attention if they have the European Health Insurance Card (EHIC). If you don't have one but can get one sent or faxed within a few days, you will be exempt from charges. Citizens of certain other countries that have a special agreement with Spain, among them several Latin American states, can also have access to free care.

Madrid's tap water is good and safe to drink. There are occasional water shortages in summer, and signs posted in hotels urge guests to avoid wasting water. If you want tap rather than bottled water in a restaurant specify that you want *agua del grifo*.

ID

Foreigners are meant to carry an ID card or a passport with them at all times, and are in theory subject to a fine for not doing so – in practice, you're more likely to get a warning. If you don't want to carry it around with you, it's a good idea to carry a photocopy or a driver's licence instead; it's usually acceptable.

LEFT LUGGAGE

Barajas airport *Terminals T1 & T4 (information 91 746 60 65)*. **Open** *24hrs daily*. **Rates** *€10 for 2-24hrs.*
RENFE train stations **Open** *Chamartín 7am-11pm daily. Atocha 5.30am-10.20pm daily.* **Rates** *from €3.10-€5.20 depending on locker size.*

LGBT

COGAM *C/Puebla 9, Malasaña & Conde Duque (91 523 00 70, www.cogam.es). Metro Gran Vía.* **Open** *5-9pm Mon-Fri; 6-9pm Sat.* **Map** *p118 J12.*
The largest gay and lesbian organisation in Madrid, with an on-site café.
Fundación Triángulo *C/Melendez Valdés 52 1ºD, Chamberí (91 593 05 40, www.fundaciontriangulo.es). Metro Argüelles.* **Open** *10am-2pm, 4-8pm Mon-Fri. Closed Aug.* **Map** *pull-out E8.*
A gay cultural organisation that campaigns on equality issues. It also runs a helpline (91 593 05 40, same times as above) and offers legal help, health advice and AIDS prevention programmes.

LOST PROPERTY

Oficina de Objetos Perdidos (Madrid City Council) *Paseo del Molino 7, south of the centre (91 527 95 90, www.madrid.es). Metro Legazpi.* **Open** *8.30am-2pm Mon-Fri.*
This office mainly receives articles found on the metro, buses, trains, at the airport or in taxis, but if you're lucky, something lost in the street may turn up here.

MONEY

Spain's currency is the euro. Each euro is made up of 100 *céntimos*. One thing to remember is that the British/US practice on decimal points and commas is reversed (so 1.000 euros means one thousand euros, while 1,00 euro is one euro). There are banknotes for €5, €10, €20, €50, €100, €200 and €500.

Banks & currency exchanges
Obtaining money through ATMs with a debit or credit card is the easiest option, despite the fees often charged.

Bank hours Banks and savings banks normally open 8am-2pm Mon-Fri. From Oct to May many branches also open 9am-1pm on Sat. Hours vary a little between different banks, and some have branches that stay open until around 5pm a day a week (usually Thur). Savings banks often open late on Thur afternoons, but are less likely to open on Sat. Banks are closed on public holidays.

Out-of-hours banking Outside normal hours you can change money at the airport (terminals T1, T2 and T4, open 24hrs daily), at main train stations (Atocha, 7.30am-10pm daily), in El Corte Inglés, in hotels and at private *cambios*.

Credit & debit cards
Major credit and charge cards are accepted in most hotels, shops, restaurants and other places (metro ticket machines and pay-and-display parking machines, for instance). American Express cards are less

frequently accepted than MasterCard and Visa. You can withdraw cash with major cards from ATMs and banks will also advance cash against a credit card.

Lost/stolen cards

All lines have English-speaking staff and are open 24hrs daily. Maestro does not have a Spanish helpline.

American Express *freephone 902 375 637.*

Diners Club *902 401 112.*

Mastercard *freephone 900 971 231.*

Visa *900 991 124.*

Tax

The standard rate for sales tax (IVA) is 21%; this drops to 10% in hotels and restaurants, and 4% on some books. IVA may or may not be included in listed prices – if it's not, the expression *'IVA no incluido'* (sales tax not included) should appear after the price. Beware of this when getting quotes on more expensive items. In shops displaying a 'Tax-Free Shopping' sticker, non-EU residents can reclaim tax on large purchases.

OPENING HOURS

Eating, drinking and shopping all happen late in Madrid. The siesta has faded to a myth, but most shops open from 10am-2pm, and 5-5.30pm to 8-8.30pm Mon-Sat, and many stay closed on Sat afternoons. Food markets open earlier, around 8am. In July and, especially, in Aug most shops and services (such as the post office and government offices) close in the afternoon. Aug is also the time when most shops, bars and restaurants close for their annual holidays (from 2wks up to the whole month). Major stores and malls are open from 10am-9pm Mon-Sat without a break.

Most restaurants are open 1.30-2pm to 4pm, and 9pm-midnight, and many close on Sun nights and Mon, and for at least part of Aug. Many businesses finish at 3pm in the summer. Most museums close on Mon.

PHARMACIES

Pharmacies (*farmacias*) are signalled by large, green, usually flashing crosses. Those within the official system of the College of Pharmacies are normally open 9.30am-2pm, 5-8pm Mon-Sat. At other times a duty rota operates. Every pharmacy has a list of the College's *farmacias de guardia* (duty pharmacies) for that day posted outside the door, with the nearest ones highlighted (many now show them using a computerised, push-button panel). Duty pharmacies are also listed in local newspapers, and information is available on the 010 phoneline (*see p183*) and at www. cofm.es. At night, duty pharmacies may look closed; knock on the shutters to be served.

There are many pharmacies open 24hrs daily in Madrid.

POLICE

Spain has several police forces. In Madrid the most important are the local **Policía Municipal**, in navy and pale blue, and the **Policía Nacional**, in darker blue and white uniforms (or all-blue combat gear). Each force has its own responsibilities, although they overlap. Municipales are principally concerned with traffic and parking problems and local regulations. The force with primary responsibility for dealing with crime are the Nacionales. The **Guardia Civil**, in green, are responsible, among other things, for policing inter-city highways, and customs.

Reporting a crime

If you are robbed or attacked, report the incident as soon as possible at the nearest Policía Nacional station (*comisaría*) or dial 902 102 112 (9am-9pm daily). You can make statements over the phone if the crime doesn't involve violence or if the perpetrator hasn't been identified. You'll still have to go to the *comisaría* within 72hrs to sign the statement, but you'll be able to skip some queues.

In the centre near Plaza de España, the 24hr **SATE de Madrid** (C/Leganitos 19, Sol & Gran Vía, information 060, station 91 548 85 37) is the main station for foreigners in Madrid. Other police stations in the city centre include **Chamberí** (C/Rafael Calvo 33), **Huertas/ Retiro** (C/Huertas 76-78) and **Salamanca** (C/Príncipe de Asturias 8). All are open 24hrs daily. You will be asked to make an official statement (*denuncia*). It is extremely unlikely that anything you have lost will ever be recovered, but you will need the *denuncia* in order to make an insurance claim. Very few police officers speak any English.

POSTAL SERVICES

If you just need normal-rate stamps (*sellos*), it's easier to buy them in an *estanco* (*see right*). Post offices now have automatic stamp dispensing machines (with a weighing system) but they do not always work.

Letters and postcards up to 20g cost 55¢ within Spain, 1.35¢ to the rest of Europe, and 1.45¢ to the rest of the world; prices normally rise on 1 Jan. Note that you will pay more for 'irregular' shaped envelopes (basically, not rectangular). Cards and letters to other European countries usually arrive in three to four days, those to North America in about a week. Normal post boxes are yellow with two horizontal red stripes. There are also a few special red post boxes for urgent mail, with hourly collections. For more information on postal services, call 902 197 197 or see www.correos.es.

Oficina Principal de Correos en Madrid *Paseo del Prado 1, Retiro (91 523 06 94, www.correos.es). Metro Banco de España. **Open** 8.30am-9.30pm Mon-Fri; 8.30am-2pm Sat. **Map** p135 N14.*
The central post office offers all manner of postal services. For express post, say you want to send a '*carta urgente*'.
Other locations El Corte Inglés, C/ Preciados 1-4, Sol & Gran Vía; Carrera de San Francisco 13, La Latina; C/Mejía Lequerica 7, Chueca; C/Jorge Juan 20, Salamanca; Terminal 1 in the airport.

Estancos

The main role of the tobacco shop or *estanco* (look for a brown and yellow sign with the word '*tabacos*') is, of course, to supply tobacco-related products. But they also sell stamps, phone cards and Metrobús and monthly *abono* tickets. *Estancos* are the only places to obtain official money vouchers (*papel de estado*), needed for dealings with Spanish bureaucracy.

Poste restante

Poste restante letters should be addressed to Lista de Correos, 28000 Madrid, Spain. To collect, go to the main post office (*see left*); you'll need to bring your passport when coming to claim your mail.

PUBLIC HOLIDAYS

On public holidays (*fiestas*), virtually all shops, banks and offices, and some bars and restaurants, are closed. There is a near-normal public transport service, though, except on Christmas Day and New Year's Day, and many museums do remain open, albeit with Sun hours operating. When a holiday falls on a Tue or Thur it's a common practice for people to take the day before or after the weekend off as well, in a long weekend called a *puente* (bridge). Many places are also closed for the whole of Easter Week. For the city's festivals, *see p45*. The usual official holidays are:

New Year's Day/Año Nuevo *1 Jan*
Three Kings/ Reyes Magos *6 Jan*
Good Friday/Viernes Santo
May (Labour) Day/Fiesta del Trabajo *1 May*
Madrid Day/Día de la Comunidad de Madrid *2 May*
San Isidro *15 May*
Virgen de la Paloma *15 Aug*
Discovery of America/Día de la Hispanidad *12 Oct*
All Saints' Day/Todos los Santos *1 Nov*
Virgen de la Almudena *9 Nov*
Constitution Day/Día de la Constitución *6 Dec*

Immaculate Conception/La Inmaculada *8 Dec*

Christmas Day/Navidad *25 Dec*

SAFETY & SECURITY

As in most major cities, street crime is a problem in Madrid and tourists are often targeted. One plus point is that pickpocketing and bag-snatching are more likely than any violent crime.

Street criminals prey very deliberately on the unwary, and their chances of success can be limited greatly by taking the following simple precautions.

• When sitting in a café, especially at an outside table, never leave a bag or coat on the ground, on the back of a chair or anywhere you cannot see it clearly. If in doubt, keep it on your lap.
• Give the impression of knowing what's going on around you, and – without getting paranoid – be alert and watch out to see if you are being followed.
• Wear shoulder bags pulled to the front, not at your back, especially in the underground. Keep the bag closed and a hand on top of it.
• Avoid pulling out large notes to pay for things, especially in the street at night; try not to get large notes when changing money.
• Be aware that street thieves often work in pairs or groups; if someone hassles you for money or to buy something, or pulls out a map and asks for directions, keep walking, as this can be a ruse to distract you so that the thief's 'partner' can get at your bag. This is often done pretty crudely, and so is not hard to recognise.
• Be extremely careful when you withdraw money from ATMs. Don't let anyone distract your attention while putting in your PIN code.
• Beware of fake policemen: if someone asks to see your ID, ask to see their identification first.

SMOKING

Many Spaniards are keen smokers, but Spain's tough anti-smoking laws mean that smoking is now banned in enclosed public places. This includes all restaurants, though there has been a marked increase in permit applications for open-air terraces as a result. Some hotels still have smoking rooms, but there will only be a handful.

TELEPHONES

Dialling & codes

Normal Spanish phone numbers have nine digits; the area code (91 in the Madrid area) must be dialled with all calls, both local and long-distance. Spanish mobile phone numbers usually begin with 6 and, very occasionally, 7. Numbers starting 900 are freephone lines, while other 90 numbers are special-rate services. Those starting with 80 are high-rate lines and can only be called from within Spain.

To call abroad, dial 00 followed by the country code, then the area code (omitting the first zero in UK numbers) and number. To call Madrid from abroad, dial the international code (00 in the UK, 001 from the USA), then 34 for Spain. Country codes are as follows:

Australia *61*.
Canada *1*.
Irish Republic *353*.
New Zealand *64*.
United Kingdom *44*.
USA *1*.

Mobile phones

Most mobiles from other European countries can be used in Spain, but you may need to set this up before leaving home. You may be charged international roaming rates even when making a local call, and you will be charged for incoming calls. Not all US handsets are GSM-compatible; check with your service provider before you leave.

If you're staying more than a few weeks, it may work out cheaper to buy a pay-as-you-go package when you arrive or buy a local SIM card for your own phone.

Phone centres

Phone centres (*locutorios*) offer cheap international calls, and are full of small booths where you can sit down and pay at the end. Find them particularly around Lavapiés, Huertas and Malasaña. Often other services – internet, currency exchange, money transfer – are also available.

TIME

Spain is on CET (Central European Time), 1hr ahead of Greenwich Mean Time, 6hrs ahead of US EST (Eastern Standard Time) and 9hrs ahead of PST (Pacific Standard Time). Daylight saving time runs concurrently with the UK.

TIPPING

There are no rules for tipping and in general Spaniards tip very little. It's usual to leave 5%-10% in restaurants, unless the service has been bad. People sometimes leave a little change in bars. In taxis, tipping is not standard, but many people round up to the nearest 50¢. It's usual to tip hotel porters.

TOURIST INFORMATION

Full information on what's on is in local papers, listings magazines and local English-language magazines.

Centro de Turismo de Madrid *Plaza Mayor 27, Los Austrias (91 578 78 10, www.esmadrid.com). Metro Ópera. **Open** 9.30am-9.30pm daily. **Map** p69 H15.* This is the largest tourist information office in the city.

Smaller *puntos de información turística* are located at: the Plaza de Cibeles; Plaza del Prado at Plaza Neptune; Atocha, next to the Reina Sofía Museum; the Plaza de Callao; Paseo Recoletas; Paseo de la Castellana next to the Santiago Bernabéu Stadium; and at Barajas Airport Terminals 2 & 4. There's also a Foreign Tourist Assistance Service (SATE) at the police station (Comisaría) at C/Leganitos 19.

Oficinas de Turismo de la Comunidad de Madrid *C/Duque de Medinaceli 2, Huertas (91 429 49 51, 902 10 00 07, turismomadrid.es). Metro Banco de España. **Open** 8am-8pm Mon-Sat; 9am-2pm Sun. **Map** p95 L15.*
Other locations Atocha train station, Barajas Airport Terminals 1 & 4.
Summer information officers
During July and Aug pairs of young information guides, in bright yellow and blue uniforms, are sent to roam the central area ready to answer enquiries in a courageous variety of languages (8am-8pm daily). They also staff information stands at Puerta del Sol, Plaza del Callao, Plaza Mayor, by the Palacio Real and by the Prado.
010 phoneline *Open 8am-10pm Mon-Sat; 10am-9pm Sun.*
A city-run information line that will answer enquiries of any kind on Madrid, and particularly on events promoted by the city council. Calls are accepted in French and English. To access the line from outside Madrid, call 91 529 82 10.

VISAS & IMMIGRATION

UK and Irish nationals will need a valid passport to enter Spain. Due to the Schengen Agreement, most other EU citizens, as well as Icelandic and Norwegian nationals, need only a national ID card.

Visas are not needed by US, Canadian, Australian or New Zealand citizens who are arriving for stays of up to 90 days. Citizens of South Africa and other countries do need a visa to enter Spain; approach Spanish consulates in your home country for information (see embassy.goabroad.com). Visa regulations do changes, so check before leaving home.

WEIGHTS & MEASURES

Spain uses metric weights, distances and measurements.

Vocabulary

Like other Latin languages, Spanish has different familiar and polite forms of the second person (you). Many young people now use the familiar *tú* form most of the time; for foreigners, thought it can be advisable to use the more polite *usted* with people you do not know, and certainly with anyone over the age of 60. In the phrases listed here all verbs are given in the *usted* form. For help in making your way through menus, *see p32*.

Pronunciation

· **c** before an **i** or an **e** and **z** are like **th** in **th**in
· **c** in all other cases is as in **c**at
· **g** before an **i** or an **e** and **j** are pronounced with a guttural **h**-sound that doesn't exist in English – like **ch** in Scottish 'lo**ch**', but much harder
· **g** in all other cases is as in **g**et
· **h** at the beginning of a word is normally silent
· **ll** is pronounced like a **y**
· **ñ** is like **ny** in can**y**on
· a single **r** at the beginning of a word and **rr** elsewhere are heavily rolled
· v is more like an English **b**
· In words ending with a vowel, **n** or s, the penultimate syllable is stressed: eg *barato, viven*.
· In words ending with any other consonant, the last syllable is stressed: eg *exterior, universidad*
· An accent marks the stressed syllable in words that depart from these rules: eg *estación, tónica*

Basics

· **please** *por favor*; **thank you (very much)** *(muchas) gracias*; **very good/great/OK** *muy bien*; **you're welcome** *de nada*
· **hello** *hola*
· **goodbye/see you later** *adiós/ hasta luego*

· **excuse me/sorry** *perdón*; **excuse me, please** *oiga* (**the standard way to attract attention, politely; literally, 'hear me'**)
· **OK/fine/that's enough (to a waiter)** *vale*
· **open** *abierto*; **closed** *cerrado*
· **entrance** *entrada*; **exit** *salida*
· **very** *muy*; **and** *y*; **or** *o*; **with** *con*; **without** *sin*; **enough** *bastante*

More expressions

· **good morning/good day** *buenos días*; **good afternoon/good evening** *buenas tardes*; **good evening (after dark)/good night** *buenas noches*
· **do you speak English?** *¿habla inglés?*; **I'm sorry, I don't speak Spanish** *lo siento, no hablo castellano*; **I don't understand** *no lo entiendo*; **speak more slowly, please** *hable más despacio, por favor*; **wait a moment** *espere un momento*; **how do you say that in Spanish?** *¿cómo se dice eso en castellano?*
· **what's your name?** *¿cómo se llama?* **my name is...** *me llamo...*
· **Sir/Mr** *señor (Sr)*; **Madam/Mrs** *señora (Sra)*; **Miss** *señorita (Srta)*
· **where is...?** *¿dónde está...?*; **why?** *¿por qué?*; **who?** *¿quién?*; **when?** *¿cuándo?*; **what?** *¿qué?*; **where?** *¿dónde?*; **how?** *¿cómo?*; **who is it?** *¿quién es?*; **is/are there any...?** *¿hay...?*
· **what time does it open/close?** *¿a qué hora abre/cierra?*
· **pull** *tirar*; **push** *empujar*
· **I would like** *quiero*; **how many would you like?** *¿cuántos quiere?*; **how much is it?** *¿cuánto vale?*
· **price** *precio*; **free** *gratis*; **discount** *descuento*; **do you have any change?** *¿tiene cambio?*
· **I don't want** *no quiero*; **I like** *me gusta*; **I don't like** *no me gusta*
· **good** *bueno/a*; **bad** *malo/a*; **well/ badly** *bien/mal*; **small** *pequeño/a*; **big** *gran, grande*; **expensive** *caro/a*; **cheap**

barato/a; **hot (food, drink)** *caliente*; **cold** *frío/a*
- **bank** *banco*; **to rent** *alquilar*; **(for) rent, rental** (*en*) *alquiler*; **post office** *correos*; **stamp** *sello*; **postcard** *postal*; **toilet** *el baño, el servicio, el lavabo*
- **airport** *aeropuerto*; **rail station** *estación de ferrocarril/ estación de RENFE* **(Spanish railways); metro station** *estación de metro*; **car** *coche*; **bus** *autobús*; **train** *tren*; **bus stop** *parada de autobus*; **the next stop** *la próxima parade*
- **a ticket** *un billete*; **return** *de ida y vuelta*
- **excuse me, do you know the way to...?** *¿oiga, señor/señora, sabe cómo llegar a...?*
- **left** *izquierda*; **right** *derecha*
- **here** *aquí*; **there** *allí*; **straight on** *recto*; **near** *cerca*; **far** *lejos*; **at the corner** *a la esquina*; **as far as** *hasta*; **towards** *hacia*; **it is far?** *¿está lejos?*

Time

- **now** *ahora*; **later** *más tarde*
- **yesterday** *ayer*; **today** *hoy*; **tomorrow** *mañana*; **tomorrow morning** *mañana por la mañana*

- **morning** *la mañana*; **midday** *mediodía*; **afternoon/evening** *la tarde*; **night** *la noche*
- **at what time...?** *¿a qué hora...?* **in an hour** *en una hora*; **at 2** *a las dos*

Numbers

0 *cero*; **1** *un, uno, una*; **2** *dos*; **3** *tres*; **4** *cuatro*; **5** *cinco*; **6** *seis*; **7** *siete*; **8** *ocho*; **9** *nueve*; **10** *diez*; **11** *once*; **12** *doce*; **13** *trece*; **14** *catorce*; **15** *quince*; **16** *dieciséis*; **17** *diecisiete*; **18** *dieciocho*; **19** *diecinueve*; **20** *veinte*; **21** *veintiuno*; **22** *veintidós*; **30** *treinta*; **40** *cuarenta*; **50** *cincuenta*; **60** *sesenta*; **70** *setenta*; **80** *ochenta*; **90** *noventa*; **100** *cien*; **200** *doscientos*; **1,000** *mil*; **1,000,000** *un millón*

Dates & seasons

- **Monday** *lunes*; **Tuesday** *martes*; **Wednesday** *miércoles*; **Thursday** *jueves*; **Friday** *viernes*; **Saturday** *sábado*; **Sunday** *domingo*
- **January** *enero*; **February** *febrero*; **March** *marzo*; **April** *abril*; **May** *mayo*; **June** *junio*; **July** *julio*; **August** *agosto*; **September** *septiembre*; **October** *octubre*; **November** *noviembre*; **December** *diciembre*
- **spring** *primavera*; **summer** *verano*; **autumn** *otoño*; **winter** *invierno*

Index

Picture credits

Inside front cover: stoyanh/Shutterstock.com. Pages 2
(top) VictoriaSh/Shutterstock.com; 2 (bottom) dimbar76/
Shutterstock.com; 3 Sergio Albert; 4 trabantos/Shutterstock.
com; 7 Curioso/Shutterstock.com; 11 (bottom) Takashi
Images/Shutterstock.com; 11 (top), 190 (bottom) dmitro2009/
Shutterstock.com; 12 (middle), 14 (middle), 84 Courtesy of
Departamento Prensa Patrimonio Nacional; 12 (top) Kiev.
Victor/Shutterstock.com; 12 (bottom) Iberfoto/SuperStock; 13
(bottom), 139 Andrii Zhezhera/Shutterstock.com; 13 (top) The
World in HDR/Shutterstock.com; 13 (middle), 58, 111 Pedro
Rufo/Shutterstock.com; 14 (top), 148 James Tye; 14 (bottom),
85, 86 © Real Academia de Bellas Artes de San Fernando; 15
(top) Press; 15 (bottom) Florentino Ar G/Shutterstock.com; 15
(middle) Chiyacat/Shutterstock.com; 16 (middle), 155 (bottom)
Alvaro German Vilela/Shutterstock.com; 16 (bottom), 120
Gabriel Lopez Perez; 16 (top), 76 Pabkov/Shutterstock.com; 17
(top) Andres Garcia Martin/Shutterstock.com; 17 (bottom), 164
Alberto Loyo/Shutterstock.com; 17 (middle) photogomezsport;
19 Matej Kastelic/Shutterstock.com; 21 Urko Castanos/
Shutterstock.com; 22, 97 (right) Museo Thyssen-Bornemisza;
24 b-hide the scene/Shutterstock.com; 26 joyfull/Shutterstock.
com; 27, 38 nito/Shutterstock.com; 29 Casa Alberto; 30
somor/Shutterstock.com; 31 (top & bottom) Emilia Brandao;
33 Goran Bogicevic/Shutterstock.com; 34 La Taberna de
Antonio Sánchez; 35 DeltaOFF/Shutterstock.com; 37 Salvador
Aznar/Shutterstock.com; 39, 59, 63, 137, 190 (top) Lord
Kuernyus/Shutterstock.com; 40 Karl Blackwell/Time Out;
41 Samantha López S Photography; 43, 104 Teatro Español;
44, 103 Lucas Vallecillos/age fotostock/SuperStock.com; 46
DAVID_NERIDA_MENDEZ; 47 Christian Bertrand/Shutterstock.
com; 49 RnDms/Shutterstock.com; 50 Marques/Shutterstock.
com; 51 (bottom), 101 (bottom) JJFarq/Shutterstock.com; 51
(top), 72, 153 Catarina Belova/Shutterstock.com; 52 (top)
Taller Puntera; 52 (bottom) Enriscapes/Shutterstock.com; 52
(middle), 190 (middle) EQRoy/Shutterstock.com; 53 (top left),
102 Salmón Guru; 53 (bottom) Museo Nacional Centro de
Arte Reina Sofía; 53 (top right) Alastair Wallace/Shutterstock.
com; 54, 127 elenaquintanarphotography; 55 David Herraez
Calzada/Shutterstock.com; 56 (top) DPimenta/Shutterstock.
com; 56 (bottom left) travelview/Shutterstock.com; 56
(bottom right) Charles Bowman/SuperStock.com; 57 Jacobo
Medrano; 61 elRoce/Shutterstock.com; 62 SelectorMarx;
64 Semmick Photo/Shutterstock.com; 65 Leonid Andronov/
Shutterstock.com; 66 ESB Professional/Shutterstock.com;
71 S-F/Shutterstock.com; 73 María Sainz Cabezalí; 75,
78, 110 Bill Perry/Shutterstock.com; 81 Alexandre Arocas/
Shutterstock.com; 87 LucVi/Shutterstock.com; 88 basiczto/
Shutterstock.com; 90 White Star/Monica Gumm/SuperStock.
com; 91 Kamira/Shutterstock.com; 92 Teatro de la Zarzuela;
93 Marcos del Mazo Valentin/Shutterstock.com; 97 (left) Pablo
Casares©2014; 98 Manuel Ascanio/Shutterstock.com; 101
(top) José Francisco Castro; 105 Carlos Crespo Gonzalez/La
Casa Encendida; 108 Christian Mueller/Shutterstock.com;
109 Angelo Cavalli/SuperStock.com; 113 M G. de Lamo/Los
Chuchis; 115 Carlos Horcajada/Centro Cultural Conde Duque;
117 Jon Santa Cruz/Time Out; 124 Javitouh/Shutterstock.
com; 125 Lozzy Squire/Shutterstock.com; 126 Fundación
Telefónica; 133 Anibal Trejo/Shutterstock.com; 141 Lisi4ka/
Shutterstock.com; 143 Visions of America/Superstock.com;
144 SuperStock.com; 145 Bertl123/Shutterstock.com; 151
catwalker/Shutterstock.com; 155 kavram/Shutterstock.com;
157 David Carrascosa; 163 Paco Gómez/NOPHOTO; 165
Manuel Hurtado/Shutterstock.com.

RED DE METRO Y ME

SIMBOLOGÍA Key

Estación accesible / ascensor
Step-free access / lift

Transbordo corto
Metro interchange

Transbordo largo
Metro interchange with long walking distance

Cambio de tren
Change of trains

Horario restringido
Restricted opening times

Metro Ligero
Light Rail

Cercanías
Suburban railway

Autobuses interurbanos
Suburban buses

Autobuses largo recorrido
Interregional bus station

Terminal autobuses nocturnos
Night bus line terminal

Autobús exprés aeropuerto
Airport express bus

Estación de tren
Railway station

Aeropuerto / Airport
Adolfo Suárez Madrid-Barajas

ZONA A Zonas tarifarias
ZONA B1 Fare zones

ATENCIÓN A LA TARIFA
Validación a la SALIDA
PAY THE RIGHT FARE
Ticket checked at the EXIT

Atención al cliente
Customer Service

Oficina de gestión tarjeta transporte público
Public Transport Card Office

Objetos perdidos
Lost and found

Bibliometro
Metro Library

Productos oficiales Metro
Official Metro merchandising

Espacio histórico de Metro
Metro historic space

HORARIO Opening times

Todos los días de 06:00 a 01:30 h.
Every day from 6:00 a.m. to 1:30 a.m.

1 Pinar de Chamartín
Valdecarros

2 Las Rosas
Cuatro Caminos

3 Villaverde Alto
Moncloa

4 Argüelles
Pinar de Chamartín

5 Alameda de Osuna
Casa de Campo

6 Circular

7 Hospital del Henares
Pitis

8 Nuevos Ministerios
Aeropuerto

9 Paco de Lucía
Arganda del Rey

10 Hospital Infanta Sofía
Puerta del Sur

11 Plaza Elíptica
La Fortuna

12 MetroSur

R Ópera
Príncipe Pío

1 Pinar de Chamartín
Las Tablas

2 Colonia Jardín
Estación de Aravaca

3 Colonia Jardín
Puerta de Boadilla

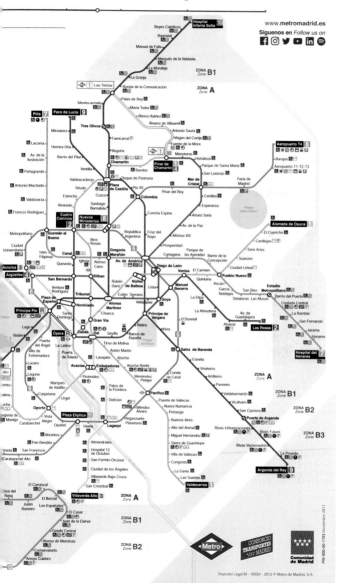

www.metromadrid.es

Síguenos en *Follow us on*

METRO MAP

Depósito Legal M - 18034 - 2013 © Metro de Madrid, S.A.

PW-000-00-1703 Noviembre 2017

Credits

Crimson credits
Editor Sally Davies
Listings Editor Mary-Ann Gallagher
Layouts Emilie Crabb, Patrick Dawson
Cartography Gail Armstrong, John Scott

Series Editor Sophie Blacksell Jones
Production Manager Kate Michell
Design Mytton Williams

Chairman David Lester
Managing Director Andy Riddle

Advertising Media Sales House
Marketing Lyndsey Mayhew
Sales Joel James

Authors
This guide was written and researched by Sally Davies, with contributions from Robert Elms, Nick Funnell, Mary-Ann Gallagher, Harvey Holtom, Simon Hunter, Michael Jacobs, Anna Norman, Nick Rider and Rob Stone.

Acknowledgements
The editor would like to thank contributors to previous editions of *Time Out Madrid* and *Time Out Madrid Shortlist*, whose work formed the basis of this guide. The editor would also like to thank Sonia Alonso, Annie Bennett, James Blick, Aida Casamayor, Alana Fogarty, Vera de Frutos, Pilar Gimeno, Fabian González, Simon Hunter, Botoa Lefe, Jordi Luque, Concha Marcos, Andrea Martín, Myriam Martín, Yoly Martín, Kate McWilliams, Tess O'Donovan, Paul Richardson, Carlota Sartorius Freschet and Ben Serio for their inestimable help in compiling this edition.

Photography credits
Front cover Bertlmann/iStockphoto.
Back cover RnDmS/Shutterstock.com.
Interior Photography credits, see p189.

Publishing information
Time Out Madrid Shortlist 2nd edition
© TIME OUT ENGLAND LIMITED 2018
May 2018

ISBN 978 1 780592 63 3
CIP DATA: A catalogue record for this book is available from the British Library

Published by Crimson Publishing
21d Charles Street, Bath, BA1 1HX (01225 584 950, www.crimsonpublishing.co.uk) on behalf of Time Out England.

Distributed by Grantham Book Services
Distributed in the US and Canada by Publishers Group West (1-510-809-3700)

Printed by Replika Press, India.

While every effort has been made by the authors and the publishers to ensure that the information contained in this guide is accurate and up to date as at the date of publication, they accept no responsibility or liability in contract, tort, negligence, breach of statutory duty or otherwise for any inconvenience, loss, damage, costs or expenses of any nature whatsoever incurred or suffered by anyone as a result of any advice or information contained in the guide (except to the extent that such liability may not be excluded or limited as a matter of law).